LIFE WITH BILLY

An Autobiography

Maurice Rowlandson

Hodder & Stoughton
LONDON SYDNEY AUCKLAND

Dedication

To Marilyn, Gary, Julian and Jacky – my long-suffering family – without whose love and support the ministries of this story would never have been possible.

Unless otherwise stated, scripture quotations are taken from the HOLY BIBLE, NEW INTERNATIONAL VERSION. Copyright © 1973, 1978, 1984 by International Bible Society. Used by permission.

Scripture quotations marked (NKJV) are taken from the New King James Version. Copyright © 1982 by Thomas Nelson, Inc.

Photographic Credits   pp1, 2 and 8 Maurice Rowlandson; p4 Picture of Cherylyn Rowlandson, Middlesex County Press; p4 Pictures of Spre-e '73, Russ Busby; pp5–7 Russ Busby.

British Library Cataloguing in Publication Data

ISBN 0-340-57691-X
Copyright © 1992
First published in Great Britain 1992

Published by Hodder and Stoughton,
a division of Hodder and Stoughton Ltd,
Mill Road, Dunton Green, Sevenoaks, Kent TN13 2YA
Editorial Office: 47 Bedford Square, London WC1B 3DP

Typeset by Phoenix Typesetting, Burley-in-Wharfedale, West Yorkshire.

Printed in Great Britain by Clays Ltd, St. Ives plc.

Contents

Foreword by Billy Graham

All over the world our ministry has been greatly helped by men and women whose gift is administration. No one has done more in Britain than Maurice Rowlandson, backed by his beloved wife Marilyn, who comes from Minneapolis, where our offices are.

Maurice would have risen to the top in the world of British business or politics had he not devoted his life to the gospel. I first met him in Westminster Chapel, London in the early spring of 1948. He had responded to an invitation which I gave from the pulpit to travel to Minneapolis to study at Northwestern Bible Schools of which, at the time, I was President. As I wrote his name on the back of an envelope I little thought that in years to come he would be a valued member of our team, working with us in our London office.

When we first met, Maurice Rowlandson was with the beloved British evangelist, Tom Rees, whom I held in very high regard. In a remarkable way, God led Maurice from one evangelist to another – but always he had the one thought in mind: to uplift and glorify the name of the Lord Jesus Christ so that others might find Him, and in finding Him, find salvation and power to live for Christ.

Maurice has been involved in many important crusades and missions, beginning with Harringay in London in 1954 where he was chief steward. His descriptions often have a light touch, for his sense of humour has been a great asset. But they make it plain that sacrifice and hard work go into preparing a crusade and following it up. Maurice is efficient, always seeking the best use of time, money and manpower for the gospel. He is positive: he never asks why something should be done. He always asks, 'Why not?'

Skilled at harnessing modern technology to the service of Christ, Maurice thought up the idea of taking our films into prisons all over the British Isles. Nearly twenty years later he put before us the plan which became Spre-e '73 – an event which affected the lives of thousands of young people, many of whom today are in full-time Christian service.

Maurice's book does not disguise problems and setbacks but he shows how closely our team and the hundreds of local volunteers, work together, motivated and bound by Christian love.

And he writes of God's omnipotence: 'Whether the sun is shining or there is a violent storm, He is in control and the end result will be for His glory. Not always is it what I would want it to be. Marilyn and I were to learn that as the years went by.' Nothing is more moving than his testimony to God's grace and comfort when their elder daughter Cherylyn was killed in a road accident. The Rowlandsons at that time of great sorrow were an inspiration to me and to many others.

Maurice has his heart in evangelism. He has devoted himself tirelessly to this ministry in many ways throughout the years. In this book you will read of the way in which God has led him: his philosophies of life and the centrality of Christ in everything he does. I commend this book because it will encourage, uplift, instruct and enthral you.

Foreword by Cliff Richard

I've posed for a fair number of pictures in my time, but one of the strangest had to be on a Billy Graham crusade platform at Earls Court back in 1966. The photograph shows me looking surly and bored – behind me, grim-faced and every inch the bouncer, is Maurice Rowlandson.

What the 12,000-strong audience didn't know is that we were filming a scene for the Billy Graham movie *Two a Penny* and, at a given signal from director Jim Collier, who had wisely secreted himself away from public view, I had to slip into character. Unfortunately for me, 'character' meant yobbing it up as Jamie, a thoroughly cynical and nasty bit of work, who, according to the storyline, was only at the crusade under duress, and on the platform by animal cunning. I took the subsequent letters of censure as a tribute to my acting.

My respect for Dr Graham is no secret, so for me to read a book which gives a unique insight not only into the man himself, but also into the team and organisation that have surrounded him for so long, is fascinating. From the outset, the Billy Graham Association's professionalism and efficiency were impressive, often in contrast to some of the other well-meaning but ultra-casual Christian organisations I encountered in my early days as a 'celebrity Christian'.

Maurice Rowlandson of course was the Billy Graham 'face' in the UK. He was the one with whom we discussed projects and possibilities, and it was he, I suspect, who persuaded Dr Graham to invite me to give that much-publicised testimony at an earlier Earls Court meeting. I can't imagine that Billy Graham, or anyone else in the American team, come to that, would ever have heard of Cliff Richard.

In many ways, that particular evening was a significant land-mark for me. Certainly I had shared my Christian testimony before, but never on such a public platform. There was no going back after that night. The press ensured that my colours were well and truly nailed. I was a Billy Graham man; more important, I was Christ's man. Thanks, Maurice, for helping me make that clear!

Acknowledgments

There are four reasons why this book has been written. First and foremost is the desire to give thanks to God for His goodness to my family and me over the years. 'He who began a good work in you will carry it on to completion until the day of Christ Jesus' (Phil. 1:6). I hope this story may help someone else to learn the power of prayer, and the reality of guidance as one's life is committed to Christ.

Secondly, I want to share the positive feeling I have about life. In all experiences, I believe God's hand is at work – be they matters for rejoicing or matters of sorrow. I can best sum up this feeling in the words of the hymn:

> Fill Thou my life, O Lord my God
>   In every part with praise,
> That my whole being may proclaim
>   Thy being and Thy ways.
>
> Not for the lip of praise alone
>   Nor e'en the praising heart
> I ask, but for a life made up
>   Of praise in every part:
>
> Praise in the common things of life
>   Its goings out and in
> Praise in each duty and each deed
>   However small and mean.
>
> Fill every part of me with praise;
>   Let all my being speak
> Of Thee, and of Thy love, O Lord
>   Poor though I be – and weak.

So shalt Thou Lord, from me, e'en me
   Receive the glory due;
And so shall I begin on earth
   The song for ever new.

So shall no part of day or night
   From sacredness be free
But all my life, in every step
   Be fellowship with Thee.

(Horatius Bonar, 1808–82)

Thirdly, I believe that people are interested in people (as my good friend and former colleague Jim Douglas used to say). Therefore there are many friends mentioned in this story. All of them had a part to play in my life, and became indirectly involved in the ministry of Billy Graham. To all of them I express my love and gratitude.

Finally, I am convinced that there are many stories about Billy Graham which will not be told elsewhere. In all of those that appear in this book, I have been involved. I have kept very careful records, including a daily diary since January 1st, 1944: never a day was missed. Hence I can pinpoint with accuracy events which have often been put into another context in stories elsewhere. My diary discloses when they *really* happened.

I have an enormous debt of gratitude to pay to Billy Graham and his team, for all that they have meant to me over the years. If you're looking for scandal . . . you'll have to look elsewhere. But if you're looking for the story of a caring organisation, an organisation in which the rules of the day were discipline, care in finances, excellence in every sphere and a lot of humour, then this is the story for you. My life with the Billy Graham Evangelistic Association lifted me to a new plain of excellence. If a thing was worth doing, it was worth doing well. That experience has given me many happy memories which I hope I can share through this book.

I wish to pay tribute to my many friends who have helped and advised me in the preparation of this book. First and foremost my thanks to Marilyn, my wife, who has read each chapter critically; she has made innumerable suggestions. She has tested the accuracy of each story. At the same time, she has pencilled in suggestions where I should be more explicit and – occasionally – has said: 'You can't put that in!' The whole story has been a co-operative family effort, and without their love and support it might never have been possible to write it. I thank God that, in spite of long absences from home at a time when our four children were in their most formative years, God has again been 'no man's debtor'.

Then my thanks to my friend Roger Hoath, whose early encouragement really got me started. Others to whom I would express my gratitude are my secretaries Marion Harris, Barbara Binder who did the final typing and checking, and Amanda Bragg. Each, at different times, was involved in typing and retyping the manuscript – as was Timothy Innes, one of the young volunteers at the Keswick Convention. I must also thank John Pollock who helped me to find a publisher and David Hayton who gave me encouragement. Especial thanks to T.W. Wilson who read through the manuscript and corrected a few errors and made a number of other suggestions. To all of them, my grateful thanks.

Finally my thanks to so many friends – some of whom figure in the stories in the book – who have helped me to recollect, and accurately chronicle, an event in which they were involved.

Prelude –

Life *Without* Billy

God has given me a wonderful life! The chapters of this book are largely devoted to telling of His goodness to me. He gave to me the great privilege of helping in the evangelistic ministry of Billy Graham.

While that involvement has been exceedingly important to me, it has by no means excluded me from a variety of other interests, all of which have been satisfying. In a remarkable way, all that I have done seems to have dovetailed together without presenting any difficulties. My involvement in other Christian ministries has been complemented by many other activities, both Christian and secular, during my years with Billy Graham.

My former professor at Northwestern College, Dean Edwin J. Hartill, laid strong emphasis upon redeeming the time. He reminded us often that we had only one life to live and that time wasted was time which God had given us for His service. He reminded us – budding preachers and speakers – that if we spoke to one person, for one minute, and said nothing worthwhile, we had wasted two minutes – one minute of his time, and one minute of mine! Therefore, if we spoke to 500 people for one minute and said nothing worthwhile, we had wasted 501 minutes. It concentrates the mind!

Without doubt, the most important other activity in which I have been involved was founding and running (for forty-seven years as it turned out) the Venturers Norfolk Broads Cruise. Because of my love of sailing, and because I realised that in the close confines of a cabin yacht there were great spiritual opportunities, I decided to bring these two elements together.

In April 1946 I rented six sailing cabin yachts on the Norfolk Broads. Then I set about finding schoolboys to fill the places, together with a competent skipper to take charge of each yacht.

Year by year, some sixty to sixty-five boys (and nowadays girls too) have sailed with the Venturers Cruise each April. The entire administrative team and all of the skippers were, for many years, senior members of the cruise who had first sailed as boys with the Venturers. There was a touch of pride in being a Venturer.

The full story of the Venturers Cruise may be told elsewhere: there is neither space nor relevance to this present story. Suffice it to say that, over the forty-seven years, the cruise has influenced the lives of many thousands of boys and girls. It has, incidentally, brought me some wonderful friendships. Not least among these has been the man who, from 1947 onwards, was to become the commodore, my good friend Henry W. Hole. He came to the Venturers almost by accident; but his arrival was good news for me, and for all those who have sailed with him throughout the years. His leadership and guidance in so many areas of life have been invaluable.

I had no intention of continuing the cruise after that first year in 1946. But everyone enjoyed themselves and were so enthusiastic that it should continue that I found myself organising the next, and the next and the next! It was a miracle to me that, in each sphere of service I entered, there was a willingness among my employers to allow me time to organise the cruise. First, when I started my Christian work with Tom Rees, I told him about the cruise and he encouraged me to stay involved. While I was at college in America, my good friend the Reverend A. Morgan Derham stepped into my shoes and continued it.

Later, when I went on to serve as the boys' administrative chief of the Christian uniformed youth movement the Campaigners, I made it a point in my interview for the job, and secured the agreement of the late Prebendary Colin C. Kerr (the clans' chief and founder) that I could organise the cruise as part of my work in the office. The same agreement was secured when I later moved to the Evangelical Alliance, and yet again when I commenced work with Billy Graham. It could not have been any other way, for one hundred per cent of my time was committed to the work of the association. There had to be an agreement, therefore, that the cruise would be part of that work.

The Venturers Cruise has brought to our family some of the happiest experiences of our lives. It has brought us many of our closest friends and supporters. It brought to me, especially, a team upon which I could count for any event with Billy Graham in which I was involved. Henry Hole was my deputy chief steward at the Harringay crusade, and chief steward at Wembley Stadium, Earls Court, Spre-e '73, and the centenary meeting at Keswick. He enrolled the help of most of the Venturers team in all of these events – and everything went like clockwork. For the part that he had played in the leadership of the cruise, he was honoured by Her Majesty the Queen with an MBE in 1980. This was initiated through our own team, but achieved largely through the good offices of a former Venturer who, at the time, was a Member of Parliament, Christopher Brocklebank-Fowler.

Although Henry Hole and I have now retired from the leadership of the Venturers Cruise, it still continues with young men who first came with us as boys. They grew up on the cruise, and are now in the positions of leadership which we formerly held. John Spradbery is the current commodore and Mark Smith the honorary secretary. Numbers continue to be maintained – and that is without a programme of advertising. The cruise has not advertised for participants for more than thirty years. Word-of-mouth propagation has ensured a continuing stream of youngsters who wish to sail with us.

Shortly after my retirement as honorary secretary a letter arrived out of the blue. It was from Tim Smith. He was one of those who had come on the cruise as a boy and had grown up to be one of our leading skippers. He said:

> I have not, to my shame, offered my personal thanks to you for your past leadership of the Venturers. I have found your enthusiastic and pro-active concern for all matters related to the Cruise to be a great source of inspiration. I am confident that your attention to detail and continuous focus on the spiritual objectives of the Cruise have left their mark on those of us who now carry on the good work. It is my hope that a small part of your leadership over my thirty-something years of Venturing will 'rub off' on me as I endeavour to serve the Lord on Cruise affairs in the coming years.

What better tribute and testimony could I have wished for! It was a testimonial deeply appreciated and gladly received.

✳   ✳   ✳

During the years, there have also been numerous small events in which I have been involved. Sometimes these have stemmed from introductions which came from the Billy Graham Evangelistic Association (BGEA) before I was invited to work full time with them. One of these was the visit of Mr Kenneth S. Keyes of which more is told in the narrative. I was asked to organise a series of preaching engagements for him. He had a set piece in which he specialised: 'In Partnership with God'. It was a series of addresses on stewardship. Wherever we went, he was well accepted and his addresses affected the lives of many.

A year or two later, I was again asked by the BGEA to assist in a series of meetings to be organised, this time for Jim Vaus. Jim had been converted at Billy Graham's first major crusade in Los Angeles in 1949. At the time of his conversion he was known throughout the United States as a criminal who had specialised in wire-tapping. His big coup was to tap the wires of the bookies on the race-course: he delayed the message long enough to enable his conspirators to place a bet on what they now knew to be the winning horse. Then he would release the message to the bookies with the resultant pay-out on the last-minute bets. Ultimately he was discovered, and went to prison for his crimes.

He and his wife were soundly converted under Mr Graham's ministry, and now Jim was touring America to tell of God's goodness to him in his life, and to preach the gospel. He wanted to come to Britain also, and I was asked to organise the meetings for him. It was a great experience to work with Jim and Alice, and we went all around the country with him.

Then in September 1960, Tom Rees asked me to be involved in a series of evangelistic rallies which he planned for Sunday nights in London's Palace Theatre in Shaftesbury Avenue. It was an effective series, and I was given full responsibility for organising them.

I had a telephone call from India in March 1985. It was Billy Graham's associate evangelist Robert Cunville. He was calling to say that his colleague Zak Patiak had been taken ill. He was no longer able to handle the administration of a major crusade planned for Robert on the island of Guernsey. Robert asked me if I could take over.

I paid an immediate visit to Guernsey. The crusade, which took place in June 1985, was a tremendous success. Robert Cunville was well received by the folk in the Channel Islands. It was the only occasion when I acted as a crusade set-up associate for a member of the team. It was an experience I enjoyed, and I found it incredibly satisfying to see all of one's planning come to successful fruition.

In all my intense activity with Christian work, I was conscious of the fact that I stood in danger of forgetting about the real world outside. That there *was* a world out there without Christ, was hard to remember when you were moving in a closed circle of people (and friends) who shared the same faith. It was easy to begin to think that everyone was a Christian: so what was the purpose of evangelism?

This concern began to exercise me in 1950, about the same time that there was considerable pressure for involvement in civil defence. These were the days of imminent nuclear warfare. East and West were building up their nuclear arsenals at a rapid rate and there was every expectation that some madman, somewhere, would push the button and we would all be annihilated. There were many advertisements in the press asking for volunteers to be trained in civil defence. I began to think that I might solve two problems at one stroke. I would be doing something for my country, and I would be involving myself in an assuredly non-Christian activity. I saw it as something which would voluntarily inject me into that outside world which my friends were already experiencing in their day-to-day life in offices.

It was effective. During the next two years I learned a great deal of practical use should there ever be a nuclear attack. We learned first aid; how to rescue people from demolished buildings; how to overcome radiation and much else. So on October 8th, 1952 it was with some confidence that I telephoned the authorities at Harrow and Wealdstone when there was an horrific railway accident at the main line station there. I offered my services as a trained member of the civil defence, and I was politely but firmly told that I wasn't wanted: they said that the matter must be left to the professionals. It seemed to me that this was exactly the kind of disaster for which we had all been trained – and now we were told we were of no use. I came home that evening quite despondent. As I relaxed, I picked up the local newspaper to find a report that a new Royal

Naval Reserve unit was being formed at Northwood. It encouraged anyone interested to apply for details.

After my abortive experience with the civil defence, I thought that the Royal Navy sounded far more attractive, so I applied. I found that the unit (to be known as HMS *Northwood*) would be a handmaid to the NATO High Command, whose Northwood headquarters were situated in HMS *Warrior*, at the same location as HMS *Northwood*.

To my surprise I was accepted, and joined as a naval rating – with the assurance that there would not be any possibility of promotion. It was a surprise therefore to discover only two years later that I was before a selection board for a commission. That was the start of twenty-seven years' fascinating service with the reserve, most of the time working with the Naval Control of Shipping, and ending up as a lieutenant commander in charge of NATO Naval Records. Shortly before compulsory retirement on grounds of age, I was awarded the Reserve Decoration.

It was a good experience throughout. Certainly it placed me in the 'world': in it . . . but not of it! On those dining-in nights, when dinner was taken in the officers' mess, it was necessary to remember that discussion was taboo on three subjects: politics, sex and religion! Sitting next to a stranger in the mess, I would often be asked what job I did in civilian life. This started a conversation about Billy Graham: not, you note, about 'religion'. And if the natural course of conversation led to the question: 'What does he really believe?', you were still talking about Billy Graham and not about religion. So there were some very helpful and useful discussions in the mess.

There were some amusing situations. Each year we would have an Admiral's Inspection. The whole unit was paraded, and the admiral would move up and down each row, talking to most of the officers and ratings. He would usually have a fairly lengthy conversation with each officer. So often, when he reached me, the admiral of the day would say: 'And what do you do in civilian life?' I would reply: 'I work for Billy Graham, the American evangelist, sir!' 'Oh yes!' he would reply, and then move on to the next officer. One day, the inspecting admiral was Admiral Sir Peter Hill-Norton, a Christian man. He asked the same question, and our conversation lasted longer than any other. All my colleagues crowded around me afterwards: they wanted to know what had interested the admiral so much.

On our retirement, Captain Glanville Hart (my commanding officer for much of the time I served) decided that it would be a good idea to keep the retired officers in touch with each other. Accordingly he has painstakingly organised a series of events each year to which we are all invited. It has enabled contacts made in the service days to be continued thereafter. It was an excellent plan.

In the middle of the time I served, I had to take two years' leave of absence when I rashly decided to contest a parliamentary seat. It was in my radical days, and I was adopted as the prospective Liberal candidate for Harrow East. A few months afterwards there was a scandal involving the sitting Member of Parliament for Harrow East and a by-election was required. My local constituency party would not allow me to contest the seat, although I felt that I had a good chance. I had many friends in the district and was fairly well known. There could have been a backlash from the misdemeanours of the present member and we might have reaped the benefit. So I fell out with my committee and moved from Harrow East to the constituency of Bedford. They had a far more active and forward-looking constituency Liberal Party and they worked very hard for the next General Election.

My opposition there was Christopher Soames, at the time Minister for War in the Conservative Government. He was Winston Churchill's son-in-law, so I had a pretty impossible task. None the less, we pulled out all the stops. I had a Christian agent, and several Christian committee members. At the time, it was customary for Liberal candidates to lose their deposit; certainly my three predecessors had all lost theirs. In the event, my deposit was saved by a comfortable margin, and I got a bigger ovation when that happened than Christopher Soames got when he was re-elected!

During the election, I was canvassing a farmer out in the fields, and I referred to the danger of World War Three. He replied: 'They cain't be expectin' no war, Mr Rowlandson, 'cos they made old Soames War Minister!' The three candidates would meet in the evening, and share the stories that each had told about the others. There was quite a camaraderie among the three of us. But all that nonsense had to come to an end when I was invited to join the Billy Graham team, because it would have lent a political image to Billy's work if I were still involved as a parliamentary candidate. It was fun though, while it lasted.

Throughout the period from 1949 to around 1983 I was also involved at arm's length in the businesses inherited from my father.

He had left an interest in the firm to his colleague, my successor Horace Dales. My father always said that I put in 50 per cent of the business, the capital aspect: Mr Dales put in the other 50 per cent, the labour. In looking after his own interests, Mr Dales also looked after mine. Throughout those years we used to meet for lunch once a week, to review plans and problems related to the business. It was a printing and stationery house (Messrs Chas Davy & Co. Ltd) with a factory in Rosebery Avenue and a retail outlet in the City. It was highly profitable, and was very well run by Mr Dales.

It was odd that Marilyn's father should also have been a printer. For Marilyn it was not at all strange to enter the premises of Chas Davy: the smell of a printshop was the same on both sides of the Atlantic. Odder still was the fact that her brother Bud also became a printer and, in due time, our younger son Julian entered the printing trade, with the Christian firm of Dudley Stationery. Sometimes we wondered if printer's ink, rather than blood, flowed in the veins of our family.

There came a time when Mr Dales's retirement loomed, and we thought about putting our sons into the business. They had expressed an interest and would, I think, have done well. I insisted that if they were to be brought in, they should start on the factory floor and learn the business from the bottom up. However, the union in the factory was very strong, and they threatened industrial action if our sons came in on the factory floor. So we determined to bring them straight in to the executive office – only to be threatened with industrial action on the grounds of privilege. It was a no-win situation, so we decided that the only thing to do was to sell the business as a going concern. Five years later, the business went bankrupt and all the union staff lost their jobs! With good management, it need never have happened. It had always been a profitable business. But through the foolishness and intractability of the staff, there were many left unemployed as a result of the bankruptcy.

My father had also a number of family companies, managing various properties in Hackney. The Hervy Rowlandson Estates Ltd were managed, very efficiently, by my cousin's son Richard Rowlandson, and he kept a tight rein on all their operations. We owed a lot to him for the excellent result which followed the disposal of the companies in the mid-eighties. On his advice, and to consolidate a situation which was likely to become unprofitable, we negotiated to sell the properties. I enjoyed the brief years of working together with Richard Rowlandson and my cousin, Christopher Lambourne. I counted those days as some of the highlight experiences of family relationships. Richard's expertise always impressed me, and I often coveted the gift he had for running the companies. Had I had but a little of his experience in my own affairs, I am sure I would have made more of them than I did.

Then, in 1971, I was nominated as a magistrate by Major-General D. J. Wilson-Haffenden, and Bishop A. W. Goodwin Hudson. My appointment was to the Gore Division of Middlesex (the Benches of Harrow and Hendon Courthouses). This was a new experience for me. In many ways, it replaced my involvement in everyday events which was no longer possible in RNR. I served until 1981 on those Benches, finishing up as chairman of the Rota Committee, and deputy chairman of the Domestic Panel. In that year I successfully applied to be transferred to the Tendring division in Essex (Clacton-on-Sea Courthouse) as we were about to make our home in Frinton, moving house from London. I had the unusual experience of sitting for the last time in Harrow on December 29th, and for the first time in Clacton fifteen days later on January 13th. Usually there was a time in purdah after an application to transfer. But Clacton was short of magistrates and they were glad to have me. I transferred also to the Juvenile and Domestic Panels, becoming deputy chairman of the Domestic Panel five years later, and deputy chairman of the Bench in 1990.

In 1960, I was invited to join the council of Trans World Radio, a Christian missionary radio station, operating from studios in Monte Carlo (using the transmission facilities built during the war by Adolf Hitler!). Their offices at the time were in Croydon. Fifteen years later, I was appointed chairman of the board in Britain. Trans World Radio had a magnificent ministry to Eastern Europe, the full results of which did not become apparent until the Iron Curtain was lifted and the separation from the Eastern Bloc countries ended in 1990/91. It then became clear that the ministry of Trans World Radio had contributed in no small measure to building up and maintaining the secret church in the Soviet Union, and in the Eastern Bloc satellites. A strong, thriving church emerged, many members of which told of the strength they had derived from the broadcasts.

The Keswick Convention appointed me as their secretary in January 1979. Billy Graham had generously said that I might accept this work in addition to the work of the London office, and that I could operate from the London BGEA office. I was to give two days a week to Keswick, but by the time the BGEA office closed in 1987, this had grown to almost four days a week.

My time with Keswick I count as some of the happiest and most productive of all my work apart from that with Billy Graham. I had a wonderful council to work with and in Canon Alan S. Neech a chairman who was supportive, gracious and encouraging. One thing struck me about Keswick over all other concerns in which I had been involved: the commitment of the council was such that we almost always had a hundred per cent turnout of the members. This was a tremendous indication of support for the secretary.

In due course, Alan Neech retired, and the Reverend Philip Hacking took his place. The pace changed; the commitment grew. Philip had an idea for a building on our site and this vision came to fruition in 1987. Gently he led Keswick into the later twentieth century in preparation for the twenty-first. The message was sacrosanct; the 'package' changed. Music progressed from a simple piano to – at first – the All Souls Orchestra. But that was too big a jump for the Keswick people and was almost a disaster. Instead, we brought in the Saltmine Band, and later Roger Mayor with a specially assembled musical ensemble. These were exactly right. We introduced soloists too: Anne Williams from Sheffield whose lovely, flowing and melodious voice was a great attraction to the Keswick people, then Frank Boggs from Atlanta, Georgia, and most recently Paul Sandberg from Huntington Beach in California. Paul is my brother-in-law, so I risked the charge of nepotism! His beautiful voice complemented the Keswick message. The average age of the council dropped, and there was a greater willingness to experiment – though always with the assurance that the message would not change.

The fourteen years I spent with Keswick (I retired after the convention in 1992, when the offices moved to the new building in Keswick) were among the most memorable of all my Christian service. This was chiefly due to those with whom I was associated among the trustees, the council, the speakers and the staff.

Marilyn and I have been blessed with a loving and supportive family. Each of them, in their own way, has come to a personal faith in the Lord Jesus Christ. Gary had many traumatic experiences in his early life. We sent him to boarding school at too young an age: he had schooling problems right through until he finished up at a comprehensive school in Harrow. He was a late developer and demonstrated his capabilities by gaining a teaching diploma and, later, his BD degree at Oak Hill College when he entered the ministry of the Church of England.

He met and married Diana English. Diana was the daughter of Peter and Rosemary English of Norwich. Peter had been one of the boys who came on the very first Venturers Cruise in 1946. The following year he was sent home from the cruise with mumps. We did not see him again until many years later when he was standing on the jetty at the Norfolk Broads Yacht Club in Wroxham. As the cruise came in to moor he hailed us: 'Do you happen to have a man called Henry Hole with you?' I told him that we did, and he introduced himself to me. It was quite a surprise. Later his family came to Frinton for a summer holiday and Diana was one of those who attended Spre-e '73. We noticed then that Gary was spending a fair amount of time with her.

Later that year we were going to America, and I suggested to Marilyn that maybe Gary would like to invite Diana to come with us. Had our daughter Cherylyn still been alive, she would have travelled with us, so it was possible to invite Diana to make up the family number. Shortly after I had mentioned this to Marilyn, I was packing to go on the STS *Sir Winston Churchill*. I had gone regularly to serve as purser on the Sail Training Association ships. On this occasion, I had invited Peter English to sail with me as assistant purser. I said to Marilyn that I might have an opportunity to broach the subject on the voyage.

As far as Gary was concerned, it was not so easy a matter to broach the subject. Marilyn was downstairs in our lounge, praying that some way might be found to talk to him. I was upstairs packing, when Gary sidled into the room. 'Dad, could I ask you something?' he said. 'Do you think that there might be a possibility of someone coming to America with us?' This opened the door for me to say that we had been thinking about that too – and what about Diana? We took these events to be confirmation that this plan was the Lord's will. I asked Peter on the voyage if he would allow Diana to come with us and he was very happy to concur. We had a happy time in the USA, and two years later Diana and Gary became engaged and they were married shortly before Christmas in 1976. A few years later, they presented us with our first grandson, Timothy James, who was born in July 1980.

Cherylyn had been a great blessing to our family, and had attended Heathfield School in Harrow. She was also deeply involved in the Girl Crusaders Union bible classes, and was a regular attender at their summer camps. She was also an active member of the Campaigners, through whom she undertook the work for her Duke of Edinburgh's Gold Award.

Eventually she went to St Paul & St Mary College in Cheltenham to qualify as a teacher, and it was during her last year there that the accident occurred which took her from us. A few weeks later, we held a thanksgiving service for her life in the chapel of the college. Many of her fellow-students took part in the service, and it was clear that her life had been a blessing to many – and in her death there were those who found life in Christ.

Julian was born while I was away at Keswick. Before I became secretary to the convention, I was there most years either with an exhibition for the Billy Graham Evangelistic Association, or running a hotel party for the Evangelical Alliance. In the hotel in which I was staying, the proprietor's daughter, Susan, came bounding up the stairs early on the first Saturday morning. 'There's a telephone call for you, Maurice,' she said. I dashed downstairs to hear that Marilyn had been safely delivered of a son.

When he was old enough, he went to my old school, Belmont, which was the junior school for Mill Hill School. He had a rough time there, to some extent persecuted because of his faith. Like Gary and Cherylyn before him, he had been deeply involved in Crusaders and had come to a real and personal faith. This showed in his life, and that influence was a problem at school. As a result his marks were rather like mine . . . pretty poor! So when it came to the common entrance exam for the main school, he did not make the grade. It was a worry and concern to us. We didn't know what was best for him.

One day, Marilyn was praying to the Lord for guidance. Suddenly it came to her: why not try Monkton Combe School in Bath? She phoned me at the office and told me of this inspiration. I replied that the school would undoubtedly be full. Nevertheless, we decided to try. To our surprise they agreed to take him as a boarder and for him it was the best thing that could have happened.

If he wasn't at a meeting of the Magic Society, it was the Printing Society. If it wasn't the music or the plays, it was the Caving Society – the last to our continuing concern and worry.

But he loved it. When he came to leave Monkton Combe, the headmaster, Richard Knight, wrote to me:

> I am sure he has learned a good deal about buckling down to the uncongenial; even though his natural exuberance convinces him that it will all come right on the night. I just hope that the examiners will not pass too harsh a verdict; for, as he must in his heart realise, he has very far to go to any pretence at literacy. I have grown very fond of him, exploited his good nature in all kinds of ways, and cannot quite think how Monkton will manage without him!

Julian grew up to be the fellow-sailor in our family. His first sail was in my little Coypu dinghy when he was two and a half years old. He loved curling up under the front counter, and on one occasion came back from sailing almost blue with cold. But he loved it – and has ever since. A year or so later, Marilyn brought him to visit the Venturers Cruise in Norfolk. Julian was let loose in a sailing dinghy and was quickly sailing up and down the dyke – single-handed! He had learned the essential technique simply from watching others.

So it was a blessing for him when he found himself a lovely wife whom he taught to sail on their honeymoon. Fiona was the daughter of a local medical practitioner in Kenton, and attended the same church as Julian. How fortunate we were to have so lovely a daughter-in-law once again, and we were thrilled for Julian. In April 1991 she presented us with our fourth grandchild, Matthew John, and we were delighted both for ourselves and for them. They introduced him to sailing when he was only three months old, and in August 1991 he spent his first day on my boat.

Jacqueline – who prefers to be called Jacky – put us through no end of a trauma when she had an accident in 1982. Before that, she had first followed her sister to Heathfield but had constantly plagued me to allow her to go to Clarendon School, which was then located in Abergele, North Wales. We thought that she had seen what a good time her brother was having at Monkton Combe, and felt that she was missing out. But we feared that if she did leave Heathfield and go to Clarendon, she might live to rue the day. We had a let-out, however: I told her that Abergele was too far away for us to send her to Clarendon School. We would never see her if she went there.

Then one day, there was news in the paper that Clarendon school had burnt to the ground! How glad we were that we had not sent her there. We were vindicated – at least, so we thought. A few weeks later, Jacky came to me and said: 'Dad, where is Bedford?' I told her that it was about twenty-five minutes up the motorway. 'Not very far away from home, then?' she persisted. I confirmed that it was not. 'Good!' she said. 'Now I can go to Clarendon: they've just bought a new property at Haynes, near Bedford!'

We learned that you can't win with a determined person. Clarendon it was – and as with Julian's choice, it was exactly right for Jacky. She loved it there and had a wonderful time. Her schooldays were certainly happy days for her.

Like her two brothers, who had been Crusaders, and her sister before her, she was deeply involved in the Girl Crusaders Union, and spent time at their summer camps. She really enjoyed her involvement, and they in turn showed a real interest in her. The bible class played a big part in her own journey into faith, which culminated at the Keswick Convention where, in 1981, she stood in testimony of her desire to go into Christian service, wherever and doing whatever Christ may require of her.

Her career was to be in nursing and she did three years at Northwick Park Hospital (and its satellite hospital in Acton), loving every minute of it. She was a good nurse, and recognised as such by the senior nurses. They were as shattered as she when the accident occurred. They tried everything to rehabilitate her to nursing after she recovered and allowed her a whole year to succeed. To some extent she did, because she took, and passed, her hospital finals, but they would not allow her to take the State Registered Nurse finals for reasons they demonstrated to her. In the end, gently but firmly they told her she could not return to full-time nursing.

It was a shattering blow and, to recover, she spent a year at Capernwray Hall Bible School (where Gary had been in earlier years). She ended her time there with the award for the student who had done most to succeed. Back in London, Julian told her that his former housemaster at Monkton, now headmaster of Luckley Oakley School in Wokingham, was in need of an assistant matron. Julian suggested Jacky might apply. She did, and was successful. She spent a very happy year in Wokingham looking after the girls in the school. It was there that she realised she liked working with the smaller girls, and decided to attempt a career as a teacher. She applied to St Paul & St Mary College in Cheltenham (where her older sister had studied), and secured a place as a mature student, with a grant, for a four-year Bachelor of Education (Hons) degree. She graduated from that course in October 1990, following her marriage on April 1st, 1989 to Jeff Davies, a lovely Welshman who attended her church. Before she could get a full-time job in teaching, she had brought us new delight by presenting us with our third grandchild – and our first granddaughter – Rachel Anwen, who was also born in April 1991, a few days before her cousin Matthew.

We count ourselves inordinately blessed, both in our children and in their spouses. We constantly ask ourselves: 'What have we done to be so singularly blessed?' God has been good to us, and we are thankful to Him for the many blessings He has given to us.

As a family we have all been blessed too, in the mother – and wife – of the household. The story of the debt which both the children and I owe to Marilyn's part in the life of the family follows later. For her it has not been easy. She is a displaced person living in England. It was an immense step of faith for her, when she agreed to leave the land of her birth and come to live in Britain as my wife. She couldn't really have known what it would cost, but she was willing to accept the consequences.

There is a difference of attitude between the British and the Americans: we notice it dramatically, because we are so intimately involved. *Why* it should be so is hard to explain. Maybe it is an innate jealousy. The Americans seem to have so much more than the British, and the British look with envy on their way of life. One thing is clear: when the Englishman goes to America he is, by and large, appreciated, welcomed, the recipient of many warm invitations, and becomes the centre of attraction. Such was certainly my experience when I first went to America, and it has been repeated on every subsequent visit (except on those occasions when my travel has been restricted to New York or Los Angeles where the big city syndrome is paramount). On the other hand, when an American comes to England, he is cold-shouldered, treated with sarcasm, and confronted with a 'Why don't you go back to where you came from?' attitude.

At times, especially in the early days, there was a great language difficulty. People do say that the Americans and the British speak the same language – but don't you believe it. Take a simple sentence like 'I was mad about my flat.' In England that means 'I was thrilled with my apartment'; in America it means 'I was furious with my punctured tyre'!

So Marilyn has not found it easy, but by 1991 she had spent seventeen years in America and forty-three years in Britain. So which could more properly be counted as home? Her salvation has been in the enormous circle of friends which has formed around her – not least in the Christian Viewpoint lunches (with which she has been involved since the very beginning) and in the Community Bible Study classes, of which, for three and a half years she has been the teaching director. These opportunities of service have been an oasis.

For me, I have always counted her American nationality as one of her greatest assets. Over all the years I have encouraged her to retain both her American passport and nationality. Cherylyn was also an American because she was born in the USA and had an American passport; actually she had dual nationality, because her father was British. In the year we married, the law had recently been changed and Marilyn did not secure British citizenship by marriage. This was chiefly due to the large number of GI brides, many of whom returned with their husbands to live in the United States, but a fair proportion of whom remained to set up their homes and raise families in Britain. The law was necessary to prevent their husbands, and in my case my wife, from gaining the privilege of British citizenship automatically. (Nowadays the law has changed again.) Shortly after we were married I had to get a special letter from the Home Office to exempt her from the normal regulations (particularly relating to employment) which apply to foreign nationals. Even then, there were years when we were first married when she had to possess an alien's certificate.

The one person who always accepted Marilyn at face value was Tom Rees. From the time he first met her he loved and appreciated her and, until his death, always referred to her as 'my favourite American'. He was a great encouragement to us.

Once more the story would not be complete without some mention of our relatives and our closest friends. I had no brothers or sisters and consequently, when my parents died there was no family left except my aunts and uncles and cousins. Our closest relatives have been on my mother's side. She died when I was ten years old and two years later my father married her sister. So there was a very strong relationship with our family on that side. My cousin, Joyce Bell, in many ways replaced the sister I didn't have. She was often invited to come with the family on holiday and regularly spent Christmas with us. It was natural therefore that, when she grew up and married, Marilyn and I should find that she and her husband George were the relatives to whom we were closest.

Joyce and George have meant a lot to us over the years. They have been ready to be involved in many of our plans and programmes, and have often helped us out at the office in moments of crisis. We have enjoyed the times of fellowship that we have spent with them, and we have appreciated their love and support.

They came with us as participants on one of our Israel tours. Shortly afterwards they were enrolled by the Garden Tomb Committee in Jerusalem, to become volunteer and part-time custodians of the Garden Tomb in the city. For a number of years they travelled to Israel to fulfil this responsibility for longer or shorter periods, and it was a service which they greatly enjoyed. From time to time, when we took a tour group to Israel, there they were – in situ – and able to welcome us to the site. It was always a delight to visit them there.

Among our closest friends we number Cannon and Rita Payne. Cannon and I were Crusaders together as boys, and Rita was a member of the Youth Fellowship at our church. We were delighted when they met and fell in love, and for the many years since their marriage they have been the closest to us of all our friends. We have done countless things together: they have been the nearest to 'family' that we have had. They have spent holidays with us. Cannon has been involved in many of my programmes and activities, and Rita has worked with me in offices from the days of the Evangelical Alliance onwards. She moved on to work in the Billy Graham Association and, later, the Keswick Convention. Both of them have readily assisted in so many ways and when volunteer help was needed at Keswick to organise the special coaches, or to prepare meals for the speakers and council, they were right there to help. They have never said 'no' to any demands that we have made upon them, and they have been a great strength to us in many ways. We have shared together our times of joy; we have mourned together in times of sadness. Our friendship has endured and it has been very meaningful.

Mention has already been made of Henry and Doris Hole. His involvement with the Venturers Cruise has kept us in close fellowship. His advice and guidance in so many ways have been invaluable. I would have to say that his advice has prevented me from some of the excesses which I would otherwise have embarked upon. Equally, he has advised me on occasion to take a certain course, and his advice has always been sound. We have appreciated the friendship of the Holes over the years.

There are many others too numerous to mention. My father used to warn me about the dangers of establishing too large a circle of friends. I know his advice was well-founded, and in many ways he was probably right. But today we have a vast address book containing the names and addresses of all of our friends. They are a rich group: Venturers, Billy Graham team members, those from the Hildenborough Hall circle, Keswick council and speakers, ex-staff members, you name them. We thank God for every one of them. They have all brought an incalculable richness to our lives, and we have appreciated the part that they have played in our family life.

So, with family, friends, and other involvements, life has always been full of interest and challenge. There has rarely been a dull moment. There have been those times of sorrow, anxiety and stress but they have been cancelled out by times of joy, confidence and freedom. In it all, we have understood what Paul meant when he said: 'I have learned to be content whatever the circumstances' (Phil. 4:11). There is such a comfort resting in God's Word. To have that behind you in every experience of life is a wonderful asset.

1

Setting the Early Parameters

In a way, it could be said that it all started at Keswick. I was a young man of twenty-one when I was taken by my parents to the first post-war Keswick Convention. My attitude was one of tolerant boredom – with, perhaps, a slightly rebellious spirit. But there was pleasant company and beautiful scenery to see.

My rebellion showed up on the Tuesday when I opted out of the holy atmosphere of Convention Keswick. Alone, I cycled to the village of Threlkeld, up and over the hill and to the valley beyond. A hound trail had been advertised, and I wanted to see one. Arthur Ransome had referred to such an event in several of his Swallows and Amazons books. I was a fan of them, so it became important that I should see a hound trail – live!

The well-signposted field at Threlkeld was a hive of activity. Almost as soon as I had paid my entrance fee and entered the gate, I found many strange men with blackboards on easels. They were shouting out to one another and making the most remarkable signs with their hands. I watched for a while and soon twigged that these men were the bookies, and the figures on their boards were the odds.

I wandered around the various sites and gradually began to understand how it all worked. Eventually, I came to a board which declared that Red Rufus was worth thirty to one. There was a half-crown burning a hole in my pocket: it was that week's pocket money, but I felt tempted to try it on Red Rufus.

It was a fascinating race. The hounds followed a trail up hill and down dale. The trail had been laid earlier by a man dragging a sack filled with an aniseed concoction. How many miles he had tramped over the hills is anybody's guess, but the hounds were off the moment the man arrived back at the field. They followed the trail, as it were, in the reverse direction, bounding off with a frenzy of barking (baying, I suppose), encouraged by their owners.

I stood and watched as the hounds disappeared from view. Shortly they were in sight again, but way in the distance galloping up the side of a mountain. From there we watched them – the farmers and owners through their binoculars – as they traversed the hillside; from time to time they disappeared again in a dip, or in a valley, but soon they were back further around the mountainside.

The owners were getting excited, and calling out the name of the hound in front. Slowly but inexorably the name of Red Rufus began to figure more and more prominently. In the end he romped home a good twenty hounds' lengths in front of everybody else. I duly collected my £3.15 – and had a hard job concealing the fact that I had joined the *nouveau riche* on my excursion to Threlkeld.

In spite of that sinful excursion, the message of Keswick must have penetrated. Friday morning was the Missionary Meeting (nowadays called Worldview or the Christian Service Meeting). As I listened, everything gradually came together and it seemed as though the speaker was speaking directly to me. I was listening intently, conscious of the fact that by my side were my parents. They seemed engrossed in the meeting, as indeed they were. The speaker ended, and asked those who felt God calling them to devote their lives to His service to stand up.

There was an inner struggle: what would my parents think if I stood? What about my girl-friend back at home? But the call was real, and the inner struggle was soon completed. With a sense that it was the most right thing I had ever done, I rose to my feet along with many others. I did not know where such a move might take me – only that the future was now open to God. There was an assurance that He would direct me and show me the way to go.

I did not realise that my decision would cost me my girl-friend – but it did. Lonely days followed. Indeed, they were to last for the next three years. (Eventually God brought me to meet His choice as a wife – even if He did have to take me across the Atlantic Ocean to find her!) Despite the loneliness I also experienced a satisfaction that I had taken an all-important step. I knew instinctively that it would lead me to where He wanted me to go. It was another fifteen years before that became fully clear.

✼   ✼   ✼

On the journey home from Keswick I had been able to reflect upon my life so far. I recalled that my parents had told me that at birth they had given me to God to use as He would. They certainly did all they could to provide a happy Christian environment in our homes at Grange Park near Enfield, Mill Hill, and Frinton.

I had a conversion experience at seven years of age. A Japanese pastor, Pastor Segawa, had come to England to attend the summer conference of the Japan Evangelistic Band at Slavanka, near Bournemouth. In between the meetings he spent much time with me. He taught me origami; he told me stories of Jesus from the bible, and he played Snap with me incessantly. One day he said to me: 'Maurice, wouldn't you like to ask Jesus to come into your heart?' I didn't reply immediately.

That night, on August 23rd, 1933, when I went to bed I said a simple prayer: 'Lord Jesus, please will you come into my heart and make it new?' Before I went to sleep, I drew a picture of myself in bed, with Jesus leaving heaven en route to my heart. I was waiting for Him to come. Childish conception, maybe; but I was seven and the concept was real to me.

In later years I was to reflect upon what Pastor Segawa had said to me: 'Wouldn't you like to ask Jesus to come into your heart?' I was talking with Tom Rees about this on one occasion and he made a surprising response. 'I'm glad,' he said, 'that he expressed it like that. So often today we tell children to "give their heart to Jesus". That means giving him a heart that is sinful and unclean. Better to "ask Him to come into your heart". Then He can make it a new one, and a proper place for Him to dwell.' As I thought about it, it was a question of control. If I 'give my heart to Jesus', then the control is from without. If I 'ask Him into my heart', then the control is from within – and so much more relevant to daily living and the consciousness of His presence.

My parents were not denominationally minded: my father would worship where the Word was preached. If that meant the local Methodist, Baptist, Anglican or Congregational churches or even (for a short time) the Salvation Army, then that was where we went. So, from childhood, I never became a denominational bigot. I was at home in whichever church my parents happened to be worshipping in.

As far as my father was concerned, if the minister departed from teaching the Word then it was time to move on! Social issues were important to him but he firmly believed that as you taught the Word, men's hearts were moved by the Spirit of God without the necessity to be explicit from the pulpit.

My father's view was borne out many years later when Dr Billy Graham preached at the Harringay Arena. He rarely mentioned social issues yet out of that crusade came many effective social agencies inspired by men who had found Christ as their Saviour at the meetings.

I was about twelve years of age when we attended Westminster Chapel for the first time. Immediately after the service had ended, a steward from the upper gallery came down and introduced himself. His name was Oliver Gilbart-Smith. He was leader of a Crusader bible class in South London and had spotted my Crusader badge from a distance. Every Sunday thereafter, I always received a friendly wave and a cheerful smile from him. It meant a lot to me as a boy to feel that he was my friend. Our friendship developed further over the years: indeed, Oliver became my deputy chief steward during Billy Graham's Harringay crusade.

We were so impressed with the preaching of Dr G. Campbell Morgan, minister of Westminster Chapel in the 1930s, that we attended there on a regular basis. I am sure that much of the groundwork and teaching which culminated in the Call at Keswick started by my sitting under his ministry. They were rich days which – even as a teenager – I appreciated.

When the war broke out, travelling to London became impossible, so we turned to our local Congregational church in Mill Hill for worship. The Reverend (later Dr) S. Maurice Watts was the minister. He inspired me with a great love of evangelism and taught me a lot about the Christian life. There were gaps in his teaching, because he described himself as a liberal evangelical. Those gaps were carefully and irrevocably plugged by the teaching I received at the Crusader class. The two ministries complemented each other: God, in His goodness, made sure that I had a breadth of teaching which was to stand me in good stead in years to come.

My love of evangelism was aroused still further when the Forces Gospel Song Team from the USA visited London. Their ministry came like a breath of fresh air to evangelism-starved young people. This was an aspect of the gospel we had never seen before. Suddenly, to lead another person to Christ became exciting. The Christian life was made to look like an attractive option!

In 1945 I enlisted to be a steward at London's first post-war effort in evangelism. The Faith for the Times Campaign was held nightly in London's Royal Albert Hall. It had been organised by an ad hoc Committee of Christian Leaders who were concerned about the godless post-war society. My father was a member of that committee and he, along with others, had invited a team of six evangelists (A. Lindsay Glegg, Alan Redpath, Stephen Olford, Dr Frederick T. Ellis, Canon Colin C. Kerr and a young, as yet unknown evangelist, Tom Rees) to share the speaking, in rotation night by night.

I felt that these meetings were stereotyped and poorly organised. I shied away from bringing my friends in case they were accosted by little old men (as Tom Rees described them) who asked all and sundry: 'Brother, are you saved?' The meetings were well attended but left many of the workers – particularly younger ones like me – frustrated.

The week after the Faith for the Times meetings concluded, Tom Rees met with the organising committee and shared with them a plan which he had conceived. He proposed a month-long evangelistic campaign in Central London, at which he would be the sole evangelist. The committee did not react favourably to the idea and told Tom Rees that if he wanted to do that, he would have to go it alone.

Undeterred, Tom Rees took an incredible step of faith by booking the Central Hall, Westminster for the entire month of September 1945. He had no idea how he was going to pay for it or whether anyone would come! But by the end of September his faith had been rewarded: the meetings were an outstanding success and all the bills were paid. I will never forget this demonstration of the power of imaginative and unlimited faith. The Tom Rees evangelistic rallies were a refreshing contrast to what had gone before.

Tom Rees captured the imagination of young London, and they streamed to the Central Hall to hear him. He led the meeting, interviewed participants, conducted the singing (from time to time he even sang a solo), preached and addressed those who responded to his invitation to accept Christ.

The singing was lively; often unexpected things would happen. Tom might stop you after the first few words of a hymn. He would clap his hands and say, 'No, no, no! You must come in at the very first word.' And he would start us all over again, until we had it right. Sometimes we would sing 'What a friend we have in Jesus' and after the second verse, he would stop us and sing (in his wonderful Welsh baritone):

> Said a robin to the sparrow
> I would really like to know
> Why it is these human beings
> Rush about and worry so.
> Said the sparrow to the robin
> I just think that it must be
> That they have no heavenly Father
> Such as cares for you and me.

Then it was back to the last verse. It was captivating and different. There was laughter, enthusiasm and, above all, real communication with the audience.

When it came to the scripture reading it was recited rather than read because Tom Rees knew much scripture off by heart. In later years, when he ran a long series of Saturday night meetings in the Royal Albert Hall, all of those invited to present the scripture were adjured to learn it by heart and to recite it. This fell to me on several occasions, and I have to confess that I had the words typed out on a five-by-three-inch card which I kept folded in my hand – in case my memory should fail me. It never did, and those scriptures remain in my memory today.

A week after the Central Hall meetings concluded I received in the mail a beautifully engraved full-colour card in which, in his own handwriting, Tom Rees expressed his thanks for my support and faithfulness. He included the reference of a text and the illuminated cover declared 'How Good is the God We

Adore'. I was overcome that a man as busy as Tom Rees should take the time and effort to express his thanks – personally – to a small and insignificant participant like me. But it made its mark upon me, and was demonstrative of the importance he attached to personal relationships.

It was in August 1946 that I told Tom Rees of my Call at Keswick. He was delighted to hear my news. Thus encouraged I added: 'I believe I've been called to be an evangelist.' Tom replied: 'That's great, Maurice. How many people have you spoken to about Christ today?' He saw my hesitation and added: 'Well, this week?' Again hesitation. 'This month?'

He then went on to give me some sound advice. 'Maurice, I don't believe God has called you to that particular ministry. An evangelist has such a passion for souls that he cannot let a day pass without speaking to someone about Christ. From what I've seen, I believe God has called you to be one of His administrators and leaders.'

Tom went on to show me Romans 12:8 and 1 Corinthians 12:28 – that each of us has a gift from God, which may be the gift of administration. It is up to us to identify what our gift may be; then we must develop it and use it to the best of our ability in His service. It was a mini-sermon just for me, and I appreciated the time and advice that he gave. We parted after he had committed me to the Lord in prayer.

About a month later Tom Rees telephoned to ask me if I had ever thought of leaving business and going into full-time Christian service. If so, he said, he would like me to consider joining him on the staff at Hildenborough Hall.

At the time, I was working as my father's assistant in his busy printing and stationery company. I told my father about the invitation. His natural reaction was one of disappointment. He had seen me as following him in his business. We agreed to 'put out a fleece' and to see if God was in this plan. He suggested that it would be appropriate to ask God to send along the right person to fill the vacancy which would be created if I left him.

My father advertised for a personal assistant, and within hours he received an application from a Mr Horace Dales, a Christian man, Crusader and chartered accountant by profession. After interview, he seemed exactly right, and an offer was made to him which he accepted.

The proof that this was God's hand did not come until many years later. Mr Dales remained with the company for the rest of his working life. He became a close friend and confidant to me. After the death of my father he assumed full control of the business in the way that my father, in his Will, had planned. At the time, however, it needed both a sense of faith and sacrifice to believe that it was the answer to our prayer, and the response to the 'fleece' we had been seeking.

Shortly after Christmas 1946 I moved to Hildenborough Hall, a large mansion in the Weald of Kent. I had first heard about Hildenborough at a Tom Rees rally in the previous year. Tom had asked everyone at the rally if they would like to spend a whole week in this sort of meeting and atmosphere. He then told how he had purchased Hildenborough Hall as a venue for holiday bible conference weeks. The property had been furnished by a miracle – and it even had its own cows! This meant that cream, a real luxury in those days, would be available for all. I can vividly recall the enthusiastic audience roaring 'yes' in response to Tom's invitation. Thus was born Britain's first bible holiday conference centre.

In the summer of 1946 for the first time ever, I had attended one of these bible weeks with a group of young people from my church. Those who came were Betty Childs, Mair John, Joan King and Joan Peppiatt. We had a remarkable week. All of us were deeply and spiritually blessed as Stephen Olford, the guest speaker, unfolded God's Word to us and shared some of his own intimate testimony. At the end of the week our group wrote a poem which we presented to Stephen:

> There was a young fellow called Steve
> Who lives to give souls their reprieve
> He led us to Jesus
> And *He'll* never leave us
> In this we all firmly believe.

Subsequently it became clear that the poem was true to experience.

Richard Bennett, now a bible expositor and evangelist, was converted during that same conference. He was so excited that he came downstairs two steps at a time and ran full tilt into Rebecca Mitchell (one of the waitresses at Hildenborough) who was coming out of the dining room with a trayful of tea dishes. The whole lot went flying across the hallway and were smashed to smithereens. Tom Rees later said that if everyone who was converted at Hildenborough was that exuberant, he would be bankrupt in weeks.

The Tom Rees I met as a boss was every bit as commanding a personality as the Tom Rees I had seen on the platform at Central Hall. One quickly developed an overwhelming respect for his methodical approach to the business of running Hildenborough and evangelistic crusades and his utter integrity at every turn. Furthermore, he trusted his staff and gave them responsibility in a manner which others would have hesitated to do.

Tom Rees was on easy terms with his staff, but nevertheless found it necessary at times to draw the line. Privately, he was 'Tom' at all times, but in the business of Hildenborough he was always 'Mr Rees' first, and as the years went by he became affectionately known as 'the Boss' to everyone, including his wife.

Tom worked hard himself and demanded the same devotion to duty from all those who worked with him. He made few mistakes, and sometimes seemed a little intolerant of those who were less careful. But one quickly learned that it was not intolerance but training he was giving – and a desire that everything should be done 'decently and in order'. Looking back today, I am extremely grateful to him for all that he taught me.

One Monday morning, I arrived for work to be greeted by the Boss, who asked how I was. I replied: 'OK – but it's Monday morning, you know!' Tom turned on his heel and said emphatically: 'Don't let me ever hear you say that again! "This is the day that the Lord has made: we will *rejoice* and be glad in it!" ' I have to admit that I've never had a Monday morning feeling since – because if ever it threatened, I remembered that, weekday or Sunday, it was still the Lord's day with cause to rejoice in all that He has done for us.

A classic example of Tom's concern and leadership came in 1948 when a party of us were about to set off by car to hear an unknown American preacher called Billy Graham. (Tom Rees had been recommended to hear this young man by Bev Shea, who had been Tom's soloist during his Winnipeg campaign earlier that year.)

It was Saturday, March 31st, 1948 and Jean Rees offered to drive a party of us up to London for the meeting at Westminster Chapel. Lex Smith (the Hildenborough pianist), two of the girls on the Hildenborough staff and myself all wanted to go. We were all sitting in the car outside the front door of Hildenborough, when Tom Rees came out and tapped on the window. Jean wound it down and Tom chastised us all over the attitude of mind in which he guessed we would be going to the meeting. He knew that we were critical: the preacher was American, the name 'Youth for Christ' offended us because it clashed with our 'British Youth for Christ' title, and there was a general feeling – could any good thing come of it? Tom wagged his finger at us and told us not to be critical, but to pray for the meeting, and for the preacher in particular. 'Now *pray* for this man Graham,' he said. 'He may have a special calling from the Lord and if you must attend the meeting, then pray for him and for those attending.' We were duly chastened!

The journey to London was certainly eventful. Jean Rees suffered from fibrositis and this caused her to lift her left shoulder sharply to relieve the pain. We were driving to London on slightly icy roads, and every time she lifted her shoulder in this way, the car swerved violently – often skidding on the ice. As we approached the outskirts of London, Jean suddenly said: 'Let's pray for the meeting.' I half-expected her to pull over to the side of the road while we engaged in this spiritual exercise, or at least to allow *us* to do the praying . . . but no! She started praying immediately and I stole a quick glance at her, to discover that she was praying *with her eyes open*! This had never happened to me before. It was literally an eye-opener. I thought that, to engage in prayer to the Almighty, you either adopted the non-conformist slouch or knelt at your chair – but certainly with your eyes closed. And it was embarrassing if you peeked to find that someone else was peeking too. You suddenly found you had a fly in your eye which you were flicking out.

But to see someone engage in a prayer meeting while driving a car was a completely new experience for me. For the first time, I realised what the hymn-writer meant when he wrote: 'when I breathe I pray'. This was natural and real. It was simply talking to our Father – as though He was present in the car with us. From that moment on, prayer took on a new meaning for me.

The meeting, in Westminster Chapel, was full to overflowing. There were four Americans on the team. Stratton Shufelt was the song leader; strangely enough, I remembered that I had met him before the war when, as a boy, I had been taken to hear Dr Harry Ironside from Chicago. He and Stratton Shufelt (who was his song leader) had come to have tea at our house. The others in the party on this occasion were Chuck Templeton, Torrey Johnson and Billy Graham. It was a lively and bright meeting, and in due course Billy Graham stood up to preach. Within minutes he had captured our full attention.

He was totally different from what we had expected. We found him thoroughly absorbing and were riveted by what he was saying. He told us that he was President of a bible school in the city of Minneapolis, Minnesota, right in the heartland of America. The Lord had laid upon his heart the needs of Britain in a very real way. 'I want to make it possible,' he said, 'for ten men to come to that college – at our expense – to take a year of special training, and then to return to Britain to work in evangelism here.' Lex Smith and I looked at each other. He, like me, had been contemplating going to the States for training, but had run into the same financial problem as myself. Suddenly it seemed that this might be the answer.

After a powerful address, and a well-responded-to appeal to accept Christ, Billy Graham turned to leave the platform. As he did so, Lex and I made our way around the podium and accosted him as he came down the steps. We told him of our desire to accept his invitation. He wrote our names on the back of an old manilla envelope which he crumpled up and stuck into his pocket. 'That's the last we'll ever hear of that,' I said to Lex somewhat cynically.

But, of course, it wasn't. The parameters were now set. The stage was ready: all the participants were in place. God's timing was exactly right, as it always is. He had us in the right place, at the right time, to respond in the right way to the right man. It was the start of a lifelong association with the world's greatest evangelist, who happens to have been alive in our time . . . Billy Graham. There was much more to follow – a whole book full!

2

The Thin Gold Line

God has His own way of planning our lives. The future is often mysterious, unknown and dark. We puzzle about the route we should take. Then, when the future becomes the past, we look back and see that there has been that thin gold line running through our life. God ties together a great many projects and we can see His hand in them all.

It was certainly like that in my relationship with the work of Billy Graham.

In August 1948, I travelled to Minneapolis via New York and Chicago. Before I left New York, I was to have my first experience of American generosity. On the ship from England, I had shared a cabin with an American dentist. His sister was with him on the ship, and the three of us did many things together. On arrival in New York, I stayed for three nights at the Prince George Hotel. One day I received a telephone call from this dentist, asking me to meet him at a store on Fifth Avenue. When we met, he told me that he and his sister wanted to give me a welcome present to the USA. He had remembered that, on the ship, I had said that the thing I would miss most at college was my typewriter. So he took me into the store and asked me to choose a portable typewriter to take with me. Typically English, I looked for the cheapest I could find. But no: 'You must have the best,' he insisted. I came away with a Royal Magic Margin portable – quite the most outstanding of such typewriters at the time.

My route from New York took me to the north of the State of New York, to Buffalo, the town in which the Niagara Falls are situated. I saw them on my twenty-third birthday. That weekend I attended my first church in the USA, the Cazenovia Park Baptist Church in Buffalo. The minister was Pastor J. Palmer Muntz.

Four experiences from that church were significant. First, I was astounded to see people sitting in church reading their newspapers. I did not know about the all-church Sunday school, and that this was the break between attendance at the Sunday school and the morning worship service. It seemed very strange – and I must say that I never saw it happen anywhere else in the USA.

Secondly, I wondered about the hymns: would I know any of them? It was a delight, therefore, to discover that the first hymn was 'O Worship the King'. The organist played the first few opening notes – C F F G A – and I felt home and dry. But the next few notes were different – not C F G E F, but F B flat B flat A G! I was later to discover that there is yet another tune in the USA starting with the same five notes but continuing A B flat C B flat A G F! It is customary in the USA for every worshipper to be given a hymnal which includes the music, so had I looked at that first, I would have known.

Thirdly, I filled in a little card: where had I come from . . . and where was I going to? Nowadays we have these in Britain too; but then, it was new and different. Later, when I was to arrive in Minneapolis, I received a letter from Dr Curtis B. Akenson, minister of the First Baptist Church in the city, to say that he had had a letter from Cazenovia Park telling them that I was en route to Minneapolis. Dr Akenson invited me to come to First Baptist Church, 'if I was wondering which church to attend'. I was most impressed with this inter-state, inter-church follow-up! Strangely enough, I was to discover that First Baptist Church was the church of Northwestern College and hence associated with Dr Billy Graham.

Finally, I discovered in later years that Dr Muntz was involved in the ministry of Billy Graham and, as an associate of the team in London, I was to meet Palmer Muntz at Heathrow Airport and entertain him while he was in town.

The journey from Chicago to Minneapolis was on the '400 Express' which did the 400 miles in 400 minutes. I had very little left of the twenty-five pounds which was all a generous post-war British Government would allow travellers to take with them outside the UK. But I needed to stay somewhere overnight in the new and strange city. I took a taxi from the station and gave the driver instructions to drop me at a reasonably cheap hotel. He took me to the Curtis Hotel – at that time, quite the best and most expensive in the twin cities of Minneapolis and St Paul! I was inexperienced and imagined that the taxi driver had taken me to a cheap hotel, although this one looked very nice. Perhaps, I thought, things were done differently in America. So I booked a room for one night and the next day found that it cost considerably more than the meagre resources which I had left. Money became a matter of urgency, and I prayed that God would show me what to do.

I did not check out when I left the hotel to go and register at Northwestern College. I suppose I thought that if the worst came to the worst the college would help – but that did not seem to be a very good start! However, on my walk from the hotel to the college, I passed a shop with a neon sign in the window: 'Loans . . . on your signature only!'

As I entered the shop I dared to hope that they meant what they said. One of the gentlemen came across to see if he could help me, and I told him that I wanted a loan of two hundred dollars. Somehow I think that must have been a rare sort of request, because he coughed and spluttered, and asked exactly what I meant. So I referred him to the neon sign in the window, and said that I wanted to take him up on that offer.

This provoked a long explanation that they did not mean what they said. Some sort of security was necessary – but with that provided, there were no other formalities: just your signature. I told him that there was nothing in the window about security and that, as an Englishman, I hoped he would stand by his offer. Upon this he excused himself, and went to talk with a colleague in the back office. Eventually, the two of them came out and the second man said to me: 'You know, we Americans are very hard-hearted people.' I told him I did not believe him – because if they were, they would not have sent the CARE packages to help war-torn Britain! This reply seemed to impress him. At any rate, he asked how much I wanted, and for how long. I told him two hundred dollars – 'though, while you are about it, you might as well make it three hundred'. I said I would need it until the subsistence allowance (which had been approved by the Treasury before I left) arrived from Britain. This would probably be in two or three weeks.

In the end, he gave me five hundred dollars 'on my signature only' – the extra two hundred was on his suggestion so that I wouldn't have to come back and see him again. So I was able to go back and check out of the hotel. The next day, the bank in Minneapolis sent a message to me via Northwestern College to say that they had received a draft from Britain, and would I come to collect the money or open an account? As I was due to receive about two-and-a-half thousand dollars (a sum large enough to last me through the whole of my schooling), I opened an account – but drew out five hundred dollars to give back to my 'loans on your signature only' friend. We remained good friends throughout my stay in Minneapolis.

When I arrived at Northwestern College I was met by the registrar, who took me to meet the business manager, a man called George Wilson. He was to help me with arrangements for my accommodation at the college. There were three weeks between my arrival and the start of school. George Wilson decided that I should go to the Medicine Lake Bible Camp for that period. It was a great decision, and I had a marvellous time getting orientated to the American way of life.

This camp was a totally new experience for me. It was in a delightfully wooded area on the shores of Medicine Lake (naturally!). Accommodation, including the dining room, shop, such lounges as there were, and the bedrooms, was in log cabin style buildings. Simple, basic, four walls and a roof: the floor was still the native earth. The weather was, of course, very hot – so the movement of air between the logs was welcome. In those cabins, that was all the air-conditioning you got. But in the vast auditorium there was good air-conditioning and it was most acceptable after the 110°F heat outside.

They taught me volley-ball at the camp, a great game that I enjoyed playing. I also learned that, by cutting the side of an individual cereal box, you could pour in the milk and sugar without the need of a separate dish! I learned to eat hot dogs, found that cold iced water was the most popular drink (sometimes flavoured and called Kool-aid), and joined the choir. Each evening we had superb bible teachers who came to address the thousand-or-so in camp. One night, towards the end, we welcomed a speaker who had just returned from Europe – Billy Graham! It was the first time I had seen him since the Westminster Chapel meeting where I had first received the invitation to come.

I spoke to him afterwards, and he said how glad he was that I was already here, and he hoped I was settling down OK. I got the impression that he had remembered me – but out of the thousands he had met since London it hardly seemed possible. I came to discover that this was a gift that he had. Certainly it made me feel as though I belonged: I was expected and the President of the college had recognised me! I was walking on air.

The registrar came often to the campsite to enquire about my welfare. He took me out several times, and on a couple of occasions George Wilson joined us. Later I was to work with that registrar in London during the 1954 Billy Graham Harringay crusade and later still we would work together when he was directing the London office of the Billy Graham Evangelistic Association. George Wilson (by then vice president of the BGEA) was to invite me years later to join the Billy Graham team as an associate. But my biggest mentor during those Medicine Lake days was Dr Harry Stam. He was the brother of John and Betty Stam, who had been martyred in China. I had read their story, and was deeply impressed with the loving, caring attitude shown to me by Harry Stam and his wonderful wife, Alma. Harry took me under his wing, and I spent much time in his company. He was then a professor at Northwestern, and responsible for the missionary training courses of the college. In years to come, my wife and I were often to entertain him in our London home.

One Saturday evening, George Wilson called at the Medicine Lake Camp and took me downtown to the Minneapolis Auditorium. He had organised one of a regular series of Youth for Christ rallies there, which attracted many thousands of young people from all over the twin cities. Always he had some special feature which would be the magnet to attract his audience. On this occasion he had one hundred grand pianos on the platform playing in concert – it was a fabulous sound! To a Britisher it was new and different, and it gave me an early insight into the mind of George Wilson. I learned the lengths to which he was prepared to go to evangelise. I never forgot that night.

There is another memory of my time at Medicine Lake which remains vivid. On a Sunday night, many of the young people piled into a large number of boats – rowing boats, motor-boats and sail-boats. In the dark, they moved out from the shore and dropped their anchors. Those of us remaining on the shore sang a chorus and, when we finished, there came an echo of the same chorus sung by those in the boats. We could scarcely see them on the starlit night: they were simply silhouettes against the moon. But the sound of their voices across the water was magic. So we carried on for about an hour, singing to and fro with a real sense of worship.

Eventually my time at Medicine Lake drew to a close and I enrolled at Northwestern. During the next nine months, I received enormous benefit from the training and the special series of courses arranged for the British students.

When I arrived at the college, it was still situated in the vast premises of the First Baptist Church. Dr W. B. Riley (who had founded the college) had been the pastor of the church, and it was natural that the college should grow up in its spacious accommodation. But by now, under the leadership of Dr Billy Graham, the college had expanded far beyond the capacity of First Baptist. During the previous year, new premises were being built and they were completed at the end of August 1948, in time for us to make the move from First Baptist to the new custom-built college in Willow Street. It was a site adjacent to Minneapolis's Loring Park (the Hyde Park of the city). The new premises and their surroundings were wonderful. They included many of the latest facilities for students, and a large and attractive chapel which doubled as an auditorium for the college.

George Wilson, the business manager, was responsible for the move. He discovered that quite the most expensive part was to transfer the extensive library some six or eight blocks from one location to the other – about seven streets away. He conceived a remarkable plan. One day, soon after the start of college, the entire student body of some 1,100 people was organised to visit the library on their way to school; there they collected an armful of books together with a coding which would correspond to the exact place on the new shelving where the books should be lodged. Having delivered the first load, the students went back and collected a second and third load – and by the time everyone had taken their three loads, the entire library had been moved . . . at no cost at all. The event made headlines in the Minneapolis paper.

When I left Medicine Lake it also meant that I now needed to move into accommodation at the school dormitories. Fireside

Lodge was the accommodation to which I was assigned, where there was a martinet of a house-mother, Miss Carey, who kept a strict and watchful eye on her charges. Furthermore, it meant living communally. This I had never enjoyed, but I realised I would have to make the best of it. So I moved all my things into Fireside – into a fairly small but not too unpleasant room.

There were many activities for freshmen during the opening week of the college year. One of these was the freshmen's concert. Lex Smith and I went together and sat next to each other. Freshmen had been invited to contribute to the programme and we had privately agreed that the Brits should not be dragging behind in this. Both of us had had experience of Christian concerts; Lex had been involved in Children's Special Service Mission beach missions and I had the Hildenborough experiences and Crusader concerts behind me. So we had been to see the organiser and each of us offered to do an item.

In the event, it turned out that we had been the first two to volunteer – so we were called first to take part. Lex was first, and he told an involved and very funny Scottish story. But the laughter was desultory and the applause at the end left me with the feeling that, somehow or other, my concert item must effect a breakthrough; otherwise we were in for a dull evening. My item was a funny song which Tom Rees had taught me (and it was often used at Hildenborough concert evenings):

A mother was bathing her baby one night
'Twas the youngest of eight – and a terrible sight.
The mother was tired, and the baby was thin
'Twas only a skellington covered with skin.
The mother turned rahnd for the soap off the rack
She was only a moment . . . but when she looked back
Her baby was gawn – and in anguish she cried:
'Oh where is my baby?' – and an angel replie-hied
'Your baby has gawn dawhn the plug-hole
Your baby has gawn dawhn the plug
The poor littl' thing was so scraggy and thin
It ought to've been bathed in a jug!
Your baby is really quite happy
And it won't need a bath never more!
Your baby has gawn dawhn the plug-hole –
Not lost, but gawn before!'

The whole song was sung in broad Cockney, a strange dialect for the Americans to understand anyway, and it was accompanied by many actions and much pathos. Normally it resulted in tumultuous applause and cheers: but at Northwestern, there was a little polite hand-clapping . . . and that was it!

Our ultimate embarrassment arose from the fact that every other item throughout the two-hour concert was spiritual! Very! There were sacred solos, testimonies, scripture recitations and prayer. Our contributions had been very much out of place. The concert after all had not been dull; it had become memorable. It was the first time we realised that we were living in a different culture – and that even though we spoke the same tongue, the language was different. There were other embarrassing experiences in the months ahead which arose from language differences.

Another important activity during that first week was the attempt to find employment. The school's employment office was ever ready to help, and sent me off on half a dozen wild-goose chases. I was not suitable for any of the jobs on offer. Many required American citizenship; others required special skills or were vacancies already filled. I came back to the employment office and, while I was waiting my turn, I picked up a leaflet entitled 'Our Students in Your Home'. It went on to describe how Northwestern students would live with a family and help with the cleaning and housework; rather similar, in fact, to the au pair situation in Britain today. I felt it was not beyond my capabilities – and it would get me out of the school's dormitory accommodation and enable me to live in an American home.

There was a vacancy! A Mrs Sargent who lived at 42 Park Lane, on the shores of Cedar Lake, wanted someone. She always preferred to have male students – and they were not easy to find. So I was despatched to her to be interviewed. Happily we immediately hit it off and later the same day I moved into her home. The next day I went to remove all my things from Fireside under the frosty eye of Miss Carey. She had been looking forward to instilling some American culture into this strange Englishman who had become part of her house!

Number 42 Park Lane was a lovely white wooden house. It had a ground floor, first floor and basement. My bedroom was in the basement, where I also had my own shower facilities. Park Lane was, at the time, one of the more exclusive areas of the twin cities, and the view across Cedar Lake from the house was wonderful. Everything in the house was of the highest standard, and Mrs Sargent was very house-proud. She liked everything to be kept sparkling and spotlessly clean, and she relied upon me to uphold her wishes in this.

Mrs Sargent taught me to clean, to cook, to wash clothes, to iron, to polish – and many other household chores. My schedule was to arise at 5.30 a.m. and leave for school at 6.15. First classes were at 7 a.m. By 12 noon all classes were ended, and the student body went off to earn money to work its way through school – a very much more satisfactory method than the system of grants which has grown up in the UK. All students in the USA are accustomed to this early start to classes, and to the expectation that they will finance themselves. Work generally finished after dinner (they always eat earlier in the USA) and by 7.30 p.m. I was ready to complete my study assignments before retiring to bed at around 11 p.m.

Mrs Sargent and her daughter Geraldine were delightful people. Mrs Sargent had been personnel officer at Dayton's department store (the Harrods of Minneapolis) but was now retired. Geraldine was in business in the city. Mrs Sargent became more than an employer – a fact which was demonstrated eighteen months later when, at my wedding in Minneapolis, she stood in the welcoming line in place of my parents who had been unable to come. I worked for her for three months before discovering that, while I was earning enough to live on, I was not able to put enough aside to buy my ticket home at the end of my college courses. It became necessary to find another job.

At first I tried supplementing what Mrs Sargent could pay me by selling magazines door to door on my days off. Then I got a job selling portrait photographs from door to door. The scheme was that I would sell a two-dollar coupon which would provide the purchaser with a twenty-five dollar colour portrait. In fact, the studio did the portrait free. They made their money on the extra copies which they felt sure their subjects would buy after they saw the finished result. So the two dollars I received became mine. I could, if I wanted, give the prospective purchaser a special offer and reduce the two dollars by as much as I wished. But then I received only the reduced amount. I sold a number of coupons at reduced prices – but the ultimate value was nil. Before I returned the book of coupons, I decided to take one for myself, and I went and had my portrait taken. It was so good that I just had to buy extra copies!

The final decision to move on from Mrs Sargent's came when she gave me a big painting job to do. Of all the things I dislike, painting was top of the list. It was the catalyst which prompted me to become serious about finding another job.

I prayed that the Lord would show me what I should do. I wanted to do what was right, and I sought His leading in this. One day, waiting for the bus to take me back to Park Lane after school, I looked round and saw a door with the words 'Hospitality House Christian Center' upon it. On impulse, I left the bus queue and went upstairs to ask if there was a job available. I was met by Verna Peterson, who was the personal assistant to the director. She listened to what I had to say, and slowly shook her head. 'Sorry,' she said, 'we have no vacancies of any sort.' Disconsolately I walked back down the stairs. Halfway down, I heard her calling me back. She told me she had had second thoughts, and maybe – if I was prepared to do *anything* – they could use me. Because I felt that this was where the Lord had led me, I instantly agreed and I made arrangements to start the following Monday.

Then I had to face the problem of telling Mrs Sargent. There were two factors. First, I felt I was letting her down; secondly, there was the selfish factor, that now I would have to move back to the school dormitory! I visualised the face of Miss Carey as I arrived back with all my things. Summoning up all my courage, I asked Mrs Sargent if I could speak with her.

As is so often the case, the Lord had prepared the way. She had already realised that I was looking elsewhere for work – and she had anticipated the reason why I wanted to see her. 'If you want to tell me that you have to stop working for me, Maurice, I quite understand. Geraldine and I had talked about this possibility, and there is no way we can pay you more – but we would like you to continue to regard our house as your home while you are here in Minneapolis!'

What more could I ask? For the rest of my time – and later, in the autumn of 1949, when I returned to get married, 42 Park Lane was home to me. As Tom Rees had said on that card in 1945, 'How good is the God we adore!'

Mrs Sargent found another young man to do the housework, and he was given the room next door to mine. There was one occasion when I was exceedingly naughty! This other young man enjoyed listening to loud music on his radio. Mostly it did not bother me, but when I was studying, it was very intrusive. I had asked him on a couple of occasions to turn it down a bit – but his memory seemed very short. He would turn it down, but the next day it was as loud as ever. About that time, I saw a mail order advertisement for a wire-free radio microphone. Basically, this microphone was the forerunner of today's radio microphone. This early model worked off a battery and could be tuned in to your radio with a little red knob at the side. As you completed the tuning, there was a squeak and a whistle – and then, with startling clarity, your voice came from the radio. It occurred to me that maybe I could tune it in to my neighbour's radio in the next room, and ask him over the microphone to turn it down. Instead, I found that the squeak and whistle so disrupted his listening that he turned his radio off altogether. One day I heard him complaining to Mrs Sargent that there was terrible interference on his radio in the basement. He put it down to the basement room, and from then on I was able to study in complete peace. If he reads this book, he may at long last discover what the interference was . . .

After school and lunch the following Monday, I presented myself for work at Hospitality House, ready to do anything. My first job? To clear out and paint the entire back office. I felt that the Lord was trying to tell me something – and I believe I got the message!

Within a week, and after that first painting job, I found early promotion accorded to me: I was asked to assist the director, George England. Here was another perfectionist. I had gone from Hildenborough Hall (HH) and Tom Rees, to Hospitality House (HH) and George England, and God was continuing the process of training me for His work. George was PR-conscious and called in the press the day I started with him, which resulted in an article in the Minneapolis *Star*: 'England comes to Minneapolis to see England'! The article started: 'England wanted England to come to England. But because of pressing duties England couldn't go. So naturally England has come over to see England.' How corny can you get! That was the first of more than a dozen articles which appeared in the next nine months, inspired by George England's promotional skills. 'All publicity is good publicity' he used to say, and he saw all publicity as good PR for Hospitality House.

If there was a similar centre in London, it would be in Leicester Square. In Minneapolis the building at 9th and Hennepin had a Christian bookshop in the basement. On the ground floor there was a Christian radio station ('1440 on your dial; the friendly family station, Minneapolis/St Paul. Stay tuned for good listening!'). The first floor housed the offices together with a restaurant (where, as George England said, you were more conspicuous if you didn't say grace), a Christian library, a film department, a chaplain in the juvenile courts, and a comfortable lounge for folk to come and relax in. On the second floor was the Christian Youth Center with a snack bar serving hamburgers, Cokes and sundaes; a juke box playing Christian music and a games room with ping-pong, shuffleboard, billiards, etc. On Sunday nights we held an after-church 'sing' in the youth centre and packed in more than a thousand kids (anyone from ten to twenty-five) week after week. To top it all off, there was a thirty-by-sixty-foot neon sign on the roof which bore a gospel text, changed each month. That was Hospitality House. It was sponsored by the Christian Business Men's Committee of Minneapolis as an answer to youngsters who wanted to be downtown, and among the bright lights. It was an ambitious and successful project.

I learned as much, if not more, from Hospitality House as I learned from the classes at school. The two together were complementary, and I felt sure that the Lord had put me there for a special purpose. They were full and busy days and I gained as many insights from meetings and film shows (which were all part of my assignment) as I did from working as head waiter in the restaurant (open all the week but where on Sundays we served more than 500 meals).

That experience taught me many things, so that today I realise how poorly we are served in restaurants. My waitresses at Hospitality House *never* had to ask who had ordered what at a table: the orders were always taken on a north, east, south, west basis (one wall of the restaurant was marked north wall). Orders were written down accordingly, north first. Simply by glancing at her order slip, each waitress always knew exactly what each person had ordered. Each waitress (we had no waiters) was trained to keep her eye open for customers who wanted more water, coffee or any extra items from the menu. 'Always look around' was the order of the day. Finally, the bill was always placed in front of the host at each table, with the final cup of coffee. You never had to wait for the bill. These simple rules would enable every restaurant in Britain to be more efficient and welcoming.

During the lunch and dinner hours I was in charge of six or seven waitresses in the restaurant. One day, passing at speed through the narrow passage between one of the dining rooms and the kitchen, I collided with one of the waitresses carrying a trayful of dirty dishes to be washed. They scattered all over the floor, and Marilyn Sandberg and I met for the first time as we retrieved them all – and we have been meeting over dirty dishes ever since, for in October 1949 she became my wife.

It was not quite love at first sight, but Marilyn was obviously flustered by the suave Englishman who was helping her. This was shortly before Christmas, and a few days later she asked me what I planned to do for the festival. I had no plans, and she conveyed an invitation from her parents to spend Christmas with them. It was one of the most delightful Christmases I ever spent. Thereafter, we spent much time together and I came to know her, her parents Ruth and Arvid Sandberg, and her brothers Bud and Paul very well. They were of Swedish stock, and smatterings of the Swedish language rubbed off on me. Swedish hospitality left nothing to be desired and Swedish coffee and cooking were magnificent! I left Minneapolis in June 1949 smitten, and shortly afterwards proposed – and was accepted – by letter. We were married on October 14th, 1949 in Minneapolis.

Meanwhile, back at school classes had begun in earnest. I had been enrolled in some seven subjects, and the lectures, study and assignments occupied most of my time at school and my spare time in the evenings. Shortly after school had started the president, Billy Graham, made an announcement that he had invited a Dr T. W. Wilson to join him as vice president of the school. He said that, because of his own heavy commitments as an evangelist, T. W. Wilson would take on the day-to-day responsibility for running the school. We met him shortly afterwards.

I didn't immediately remember that I had met him previously in London. During the days of the Gospel Song Team, he had been there as leader of a singing group known as the Couriers for Christ. I remembered his ministry, and was glad to know that he was now to be my vice president.

One weekend Lex, Dave Harrison (another student from Britain) and I had attended a meeting in a suburb of Minneapolis at which Billy Graham was the speaker. At morning chapel on Monday, T. W. Wilson reported to the school student body that it had been an exceptional meeting with people packed and jammed into the building.

Now we knew that was not true. There had been many empty seats. Already we suspected our American brethren of exaggeration. Lex said: 'Maurice, we've got to go and confront him about that statement.' Lex said that he could not go through a whole school year making mental adjustments to any report he heard. If he did, he would become cynical and stop believing anything. So we made an appointment with the vice president, and the three of us went to confront him.

He listened graciously to what we said, and was quite broken that we should have found it necessary to come and see him. He promised us that he would try to contain his enthusiasm in the future. During our time in Northwestern, we never felt concerned about this again. Later, T. W. Wilson was to be part of the Billy Graham team, and a valued and respected colleague. In my hearing, he never again fell into the trap of exaggeration – so maybe the British students at Northwestern had a contribution to make that would inadvertently shape the future ministry of the Billy Graham team.

Northwestern College had been founded by Dr W. B. Riley. On his deathbed, he had personally invited Billy Graham to succeed him. Dr Riley's widow remained on the faculty and taught regularly at the school. She was tall, commanding, had steel-blue flashing eyes and the student body generally lived in fear of her. On one occasion, both Billy Graham and T. W. Wilson were away from the college for an extended period. On their return they discovered that there had been some griping about some insignificant thing during their absence. T. W. Wilson (or simply T.W. as he became known) wanted gently to chide the student body. He told us the story of a visit Billy and he had made to a sideshow in a fair in Florida when they themselves were at college. The sideshow was billed as the 'cat with three eyes'. He described how the cat was asleep, with its front two eyes tightly closed, but on top of its head was the third, freakish, eye which was wide open and was taking everything in. 'You know,' he said, 'I feel that cat was a picture of Northwestern. Billy and I were away, and rather like the two closed front eyes, but the old grey cat still had an eye open and was taking everything in!' He could not understand the ripple of amusement which passed through the student body.

The spiritual tone of Northwestern was very high. When Dr J. Edwin Orr came to address the student body during one of the daily chapel hours, he gave a powerful challenge to the students about their lifestyle. At the end of his address, he closed in prayer and we should have been dismissed to classes. But before that happened, one of the students in the hall started praying. He was followed by another, and another, and another. At noon, T.W. came to the platform to announce that all classes had been cancelled for the day, and that as long as people wanted to pray, the chapel would remain in session. We were there until late in the evening – without any breaks for food. There was a powerful sense of the presence of God; it was not emotional, but simply realistic. From then to now, I have never been in another prayer meeting with such a sense of the presence of God as we had that day.

What particularly surprised me was the large number of students who were coming to Christ for the first time during that prayer meeting. The comprehensive application forms to get into college should have precluded any who were not already committed Christians. The questions were penetrating and deep. I did not see how anyone could be at college who did not already know Christ. But I was to learn in conversations following that day that many parents had completed the application forms in fond hope that their offspring were all that the parents claimed. In that sense the students had been sent by their parents: their own commitment to Christ was nil. Hence, as the Spirit of God began to work during that prayer meeting, there were many who came under a conviction of sin and, for the first time, gave their lives to Christ.

Mid-term, I began to have thoughts about the future, and my return to Britain. As I prayed about this, I felt convinced that God wanted me to extend the work of Hildenborough Hall by setting up a new bible conference centre – but at the seaside rather than in the country. Round about this time, Tom Rees came to Minneapolis on a visit. T. W. Wilson kindly took me to the airport to meet him, and he invited Tom to address chapel at Northwestern during that week.

Our American friends love a title, and on the first day in chapel, Tom was introduced as 'The Reverend Tom Rees'. After the service he took the dean aside and said: 'Just simply "Tom Rees": I'm not a rev.' Day number two came and he was introduced as 'Dr Tom Rees'. 'Not doctor,' said Tom, 'simply "Tom Rees".' On day three it was 'Evangelist Tom Rees' and on the final day 'Brother Tom Rees'! They never did manage the simple introduction: 'Tom Rees from London, England'.

One evening Tom took the British students out to dinner. As we sat next to each other he asked me what I planned to do when I returned home. 'Just don't think of starting another bible conference centre,' he said. He explained to me the enormous pressures and burden that Hildenborough Hall was to him. So it was with some diffidence that I shared my vision with him. As he listened, he too became convinced that this was a call from God and he gave me every encouragement to go ahead.

From Minneapolis, I wrote to my father and shared this vision with him. He, in turn, spoke to his brother who said that he would be willing to put up the money to buy a suitable property. Thus, during the remainder of my time in Minneapolis, my thoughts were concentrated on this future ministry. It did not detract from my schooling, and at the graduation ceremony, I was one who received a special certificate to commemorate my time at Northwestern.

At that graduation ceremony, my time at Northwestern ended as dramatically as it had begun. The final activity of the school year was the Commencement Exercises and Banquet. Commencement implied the commencement of your life's work after graduating.

It was the accepted custom for each student to invite another to be their guest at the banquet. As there were more girls than fellows, each male student was expected to invite one of the young ladies to be his guest. Any man without a lady partner had to attend on his own. The remaining girls paired up and came together.

I knew very few of the girls in my class. Most of my friends were among the young people who frequented Hospitality House. Just one or two were both at school and at 'Hop House'. One of these was Betty Halbersma, who was also in my classes at

Northwestern, so she seemed the most likely candidate for my invitation.

One day, in trepidation, I approached her and asked if she would accept an invitation to be my guest at the Commencement Banquet. I'm sure she replied: 'I'm very sorry, but I've already promised to go with someone.' Having used up all my courage on this one invitation, I resigned myself to being one of the odd-balls, the men who couldn't find a partner.

The day came. It was a tuxedo, evening dress, affair. All the men bought a corsage for their partners, most of whom were already wearing beautiful flowers in their hair. The secret was to find out from a friend the colour of the gown your partner would be wearing and to get either a gardenia, or an orchid to match. I was not saddled with that problem because I was on my own. Furthermore, I had brought no money with me, except enough for the bus fare back to Park Lane.

The first course of the dinner had been served when I was called away from the table to take a telephone call. It was Betty Halbersma: 'Are you coming to get me, or should I find my own way there?' I can scarcely describe the sense of shock which permeated my whole being. Quick thinking was the order of the day. Without giving any clue that I was not expecting her (because I had believed she was already committed), I apologised for my lack of communication and said that I had thought we were to meet at the banquet. She in turn apologised and rejected my offer to come and collect her. She said she would be right down in a taxi.

That gave me just enough time to talk to the head waiter and explain to him what had happened. There was a quick re-adjustment of the tables, and my seat was moved to the end where there was room for another alongside. Then I found a friend of Betty's and asked her if she knew the colour of her gown. Peach, I was told; it was an easy colour to match with an orchid from the hotel flower-shop! All this had just been completed when Betty came in through the door and I proudly escorted her to her seat. She brushed off my apologies and said that it was all her fault. We caught up in the meal and enjoyed each other's company. Later, the Commencement Exercises (the programme that accompanied the banquet and at which the graduation certificates were presented) included a musical programme by the numerous groups in the musical department of Northwestern. This was the first time I ever heard a choral rendering of 'Mine eyes have seen the glory of the coming of the Lord' and it sent cold shivers down my spine. Since then, I have heard many choral renderings, but none approached the memory of that first presentation, arranged and conducted by Bill Bernsten, who was later to succeed to the President's chair at the college. So, in spite of the traumas, all went well . . . until the time came to go home.

It was an expected courtesy that you would take your date home in a cab. Conscious of the twenty-five cents or so that I had in my pocket, I escorted Betty to a cab and prayed that she did not live too far away. But the cab driver came to my rescue. As Betty got out of the cab and we said our goodbyes, the cabby looked over his shoulder and said: 'Where do I take you to, bud?' That was the solution! He could take me back to Park Lane where my wallet was, and all would be well. Betty never knew of the drama that surrounded her visit to the Commencement Banquet.

As I left Northwestern, I also took my leave of Hospitality House, and they gave me two magnificent pictures to take home to hang in the new bible centre. In June 1949, I returned home on the *Queen Elizabeth* after a wonderful time in the United States.

My father had told me that a suitable property had been found and purchased (in faith!) at Frinton-on-Sea in Essex. It was right on the sea front, and upon examination I knew he had made the right choice. There was, however, one problem. The property was secured with covenants which said it could only be used as a private home. It became necessary to apply for change of use – and in the event, there were sixty-five objections from residents of Frinton. Frinton was notorious as an exclusive town, and the idea of the intrusion of a Christian conference centre was more than the residents could stomach. This meant that an arbitration hearing would have to be held, and this was scheduled for late September 1949.

On September 8th, my future wife arrived at London Airport for a short visit before we were to be married on October 14th. What a different London Airport it was! In those days it was simply a Nissan hut on waste ground, and the aircraft came virtually to the door. My father had exercised his wisdom to say that Marilyn should pay a visit to her adopted country before we were married – to see if she could cope with that as well as me. Towards the end of her visit, we were involved in the Frinton arbitration.

It was held at Kelvin Lodge – the property in question – and the proceedings were very formal. There were counsel for ourselves, for several of the residents, one for the local council and one on behalf of the government department. It lasted all day, and I spent long hours in the witness box being cross-examined by the various counsel. At the end of the day, no one could have said how it would go and what the decision of the arbitrator would be.

One thing was clear – the press were very interested in the arbitration, and covered the story with dramatic headlines the next day: 'They Dread it Being an Abode of Love' (*Daily Express*); 'Consecrated Fun at £7.7s per week' (*Evening News*); 'Objections to Bible Centre at Mansion' (*Daily Telegraph*); 'They Don't Want His Holy Fun' (*Daily Mirror*). The local newspaper, the *Frinton Gazette*, printed this poem:

It simply isn't Frinton, it really can't be done
A xylophone to start the day of consecrated fun!
Marilyn and Maurice we all agree with you
That if we don't reach Heaven we won't know what to
        do.
But why should we have pep talks to help us on our
        way?
Remember, this is Frinton and NOT the U.S.A.!
Grand choruses and laughter to break the evening still
(No baccy, beer or bebop which seems a bitter pill!)
    Will our redemption be complete?
    Shall we secure a forward seat?
    Shall we be sure to land in Heaven?
    If we pay eight instead of seven?

(Constance Wells, Crown Hotel, Thorpe)

One factor which led us to believe we were in the centre of God's will in the establishment of Kelvin Lodge as a bible conference centre was the flow of equipment which came to us. These were still the days of wartime shortages and it was almost impossible to obtain china and glass, furniture, cutlery and all the multitudinous items needed for such a centre. But, by a miracle, we not only managed to find sources of supply for what we needed, but some of it was donated to us without expense. So we were in high hopes – but we still had not had the result of the arbitration.

With all that hanging over us, we went off to the USA to get married. My old Hildenborough buddy, Lex Smith, was my best man at the wedding which followed American custom and was held at nine o'clock at night. One of our great delights at the wedding was the presence of Dr C. T. Cook, then the editor of the British Christian newspaper the *Christian*, who happened to be visiting Minneapolis at the time. In later years the *Christian* was to be owned by the Billy Graham Evangelistic Association and came under my jurisdiction as director of the London office.

Our honeymoon was to be on the *Queen Elizabeth*, travelling first class – a wedding present from my father – across the Atlantic on the way home. In the event we suffered a fearsome crossing with waves of seventy-five feet. Even forty-one years later that crossing is still referred to as the roughest ever. Somehow we managed to stagger to our feet at tea-time each day. But the rest of our time we spent in bed with seasickness.

There was a panic before we left New York. We had sent all of our wedding presents in big strong trunks, by carrier from Minneapolis to New York, to meet us at the boat. By the time we went aboard, they had not arrived. Consequently I had to make last-minute arrangements with shippers in New York to forward them to us in England when they arrived. These taxi journeys used up the last of my American currency – except for about twenty-five cents.

We were due to sail at about 11 p.m. At 3 a.m. the telephone in our cabin rang and the purser said: 'We have two large trunks which have just arrived: we plan to bring them to your cabin, because it is too late for the hold.' I said that I thought we had sailed at 11 p.m. He replied that there had been a delay – and it had been just long enough for our trunks to arrive. How well the Lord looks after us! The carrier's men brought the trunks to us in our cabin and all I had with which to recompense them was the twenty-five cents left over from my taxi drive. The air was blue with their comments! During the rough sea crossing, those wretched trunks slid from side to side of the cabin, crashing first this way, then that. It was remarkable that nothing inside was broken.

We were met at Southampton by my father with the news that the arbitration had gone against us, and that there was no appeal. We were, of course, completely shattered. We were not to know the plans that the Lord had laid for us were quite different. Had Kelvin Lodge materialised, we would probably not have been involved in the ministry of evangelism with Billy Graham. So, although it was a disaster to us at the time, upon looking back we can see how it was the guidance of the Lord.

Later we received information that the arbitrator, the leading counsel, several of the residents and, indeed, our own counsel were all Masons. The property was sold: it was bought by the Masons who had no difficulty in securing change of use for a convalescent home! Those are simply the facts as reported to us.

Our married life started, therefore, with the bottom falling out of the job we planned to do. We had made no alternative plans, because we had felt sure that this project was God's will for us. For the next nine months I was in purdah. I applied for various Christian openings: I even considered the pastorate. The Reverend Arch Palmer who, at the time, was pastor of Walton-on-the-Naze Baptist Church invited me to work with him as an assistant pastor. It was an unpaid post, but it enabled me to experiment with the calling of a pastor. I soon learned it was not for me. Some of the time I spent writing my first book, a children's novel entitled *Unexpected Adventure*. It became a popular volume to use as a Sunday school prize, and was well received. I wrote a sequel, but it was never published.

Then one day I had a letter from Tom Rees. He suggested that I should approach the Reverend Colin C. Kerr, vicar of St Paul's Church, Portman Square, and founder of the uniformed youth movement, the Campaigners. 'It won't be a gold-mine,' said Colin Kerr when I had an interview with him. 'We can pay you three hundred pounds per annum.' But it was all there was, and I felt I was stagnating doing nothing, so I accepted it.

By then, our first baby was on the way, and work of any sort had become imperative. For the next two years I became the boys' administrative chief of the movement and editor of their magazine, the *Lifeline*.

The new job meant moving to London. Marilyn was still in the nursing home, Gary having just been born. So I came to London to house-search alone and eventually found a semi-detached house that we could afford (with a mortgage) in Canons Park, Edgware. With a one-month-old baby, we made the move to our new home.

My work involved a great deal of travelling. I visited churches all over the country and met with various chiefs and clans. It was interesting work, but not something which challenged me. I was glad, therefore, to take part in any other opportunities for evangelism which arose, and it was with great delight that I accepted an invitation from Tom Rees to help him (in my spare time) with his next series of Get Right with God rallies in London's Royal Albert Hall. It was always a good feeling to get involved with Tom Rees in evangelism.

Early in March 1952, his good friend and former colleague Roy Cattell approached him to ask if he would extend an invitation to the American preacher Billy Graham to speak at one of the rallies. It so happened that the BBC had invited Tom Rees to provide a *Songs of Praise* programme from the Royal Albert Hall on March 16th. He discussed it with me and decided that his own involvement with the broadcast would be quite exhausting. He felt that it would be an appropriate night to invite Billy Graham to be the guest speaker.

The previous Saturday, March 8th, 1952, one of the Billy Graham team came to the Royal Albert Hall to spy out the land. He wanted to see how Tom Rees ran his meeting and he was deeply impressed. What astounded him most was the way in which Tom Rees did everything, song leader, interviewer, speaker and counsellor. It was a different concept to what he had been used to. But he felt that the context of such a rally was exactly right for Billy Graham to speak. In effect, it became his first introduction to the people of London in preparation for any future crusade.

On Sunday, March 16th, Tom Rees introduced Billy Graham to Londoners and the broadcast programme was recorded. Immediately afterwards he turned the meeting over to Billy to bring the main evangelistic message. Those who were present in the Royal Albert Hall were deeply moved by this powerful address. It set the stage in a very real way for the consultative meeting, held four days later on March 20th, 1952, in Church House, Westminster.

The World Evangelical Alliance (as it was then called) had invited some 250 Christian leaders to the meeting. They came from all over Britain to hear an address by Billy Graham. He gave the masterly address on evangelism which was later published as *The Work of an Evangelist* and sent to every clergyman and minister in the United Kingdom. The purpose of the meeting was to determine whether or not it would be appropriate to extend an invitation to him to come and conduct one of his crusades in London. From that meeting stemmed the invitation to conduct a crusade in London in 1954.

Although I found the work at Campaigners challenging and interesting – I enjoyed working with young people – the increasing 'military' emphasis of my senior chiefs at the time did not appeal to me and in September 1952 I prayed that the Lord would show me His next step.

I came home one Tuesday night and said to my wife: 'I am going to write to Roy Cattell at the World Evangelical Alliance, to ask him to remember me if ever there should be a vacancy on his staff.' I wrote the letter that night, and went out and posted it. On Wednesday morning, there was a letter from Roy Cattell to say that, if ever I thought of leaving Campaigners, would I let him know as he had a vacancy on his staff! On Thursday morning, another letter came from Tom Rees. He told me that I had been on his mind recently, and that he felt led to suggest that I contact Roy Cattell at the Evangelical Alliance to see if I could join him! I was beginning to learn what guidance was all about, and how one could expect an answer to prayer.

I was called to an interview with the formidable Lieutenant-General Sir Arthur Smith, chairman of the alliance at that time. 'Well, Rowlandson!' he barked at me. 'You don't seem to have stayed very long at one place. How do we know that if you come to us, you'll stay?' I assured him that any change I had made was directly upon the leading given to me by the Lord. 'I will stay,' I said, 'until He tells me it's time to move.' That answer seemed to satisfy the general and I was appointed.

In Isaiah 30:21 we read: '*Whether you turn to the right or to the left, your ears will hear a voice behind you, saying, "This is the way; walk in it".*' In other words, so long as you are in God's will, you will not necessarily be aware of guidance. If you are unaware of the voice behind, you are probably where God wants you to be, and you are doing what He wants you to do. If you move away from His plan for your life – that is, to the right hand or to the left – then He gently nudges you back into His will with the voice behind. This was my experience not only in this event when I moved from the Campaigners to the Evangelical Alliance, but was to be equally true in many subsequent situations in my life. I started with the alliance on September 29th, 1952 and remained there for nine years.

Billy Graham's first crusade had been held in 1949 in Los Angeles. His biography has recorded how that crusade took off and, within weeks, invitations were flowing in from all over the United States and abroad. One of those responding to Billy Graham's invitation to accept Christ was a famed US newscaster named Stuart Hamblen. He was listened to all over the United States. In the way of American TV, the newscaster often read a commercial as well as giving the news. Stuart Hamblen was retained by Camel Cigarettes for this purpose. The day after his conversion, he went on the air and said: 'Well, folks, here we come to the commercial. Last night at Billy Graham's crusade I became a Christian, and I believe that Christians don't smoke. So I don't really know what to do – except to say that if you must smoke, then smoke Camel Cigarettes – they're the best of a bad bunch!' That sort of news travels fast. Billy Graham became an evangelist of renown overnight. Stuart Hamblen later wrote the famous song 'It is No Secret (what God can do)'. There were other notable converts from that Los Angeles crusade including the notorious wire-tapper, Jim Vaus.

In 1954 a special Crusade Committee was formed and Major-General D. J. Wilson-Haffenden was invited to be the chairman. The participants were drawn from significant Christian leadership at the time, including the Right Reverend Hugh Gough, then Bishop of Barking. The honorary treasurer was a future Member of Parliament, Mr John Cordle. It was he and Roy Cattell who had been the prime movers for the invitation, having travelled to America to participate in one of the 1952 crusades. They came back on fire for the project and convinced that London was ready for such a programme.

Roy Cattell was appointed crusade secretary, and I was to be his assistant. From America, Billy Graham appointed one of

his team to act as a liaison officer between the Billy Graham
Evangelistic Association, the World Evangelical Alliance and the
Crusade Committee. He turned out to be the former registrar
at Northwestern College. God was keeping me in His thin
gold line and was directing me into the orbit of the work
of Billy Graham. I marvelled that the man appointed should
be the one I knew so well from Northwestern College. From
his point of view, he was delighted to find that there was
someone in London who spoke and understood his language.
There were many occasions during the next three years when I
found myself acting as 'interpreter' between the American team
representative and the London committee.

3

Crusades – and Prison

The first task was to find suitable offices from which the crusade could be organised. In a remarkable way we were led to offices in Gate Street, just behind Holborn underground station. They were dark, but adequate for our needs. The recruited staff were soon in residence there.

Nothing of this nature had ever been undertaken before by any of us involved, so we leaned heavily upon the experience of our American brethren. In the early days, they were busy making arrangements for the publicity, counselling classes, rehearsals and the hundred and one other things which go into the launch of a successful crusade.

It was decided that part of the preparation would be to create an awareness both of the evangelist and of the type of crusades which he ran. To do this, we imported from the USA the latest Billy Graham full-length colour feature film, *Oil Town USA*. The association had been involved in making Christian films since 1951. Many documentaries and a long line of feature films have since come from the Burbank studios (near Hollywood) of World Wide Pictures. In the United Kingdom, World Wide Pictures used the name World Wide Films, because there was already a company of that name producing less than acceptable films. We wanted to avoid confusion, although we often got telephone calls from would-be actors and actresses.

Oil Town USA was one of the earliest Christian feature films to come to Britain. This was a Texas oil country film, full of brash Texas experiences, but it had a great story and some excellent music. Above all it was a powerful vehicle for communicating the gospel. Many Christian leaders today trace their conversion back to this and to other Billy Graham films.

Colleen Townsend played the female lead in the film. Today she is the much-respected wife of Dr Louis Evans, who has been minister of one of the largest churches in Washington. In the film she was exceedingly glamorous. This was still in the days when, in Britain, make-up was an invention of the devil, and never used by sincere Christian folk. Colleen was *very* made-up. We had a letter after one of the showings: 'I greatly enjoyed the film, but I hope before you show it again, you will ask the young ladies to remove their make-up.'

For almost six months, the film was shown in every district of London and as far south as Southampton; west as Bath and Bristol; north as Leicester and in East Anglia. Two film teams were used: the writer was assisted by Cannon Payne and Heini Sheldon, and a second team comprised Gordon Ingram and Paul Stark. We had one enormous arc projector, and two ordinary 16 mm projectors which were rigged up, night after night, in a wide variety of locations. Moving the arc projector was a back-breaking job, and by the end of the series we were all heartily sick of it. But as the film was shown, men and women, young and old, responded to the appeal and hundreds accepted the Lord Jesus Christ as their Saviour. It was an exciting run-up to the crusade.

There was a short series of central London première showings of the film in the Gaumont British cinema in Wardour Street. These were significant for the presence of Redd Harper, one of the stars of the film, who put in a nightly appearance – plus his guitar – for the whole three weeks. As a team, we would go out afterwards and have supper together at the Lyons Corner House in Tottenham Court Road. In his cowboy hat and boots, Redd created quite a stir.

My blood runs cold when I think of some of the things we did in those film shows. After two or three weeks of showing the film (we had consolidated two full-length reels on to one specially made giant reel, with special extension arms for the projector) we would set the film going, and then go out to a nearby restaurant to get some supper. We knew we had an hour and a half of clear time, and it seemed to be the only opportunity we had to eat. But God was good to us! Throughout that time we never had a single film or projector breakdown. It really was a miracle.

In those locations where we were unable to use the giant reels, we devised a method of showing two reels on one projector, without ever stopping the projector during the run. We would have the end of the first reel scraped and ready for splicing with a short six-inch plain black trailer. The beginning of the second reel was also prepared with a scraped short six-inch black leader. As we reached the end of the first reel, we would unwind the last fifty feet by hand, and drape the loose film over the top and back of the projector. Then we removed the empty reel from the top arm and replaced it with the new full reel. A quick splice, and a careful feeding of the draped film through the projector followed until the splice had been taken through the gate and appeared at the take-up end. There, we broke the splice, removed the full reel from the rear arm, replaced it with an empty reel, threaded up the loose end — and away we went. It was all very hair-raising stuff and required supremely good teamwork. But we had it down to perfection, and the only bit the audience was conscious of was when the twelve-inch black strip appeared on the screen.

Nearer to the start of the crusade, there were several series of counsellor training classes in six or seven centres around London. These were taught by Lorne Sanny, Dawson Trotman and Charlie Riggs, all of them Navigators. This training presented a very different concept from the personal worker training which had been the mainstay of the Tom Rees campaign meetings of the late 1940s and early 1950s. These counsellor training classes went on over a period of four weeks, one night per week. You had to attend all four classes in order to qualify as a counsellor. There was then a careful selection procedure, the like of which had never been seen before in London.

Then the blow fell! Shortly before Billy Graham was due to arrive in England, some journalist spotted a remark in the annual Billy Graham calendar, sent out to all his supporters world-wide. Somehow a copy had fallen into the hands of this unsympathetic journalist. The calendar remarked: 'What Hitler's bombs could not do, socialism with its accompanying evils shortly accomplished.' The Labour Party was up in arms: questions were asked in the House of Commons, and plans were made to prevent Billy Graham being allowed to land when he arrived in the UK.

Our American colleagues were under pressure. They sat looking at the offending remark on the calendar while we stood glumly around. Suddenly one of them stabbed the air with his finger: 'We didn't spell "socialism" with a capital S,' he said. 'We were not referring to the political party but to secularism' (of which socialism was a synonym in America). A press release was issued, and the entire furore came to an abrupt halt – but not before the most widespread publicity (in practically every newspaper) had emblazoned the unknown name of Billy Graham before the British public. Sometimes the devil overstretches himself and the attack is reversed by God, and used to the destruction of evil. The name of Billy Graham was upon everyone's lips, just as our publicity programme hit the buses and hoardings of London. The Lord, once again, had rewarded our faithfulness.

Billy Graham arrived on the SS *United States*. He was asked at the press conference after his arrival why he had not followed Christ, who rode into Jerusalem on a donkey. Grady Wilson, who was with him, replied: 'Show me a donkey that can go across the Atlantic, and Billy will!'

From Southampton he took the train to Waterloo Station. Through the Christian press we had alerted our supporters and told them the day and time of his arrival. When we arrived at Waterloo about an hour ahead of time, the station was already full to overflowing. I went to see the station-master and asked him if the crowds could be allowed on to the platform to meet Mr Graham. He stoutly refused: 'I've had film stars and Presidents arrive at this station, and there's never been an occasion when anyone has been allowed on the platform.' I warned him that the crowds were already enormous, and that within the next hour there would be hundreds more coming. My pleading did not move him. 'Most of the crowds are the travelling public,' he said. 'You'll find you won't have as many as you expect.'

The next fifteen minutes were to prove him wrong. Ten minutes ahead of the boat train's arrival time, it was impossible for anyone to move on the station forecourt, as the whole crowd surged around the platform at which the train would arrive. Just minutes before the train came in, the station-master relented, and announced that the boat train would be diverted to Platform 10 – the platform which, in those days, ran alongside a roadway through the station. It would adequately accommodate the large numbers of supporters.

As the train steamed into the station, the whole crowd spontaneously burst into song. 'Blessed Assurance, Jesus is mine' filled the vast concourse. As Billy Graham appeared at the train doors, an enormous cheer went up, and the crowd sang another hymn. They were good-natured and well disciplined. There was no sense of disorder. Roy Cattell and myself, with one of the team members, accompanied Billy and Ruth Graham along the whole length of the platform and into the waiting car. Billy said a few words of thanks to the crowd for the welcome they had given him – and I went to say a word of thanks to the flustered and embarrassed station-master for his last minute co-operation.

The news of the crowds at Waterloo Station spread like wildfire, and before Billy Graham was driven away, the newsreel cameras and newspaper photographers had gathered for their pictures. The arrival made headline news in the national press, and there were pictures on the TV news programmes that evening.

At a meeting of the Crusade Executive Committee, which Billy Graham attended shortly after he arrived, he was urged by the members not to focus his addresses upon the atomic bomb. It was, they said, a subject not discussed in London and it would be better not to mention it at the meetings. Then, during the week before the commencement of the meetings at the Harringay Arena, the world's first hydrogen bomb was tested by the Americans – and the subject was on everybody's mind. It would have been strange if Billy Graham had not referred to it in his opening address.

From the very beginning the Billy Graham team, through the office in Gate Street, had issued rather more tickets than there were seats. Admission was free, and the tickets were really no more than invitations. They guaranteed neither admission nor any specially numbered seat. From past experience the Billy Graham team knew that, when tickets were not paid for, a large number were not used. By trial and error, they would issue excess tickets to guarantee a full hall.

It is significant that, apart from the first two opening nights, the Saturdays and the last three nights, we always *exactly* filled the arena. We felt God's hand in this, because there could have been a riot had people turned up with tickets and been denied access because of insufficient room. This is even more remarkable when you consider that, in the first ten days, the arena was said to hold around 12,500 people. However, as the management discovered that our people were well behaved and considerate, they gradually allowed this number to creep up until, by the end of the crusade, we were packing in some 14,500 to 15,000 people. Such an escalation of numbers would never be allowed today. We were able to do it at that time because they allowed us first to sit people one to a staircase step (later increased to two), and eventually to establish one row (later two) standing behind the rows of seating. But always just enough people turned up to fill the space we had – and if that space increased, more people came to fill it.

The first two nights there was a considerable excess and at first people outside were inclined to be belligerent, saying: 'I've got a ticket – you've got to let me in,' when the Harringay management had already declared the hall full with 12,500 inside. However, the problem was solved when Billy Graham climbed out of a window and, from the parapet, addressed the crowd outside. Several responded to the invitation which he gave – and the crowd melted away without further complaint.

By the Saturday, news had spread that the possession of a ticket did not necessarily guarantee admission to the meeting. By 2.30 p.m. there was an enormous queue outside for a 7.30 p.m. meeting! They came by the coachload from far afield and were arriving early to be sure of a seat. A quick telephone call to Billy Graham at his hotel secured his agreement to our plan to open the doors and let everybody in. The hall was completely full by 3 p.m. and an unscheduled full-scale crusade meeting was held. By the time it was over, another crowd had gathered and we repeated the ad hoc arrangements with a second crusade meeting at around 5.15 p.m. That still left us with enough people to fill the arena for the 7.30 p.m. meeting! These Saturday arrangements continued as long as we had the early overflow crowds.

The last three nights were impossible. We could not organise extra early meetings, because the crowds did not turn up until the prearranged time. But we could have filled the arena twice over. Emergency relay arrangements were made and the overflow audience was accommodated in the adjacent Harringay greyhound stadium.

I was allotted the task of chief steward, and my work would

have been impossible without the wonderful back-up of a team of deputy chief stewards. Henry Hole (who was to succeed me as chief steward at Wembley in 1955 and at Earls Court in 1966/67 and at Spre-e '73) became my assistant with David Rennie, George Andrews, Heini Sheldon, Percy Sprowson and Cannon Payne to assist him. Later, John Baldock joined our team as we needed additional help.

The tale of Harringay has been told in *The Harringay Story* and in *London Crusade* and other books have been written about many of the converts. It is hard to imagine just where the church in Britain would be today if there had not been the meetings at Harringay. So much of what has been achieved by the 1990s can be traced back to that series of crusade meetings at Harringay.

Tom Rees, who in Winnipeg in 1948 had first been told about Billy Graham by Bev Shea, came to the opening meeting. He had already committed all his resources to the crusade by passing on lists of names and addresses of potential counsellors, choir members and stewards. He had also cancelled any evangelistic programmes which he had in mind for the London area. But he felt it important that he should continue to be involved in active evangelism and spent the next three months in evangelistic meetings in other parts of the country. That first night, however, he was disturbed by Billy Graham's form of appeal. There were one or two aspects of it that Tom Rees felt were slightly dishonest. He wrote at length that same night to Billy Graham, and Billy took note of what he said. He slightly changed his appeal from the second night onwards, and he has followed the same pattern ever since.

Another area where Tom Rees and the ministry of Hildenborough Hall had an enormous influence upon the crusade was the adoption of the Operation Andrew plan. This was a plan devised by Jean Rees in 1945, to encourage Christian people to bring their friends to Jesus. The team heard about the programme from Jean Rees and decided to adopt it in its entirety, and it has been used by them ever since. Only eternity will reveal just how much the Harringay crusade owed to the support and co-operation of Tom and Jean Rees. There were so many areas in which their influence and support were invaluable.

It was clear that those churches which benefited most from the crusade were those who put a lot into it. This was epitomised very clearly by the experience of two churches in north-west London. At St Margaret's the rector gave every support to the crusade: he encouraged participation by his people as counsellors, stewards and choir, and ran a coach two or three nights a week to take invited guests. At the end of the crusade, so many people had been referred to the church, and had started attending, that he had to run two evening services (that was in the days before television!) to get everyone in. That situation continued until early in the 1960s, when the church built a daughter church in a new housing estate and hived off part of their congregation to the new church.

Nearby was the parish church of St Lawrence. The vicar there was very critical of the crusade at the start. 'Can any good thing come from America?' was his attitude, which prevailed throughout the Harringay days. At the end of the crusade, he asked, 'Where are the converts? We haven't seen any!' Of course not – the converts were all up at St Margaret's!

It reminded me of a story which my father used to tell. It concerned a Methodist minister, on holiday at the seaside with his son. On the Sunday they went together to the Methodist Church, the father wearing his clerical collar. On the way in a steward stopped him and took him aside. 'I see you are a minister,' he said. 'I wonder if you would be prepared to preach for us? Our own minister has suddenly been taken ill.' The father said he would be glad to. His son noticed that when the offering was taken, his father put ten shillings in the bag.

After the service, the steward approached the minister with an envelope in his hand which obviously contained money. He thanked the minister and went to give him the envelope. The minister said, 'No, I have been glad to preach for you.' The steward then said that it was the practice of the church to give the morning offering to the preacher. They would be offended if he did not accept. 'In that case, I'll be glad to accept it,' said the minister, whereupon his son turned to him and said: 'Dad, if you'd put more in you'd have got more out!' Those churches that put a lot into the crusade got a lot out in return.

There were a number of significant things about the Harringay crusade which have not been recorded elsewhere. There was the fact that the agreement between the London Crusade Committee and the Greyhound Racing Association (the owners of the Harringay Arena) was simply a two-page exchange of letters in which the committee agreed to rent, and the association agreed to make available, the facilities of Harringay. This contrasted dramatically with the document and agreement of over two hundred pages which was required by the Earls Court management ten years later. Significantly, we had not a single argument with the Harringay owners, but there were endless small disputes over the multitude of clauses in the Earls Court agreement. That agreement with Harringay was signed by Roy Cattell on behalf of the committee, and pledged them to the payment of thirty-three thousand pounds for the use of the Harringay Arena for the crusade – when they had nothing in the bank!

Then the financial situation was significant. An incredibly expensive book was prepared to circulate to top men in industry. Surprisingly this book produced a large chunk of the budget for the crusade. A direct appeal to many thousands of individuals produced further contributions – but, as the crusade started, we were left with a gap to be filled. Amid criticism, it was agreed to take a nightly offering. To those who criticised this move, the team would say: 'The money is all the Lord's – it's just that some of it is in the wrong hands. We have to get it back!' I couldn't help my own private reflections that the rent was then paid back to the Greyhound Racing Association! It seemed that the money had gone full circle. In the end, the committee arrived at a compromise and agreed that, when the budget was reached, the offerings would cease.

The first two or three nights, the stewards were given the task of counting the offering, most of which was in coinage. This kept them busy until 3 a.m., and it was clear that they could not go through three months with this schedule. First, we obtained a coin-counting machine, and this helped a bit. But it was still 2 a.m. before everything was counted and bagged. David Rennie went to talk to the crusade bank manager, and came away with a promise that the bank staff would count the offering daily, if we would deliver it to them. We were left simply to count and bag the notes. Night by night, the counted notes would be bagged, the uncounted bags of coins sealed, and all of it would be placed in the boot of my car. I would drive home with it overnight, and the next morning deliver it to the bank for counting . . . and that was a schedule that went on for the full three months, often with amounts in excess of ten thousand pounds in the boot of my car left overnight in my garage at home in Edgware. No security!

No guards! No safe! Indeed, no one raised any question about it. Today it would be impossible to do that for it would be far too vulnerable. We live in a different world. In some ways my experience reflected the way in which Grady Wilson had taken the offering at one of the first Billy Graham meetings, and had placed it in a shoe box under his bed until the next morning.

There was one small blot on the story. We had divided the stewards into groups and the groups into areas. Each area had an area captain who was responsible for that part of the arena. Part of his duties consisted of collecting the offering from the group captains, who had already collected it from the stewards. Area captains were essentially people we knew and who were in positions of responsibility and trust.

One night, one of the area captains came to me and said: 'Maurice, do you know that "Peter" is taking money out of the offering?' This seemed unbelievable because Peter (whose name I have changed) was well known to us all. However, it was impossible to ignore this accusation, and we agreed between us that we would put some marked one-pound notes in the offering buckets in his area. With the deputy chief stewards in the area alerted, we met together to empty the offering buckets. It quickly became clear that the marked one-pound notes were not there.

I found Peter and walked him around the arena. I told him of the accusation that had been made, and gave him an opportunity to confess to me if he had been taking the money. I did not tell him about the marked notes. He stoutly denied everything and seemed very affronted that I should even have suspected him. We repeated the experiment again the next night with the same result. This time, I had no alternative but to inform the police who duly arrived. I then asked Peter if he would mind answering a few questions from the police. He immediately assented, and we took him to a small room under the stands. The police asked him if he would agree to be searched and he readily agreed. They went through his pockets and searched all likely hiding places – without result. By then, we were beginning to be ashamed that we had ever doubted his word.

Just as they were ready to let him go, one of the police officers let his hand feel the bottom of Peter's jacket. The ensuing five minutes were a nightmare. The police literally ripped Peter's coat off him, tore out the lining, and out fluttered some twenty banknotes — including our marked notes. Peter was arrested and charged. Later he appeared before the local magistrates, and Major-General D. J. Wilson-Haffenden appeared to speak a word on his behalf. Peter was given a conditional discharge and ordered to stay away from the meetings in future. It was a very distressing event, and one which we would have been glad to have avoided. The temptation was real, and Peter succumbed. There, but for the grace of God, go I.

Night by night there were significant conversions. Their stories have been told elsewhere — but three must be mentioned. First was Ernest Shippam, a well-known name whose company produced fish pastes and food products that were on many a household table. Ernest was saved from a life of alcoholism — and his family with him. He never afterwards let his light dim, and until his recent death in 1991 was an inspiration to countless thousands.

Another was Major Richard Carr-Gomm. As a result of his conversion, he was given an enhanced social conscience, and shortly afterwards founded the Abbeyfield Society to house elderly people. That later separated from him, and he founded a second and similar society called the Carr-Gomm Society. To those who criticise Billy Graham for failing to preach a social awareness, the reply is always clear: there are those whose lives are changed, and who themselves become involved in social action.

The third was a young London actress, Joan Winmill. She was appearing in the London production of *The Chiltern Hundreds* when John T. Mercer Jr, the insurance agent for the Billy Graham crusade, invited her to come to Harringay. She responded to Billy Graham's invitation; she was counselled by Ruth Graham, and became a shining star through the message of her changed life. Later, she was to marry Bill Brown, a member of the Billy Graham team who was to set up the 1966/67 Earls Court crusades and eventually become head of World Wide Films, the company in America producing evangelistic films which centred around the ministry of Billy Graham.

Those who respond to Billy Graham's invitation at the end of a crusade meeting are always referred to as enquirers. It is the press and the media who often refer to them as converts. To the Billy Graham team, they are asking more about the way in which they can respond to the evangelist's message. Some, quite clearly, have made a definite decision to commit their lives to Christ, and to accept Him as their own personal Saviour. But some do not understand, and need counselling and further guidance. For some, it is a matter of rededicating themselves to Christ. They have responded to Him before, but have drifted away; now they are coming home. Some come just to be with a friend who has come, and some come simply out of curiosity. They are not all converts; they are enquirers.

Among those working with the team was Bob Benninghof, a young radio producer, seconded by CBS Radio in the USA to the Billy Graham organisation to help in the production of the weekly radio programme *The Hour of Decision* with Billy Graham. One night, in his hotel room, he was scribbling some thoughts on paper as a result of reading an article in a wire-less technical magazine. He had become aware of circuits of land-lines in the UK which had been installed by the Post Office during the war and which today were lying idle. Bob Benninghof came up with an idea which would allow this land-line network to be used to carry the meetings at Harringay to other parts of the country. These would not be 'broad-casts' which were not legally permitted; they would simply be an extension of the public address system in Harringay, but carried by direct line to other places. At the receiving end, there would be similar public address equipment to that in the Harringay Arena, and the local audience would be able to take part in the Harringay meetings as though they were there.

It had never been done before, and the idea was greeted with scepticism. However, it was tried out in London itself, with relays to the Trocadero Cinema at the Elephant and Castle. It was an immediate success. During the last weeks of Harringay, there was an increasing number of land-line relays to other parts of the country. Those in remote areas simply sat in their local halls, and listened to the service being relayed and heard the proceedings through local loudspeakers. It was astonishing to those involved to see people get up out of their seats, and come to stand in front of a black box (the loudspeaker) to indicate their desire to find Christ. In these days of closed circuit television, satellite relays and videos, it is hard to understand the impact of that simple black box! Locally, counsellors were trained in the same way as at Harringay, and there are thousands across Britain who trace their spiritual pilgrimage back to one of those relays.

At Harringay, the offerings were halted after the third week, as the budget had been met. But the break became token only, as the demand to have an opportunity to give was considerable. The offerings were started again the following week, ostensibly for future evangelism in Britain. In the event, the extension of the ministry of Harringay (including the land-line relays) resulted in a significant increase to the budget, and much of the later offerings went to defray that cost.

It was on Good Friday that Cliff Barrows was rehearsing the choir when he was puzzled by their reaction at a certain point. They were singing his arrangement of the hymn 'Man of Sorrow, what a name' and he was trying to get the men to hold on to a note in the last line. Every time they came in too quickly until, in desperation, he said: 'Men, men, men! In that line "Hallelujah, what a Saviour" sing out the "Halle . . . " but then hold it until you get to the "loo"!' He couldn't understand why the choir burst out laughing.

In addition to the meetings at Harringay there were other opportunities for evangelism. There was a meeting in Trafalgar Square and another in Hyde Park. There was also a meeting in Victoria Park in East London. Then in 1955, through the good offices of John Cordle, the door was opened for Billy Graham to preach before the royal family – the first of many occasions when Billy was able to accept an invitation from Her Majesty the Queen. In all these instances he has been very discreet, and has never talked about them. His restraint stems from a difficult experience he had as a young evangelist when he acted unwisely after a visit to President Truman in the United States. He never makes the same mistake twice!

During those twelve weeks from March to May 1954, Harringay became a way of life. There were those who had responded to the call of Christ during the early weeks, who were now coming back with their friends. Some were even organising parties to come to the crusade meetings, and some had gone through special counsellor training classes, and were themselves being used as counsellors in the final weeks. Some had enrolled in the choir; some had become stewards. Homeward-bound crowds, night by night, sang the crusade hymns on the trains; radio programmes referred to the crusade; cabbies knew all about it and asked, 'Been to Harringay yet, guv'nor?'

Several London stage plays (which depended upon contemporary news for parts of their script) included references to Billy Graham and the crusade. Cartoonists had a field day and the whole crusade became a talking point among Londoners. Years later, they were to refer to 'the Harringay experience' – and the Encyclopedia Brittanica even included the word Harringay – which it described as 'a religious event leading to the Harringay experience of Conversion'.

It was clear that Harringay Arena would be altogether too small for the crowd that would want to attend the last meeting. Accordingly, negotiations were commenced with Wembley Stadium for the final meeting to be held there. For me, as chief steward, this presented a nightmare. Communication between the various stewarding groups was hard enough in the closed confines of Harringay; in the vastness of Wembley, we had to devise a different method of briefing and control and we lacked the radio walkie-talkie equipment which would be available to us in future years.

A week before the Wembley meeting was to take place I was called in to see Roy Cattell. He told me that there were so many applications for tickets at Wembley that he had asked them if we could hold an afternoon meeting as well. They had said that this was impossible, so I was given the job of negotiating with the White City Stadium, to see if an afternoon meeting could be held there.

The logistics of such an operation terrified me. We would have to set up the full administration for stewards, choir, counsellors and the platform arrangements which, at best, could only end around 5 p.m. Then everything would have to be moved, lock, stock and barrel, to the final meeting at Wembley Stadium. In my heart I hoped that the White City would be unavailable.

The Greyhound Racing Association also owned the White City and after their experience with us at the Harringay Arena, they were only too happy to make the White City Stadium available. I returned to Roy Cattell to report that it was a possibility. The decision to proceed was taken the same afternoon.

As soon as we knew that both meetings were going ahead, we had booked a fleet of coaches to move all the workers from one location to the other. We contacted the police, and they arranged a police escort which hurried us from the White City to Wembley Stadium.

In the event it was quite remarkable. Everything went like clockwork. We spent most of the final Saturday morning at Wembley Stadium, getting everything ready for our arrival there. Then around twelve noon we went to the White City. When we arrived there the choir was already rehearsing and the counsellors were being briefed. We immediately set about briefing our own team of stewards. Henry Hole was put in overall charge of the stewarding operation and he prepared a plan which worked very well.

As expected, it was around 5 p.m. when we all left the White City; half an hour later we swung into action at Wembley, ready for the doors to be opened at 7 p.m. It was certainly one of the most hectic and energetic days I have ever experienced. But it had been worth it. White City was filled to capacity.

At Wembley the day was saved by the unexpected co-operation of the Wembley Stadium authorities who, at the eleventh hour, opened the gates to the turf and allowed some 10,000 people to pour on to the sacred ground and stand in front of the platform. That meant that in excess of 110,000 people were present in the stadium – a record which still stands to this day. Between the two meetings, Mr Graham had addressed some 160,000 people on the one day!

The Archbishop of Canterbury, Dr Fisher, was on the platform and pronounced the Benediction at this final meeting, and it became clear that this could not be the end of Billy Graham's preaching in Britain. He had already accepted an invitation to conduct a crusade at the Kelvin Hall in Glasgow in the spring of 1955. Now, he was able to announce that he would also return to London after that crusade, to conduct a week of meetings at Wembley Stadium. The news was received with acclaim by those who were present at the final meeting.

Shortly afterwards, the Evangelical Alliance were able to announce that land-line relays would be available from the meetings in Glasgow to anyone who wished to receive them. We worked out a package deal. For a fixed cost the land-line would be provided; counsellor training material would be available and would have to be used; and a unified publicity programme was designed with material including posters, handbills, newspaper matts (from which newspaper advertisements can be printed) and film trailers. All this was offered to a centre wishing to hold a land-line relay. The Evangelical Alliance thought that there might be 200 takers, and I was appointed to administer the programme. In the event there were 2,000! In fact, when the Post Office later gave me a large wall-map with every location marked, it was on my office wall for several days before my secretary pointed out to me that the outline of the British Isles was not even drawn on the map. The locations were so all-encompassing that the outline of the country was clearly delineated simply by the towns and villages to which the relays were going.

Lorne Sanny, of the Navigators (who had conducted one of the series of counsellor training classes before Harringay), was due to come from the USA for a flying visit, to record tapes for the counsellor training classes. Copies of these tapes would then be sent to each relay centre for counsellors to be trained locally. On the day he arrived, I went to London Airport to meet him. He was clearly suffering from a bad case of laryngitis. He could only whisper, and expressed the hope that he would be in good voice for the marathon recording the next day. We had arranged for students of the London Bible College to be an audience for him so that there would be a warm atmosphere for the tape recording, and Lorne would feel some response to his teaching.

The next morning I collected Lorne from his hotel, and his voice was no better. He could not speak, simply whisper. On our way to the studios, where the LBC students were already gathered, we prayed that God would work a miracle and give Lorne a good voice. At the studios he lectured for four hours, his voice strong and normal. The students received a great blessing from the teaching. But when it was all over, and I took Lorne back to his hotel, he could do no more than whisper again. So it remained for the last two days of his stay in London. Just for those few hours at the studio, his voice had been as strong as normal. It was a real and significant answer to prayer. Those tapes were to become the 'standard' for counsellor training for many years to come. They were used in the preparation of the land-line relay programme to great effect, and there are those today who look back to that time of training – by tape – as a highlight of their life.

The organisation of the 2,000 land-line relays was an exercise in co-operation between ourselves and the Post Office representatives in Glasgow. It was they who had to find the facilities for the ever-increasing numbers of relay requests. Towards the end, I had to put some pressure on them to add yet another – but there had to come a cut-off date after which we agreed we could no longer accept any further requests. It was a sad commentary that the Post Office official in Glasgow had to report to me that the pressure put upon him after the cut-off date — by, we assume, Christian people — included threats, offers of bribes and even abuse. He told me later that, if it hadn't been for the graciousness of the Billy Graham team whom he had come to know in Glasgow, he would have written Christian people off as a bad lot. It is a salutary thought and one we should note. It is important how we can appear to non-Christian folk.

As administrator to the land-line relay programme I felt that charity begins at home. The land-line relays were to take place during the same week as the Venturers Norfolk Broads Cruise for schoolboys which I had founded in 1946. This sail-holiday cruise, held on the Norfolk Broads each April, was intended to combine a sailing holiday with the gospel message. It occurred to me that to include a land-line relay to Repps Methodist Chapel in Potter Heigham, Norfolk, near to where the cruise would be mooring would be something different for the boys. Our cruise padre normally gave a gospel address each evening; on this day, we would 'attend' the Kelvin Hall instead.

The plans were duly laid and when the day arrived I went in advance of the cruise to make sure that all arrangements were properly in hand. I arrived at the chapel at around 4 p.m. and found a long queue waiting outside! I told them that this was a private relay, but said that any seats not used by the boys could be filled up by the public. Certainly only a third of the queue would be able to get in. The Post Office engineers suggested rigging up a loudspeaker outside the chapel, and to this we agreed. By the time we arrived for the relay the queue had grown to enormous proportions and when we had seated our boys we managed to cram in about another fifty to sixty people.

We had spent some time talking about, and planning for, this relay. It was our considered opinion that, because of the programme of the cruise, it would be inappropriate to continue the relay to include Billy Graham's appeal. We felt that it would be wiser to fade out the land-line relay and allow the follow-up of our own boys (for whom the relay was primarily intended) to continue aboard the boats. Normally, Billy Graham gave a clear indication of the moment when he would be moving into the appeal; on this occasion he didn't. So whether we had planned

it or not, we moved directly into the appeal in the chapel. To our
astonishment about three or four of our boys and some ten to
twelve local folk (including some who pushed their way through
the crowd from the relay outside) came and stood in front of the
black loudspeaker box. So we were faced with the necessity of
counselling those who responded. One of our boys who came
forward is today an ordained priest in the Anglican Church
and has served many years overseas as a missionary. Others
too have gone on to Christian service from that remarkable,
unscheduled, and highly unofficial relay.

The Good Friday crusade meeting in the Kelvin Hall became
the first ever Billy Graham crusade meeting to be carried live
on television by the BBC. It was simultaneously on both the
radio and television in its entirety and the programmes reflected some of the spirit and excitement which pervaded the
whole of the Scottish crusade.

Meanwhile, London was looking forward to, and preparing
for, the second Greater London crusade. Wembley Stadium had
been booked for a whole week in June 1955. In those days there
was no cover to most of the stadium and people in the terraces
at each end, as well as those in the front sections of the grand-
stands, were exposed to the elements. And it rained! Oh how it
rained! Night after night, except for one night in the middle and
on the last night, the rain poured down. But still people stayed
. . . and responded. They walked out from their seats, many
of which were dry and under cover, across the turf – often in
ankle-deep mud – to stand in the pouring rain just in front of the
platform. Counsellors were there, plastic bags over their shoes,
their bibles open inside another plastic bag. And with water
dripping off their hair, they counselled those who came forward.
Many of those water-stained bibles have become precious possessions to those counsellors who took part night after night.

Wembley was well filled each night in spite of the extra-
ordinarily bad weather. We had devised a new system for the
control of stewards and, for the first time, employed walkie-talkie
equipment to link all the chief stewards. The same team as at
Harringay came together, this time again under the leadership
of Henry Hole. Each of the men was given a radio unit.
In those days such things were very cumbersome and had
to be carried in back-packs with long aerials sticking out
of the top. Their carriers were dubbed by the team 'The

men from Mars'. One of Henry's deputies, Heini Sheldon, used the walkie-talkie equipment on the Saturday afternoon to announce to all his chief steward colleagues that he had – that day – become engaged.

Pro rata, more people attended Wembley than had attended the Harringay crusade. The number of enquirers amounted to 38,477 over twelve weeks at Harringay, and to 23,806 in one week at Wembley. In many ways, Wembley was the consolidation of what had happened the previous year. Strangely, that one week at Wembley in the rain was more effective and has become more famous than the twelve weeks at Harringay. This was chiefly because of the quality of those who responded to Billy Graham's invitation.

During the Harringay crusade life had been so busy that there was no opportunity to take pictures of all that happened. So I was determined that, at Wembley, I would carry my camera at all times. I ended up with a useful series of pictures. Our friends called round to see them, and I found myself telling the same story over and over again. One day I decided to speak into a tape recorder when I showed the slides and told the story. Then, I figured, the next time I could just show the pictures and let the tape tell the story.

Gradually this developed. I added a little bit of music, some of Billy Graham's preaching, a testimony or two and background noises – all of which began to bring the tape recording and slides to life. Eventually the inevitable happened. I decided to do it properly and put together a carefully prepared script, with speech and sound effects, to a selected series of slides to tell 'The Wembley Story'. Until that time no one seems to have conceived the idea of using a tape recording with a series of slides. I coined the name 'soundstrip' which everyone uses today, but I still believe that 'The Wembley Story' was the first ever.

Those who saw it were moved by it. It was indeed a moving story. Soon I was being asked to take the programme to churches elsewhere. The Evangelical Alliance (for whom I still worked at that time) decided to sponsor it, and made copies available for those who wished to purchase them. They also offered my services to show the programme wherever it was wanted. The next few months were busy ones as I travelled the length and breadth of Britain with 'The Wembley Story'. It was an extension of the crusade, for on each occasion one or two came to Christ. We had to take counselling packs with us wherever we went, and we were prepared to counsel those who responded. Some 500 copies of the slides and tape were sold, and I took the programme to make a personal presentation at more than a hundred locations.

Winding up affairs after Wembley was painful. The Evangelical Alliance had used up all its resources in promoting Harringay and Wembley. There came a time when the reckoning had to be done. At Roy Cattell's suggestion, the EA Council invited three businessmen to join their finance committee – Tony Kimpton, George Goyder and Peter Hemery. They looked at the EA affairs through the eyes of business people, and found it hard to reconcile the way in which this charity was run with the way in which their businesses would operate. Sadly they found that Roy Cattell had spent more extravagantly than they felt was justified and they called for his resignation. They were concerned that the EA had no reserves, and yet still maintained a large staff – a legacy from the two crusades. Roy Cattell had done nothing to reduce this expenditure and they felt that he was responsible. They appointed Peter Hemery as supremo, and gave him the task of sacking all the staff.

Roy raised no protest, but humbly submitted to their request and left without a fuss. Later events were to prove that Roy had operated far more economically than he was given credit for. In fact had things been allowed to continue as they were, the traumas of the next few months might have been avoided. Having set all this in motion, Tony Kimpton and George Goyder both resigned from the EA finance committee, leaving Peter Hemery to fulfil the task of reshaping the alliance. Peter called together all of the former crusade staff, and gently explained to them his need to terminate their employment forthwith. He did this so graciously that the large number of staff involved clubbed together and presented Peter Hemery with a mantelpiece clock as a token of their appreciation!

My own employment with the EA was also in jeopardy and on August 27th, 1954 I was called in to see Sir Arthur Smith. He started to explain why I would have to leave, when I interrupted him and asked if he remembered our conversation two years previously. He had then asked how sure the EA could be that I would stay with them, and I had replied, 'Until the Lord tells me to leave.' Now I simply said that I did not feel that that time had yet come, and that the Lord was still calling me to the work of the EA. Sir Arthur coughed, then he said: 'I like that, Rowlandson! You can stay.'

The traumatic days between the departure of Roy Cattell and the appointment of Gilbert Kirby as his successor were hard to understand. In the middle of them came the news that the land-line relay programme had produced a surplus of more than twelve thousand pounds. This was largely due to the fact that our budget had been based upon 200 relays whereas more than 2,000 had been arranged. None the less, this came as very welcome news to the EA in the financial stringency which they were presently facing. In fact, it put the EA back on to a sound footing. Gilbert Kirby appointed an ex-army colonel (who knew all about logistics) to supervise the EA finances and to conserve this nest-egg. Colonel Pugh became a byword in EA history, and without his wise guidance the alliance might never have survived.

The dear colonel was a good Anglican. He was a little mystified by the intensity of bible-believing Christians. There came a day when the Council of the Evangelical Alliance was in session. Sir Arthur Smith was in the chair, and all of the hierarchy of the evangelical world was sitting around the table. You name the heavyweights of those days, and they were there! The discussion was on some form of follow-up to the crusades, and a budget of some one hundred and fifty thousand pounds was being contemplated. While the members of the council were getting more and more enthused, Colonel Pugh was reaching exploding point. Eventually he could stand their financial nonsense no longer, and in his best and most expressive colonel's voice he burst out: 'I don't know where the hell you're going to get the money!' There was spluttering and confusion around the table, but Gilbert Kirby, in his masterly and diplomatic way, managed to smooth things over. The proposed programme never went ahead.

By the end of the two years, with Harringay, the relays, and the Wembley crusade, Marilyn and I were tired. We decided that the time had come to visit Marilyn's parents in Minneapolis and the Evangelical Alliance Council was happy to free me for three months. So in June 1955 Marilyn and I with our two young children, Gary aged five and Cherylyn aged four, travelled to Minneapolis. We went on the *Nieuw Amsterdam* and returned on the SS *United States* – sea travel was still cheaper than air in those days!

I had been invited to work at the Billy Graham office in Minneapolis. This was a great blessing to me as it enabled me to earn some money: at that time you could still take only twenty-five pounds per person out of Britain because of exchange control restrictions. I spent three weeks in the BGEA office, and it gave me some very useful experience. There was also enough spare cash to see us through. George Wilson was very generous to us.

Towards the end of our stay, I learned that Billy Graham was to conduct a crusade in Toronto. Marilyn said that I should go and visit it. She felt that it would be a bit too much travelling for her to come with the children. So I travelled by train to Toronto alone. At that time, as far as the team was concerned, I would have fallen over backwards to avoid pushing myself forward, so I chose a quiet hotel where I would not appear to be dogging the footsteps of the team. My surprise can be imagined when I discovered that, by chance, I had chosen the same hotel at which all the team were staying! I was covered with embarrassment, but they were all very kind to me.

The evening of my arrival I went to the arena where the meetings were to be held, and was immediately struck by its similarity to Harringay. During the crusade at Harringay Arena, there had been two people who were always in the same place, night after night. One of these was Willis Haymaker, a member of the Billy Graham team and responsible for the physical arrangements in the arena; the other was a Christian businessman, Francis Horsborough. He was not on any committees arranging Harringay but he was a keen prayer supporter who came every night and always sat in the same seat on the platform near to Billy Graham.

Willis Haymaker – given the nickname 'Sunshine' by the stewards' team (because you only make hay when the sun shines) – was one of the most saintly men I ever met. He had worked with many famous evangelists, including Billy Sunday and Gypsy Smith (for whom he had set up many of his meetings), and his heart was totally committed to this ministry. He was always smiling; he always had a cheerful word for everybody, and when problems arose, it was he who was a steadying influence and solved the problem in a straightforward way. We all loved him dearly. As chief steward, I was in close liaison with him day by day and often joined him in the left hand tunnel alongside the platform. When I needed him I always knew I would find him there.

We used to share many experiences together, and it was his custom to say to me: 'The meeting can start now: Francis Horsborough has just taken his seat!' Mr Horsborough himself had been deeply involved in many evangelistic enterprises, and when he became involved he was always fully involved. It was no different with the Billy Graham crusade.

Because the arena in Toronto was so like Harringay, I wondered if Willis Haymaker would be in his accustomed spot. I made my way to the left hand tunnel and, sure enough, there he was! He greeted me like a long-lost brother, warm and welcoming.

'Isn't this place exactly like Harringay?' I said, and he agreed. 'The main difference,' I added, 'is that Horsborough won't be on the platform!' Willis smiled. 'Oh yes, he is!' he said, pointing. There was Mr Horsborough in precisely the same seat that he had occupied for all those nights at Harringay. Willis later told me that Mr Horsborough didn't miss a night in Toronto either: a remarkable man.

Two months in the USA were enough to give our two children American accents. A tape recording of their voices at that time is dramatic evidence of the difference. Gary, explaining about our return trip on the SS *United States*, remarked: 'Gee, man! That ship was so noisy,' in an accent that was anything but that with which he had been brought up. On that homeward trip, on Sunday, October 16th, 1955, I was invited by the captain to conduct Morning Worship aboard – a unique experience. I spoke on the story of 'the stilling of the storm' and reminded the congregation that when Christ stilled the storm for the ship He was on, there were also with Him 'other little ships'. It must have been dramatic for them as their storm was stilled too. But then it is always dramatic for those around us, when our lives are changed by the power of Christ.

On our return to England there was, almost immediately, a meeting of the Evangelical Alliance Council. One of the members, Mr Oliver Stott, was a businessman from Southampton and he had become deeply involved in an evangelistic film ministry in prisons. He used the Billy Graham films. Not only had he found the films to be well received by the prisoners, but many of them had accepted Christ as their Saviour as a result. He proposed to the EA Council that they should initiate a programme of film evangelism in prisons.

The EA Council decided to test this as God's will, and sent out a letter to their constituency explaining about this possible ministry. The letter sought support for the plan: if the response was encouraging, the council would give further consideration to implementing it.

The response was not only encouraging, but overwhelming! A large bank balance was built up to finance this new ministry. Oliver Stott was prompted to say: 'Whenever the Evangelical Alliance turns its hand to evangelism, God always blesses!' He was given the task of setting up the ministry, and his first act was to appoint me to organise and maintain it.

Together we approached the prison chaplains' department at the Home Office, and found an immediate response from them. We were virtually given an open door to any prison in the UK. They sent us the names and addresses of every prison chaplain in England, Scotland and Wales and I set about making contact with them. During the next six years, I visited every penal establishment in the UK (except Northern Ireland) with one or another of the Billy Graham films. Quite the most effective, and the most popular, was *Souls in Conflict* – the film which had been made during the Harringay crusade, which told the conversion story of three people (including the actress Joan Winmill).

For our family, my long absences from home were distressing. I was travelling more often than not. Marilyn was given heavier responsibilities than she should have had in bringing up the children. Her input in those formative years when the children were small is vividly demonstrated in the blessing we both share today in a family that not only loves the Lord and His work, but is actively involved and supportive in so many ways. My absences could have been disastrous; that they were not is all credit to her.

There were occasions when my children were asked by their school friends: 'Where's your father?' The reply, 'In prison,' was not always understood in the way it was meant! I once went to speak at a church fellowship meeting. I had been asked to talk about the prison ministry of the EA, but I found the meeting billed outside the church as: 'Maurice Rowlandson will talk about his experiences in prison'.

God does things in odd ways sometimes! For example, when the film *Souls in Conflict* was being made, there were a couple of parts where I was asked to stand in as a film extra. As a result, when I showed the film in prison, prisoners would often come and ask me: 'Sir, was it you I saw in that film?' It gave a point of contact which otherwise would have been difficult to make. (David Rennie and his wife Ruth were also invited to act as extras in making that film. In later years he was to become chairman of the Billy Graham London board.)

Encouragements along the way were numerous. There was, for example, the letter received from Stanley Holland. He had seen the film as a prisoner in Dartmoor prison and later wrote to me:

It is now quite some months since you visited this prison with your film unit and the film which has led to a lot of happenings in my life. I shall never, as long as I live, forget *Souls in Conflict*. It has taken all this time before I could feel justified in writing to you. You see, I wanted to make really sure that I had found God before I started making any commitments. So I purchased Billy Graham's two books *The Secret of Happiness* and *Peace with God*. Since then I have read many books by many authors and as I read so I seemed to come nearer and nearer to God; but it was when I first picked up the greatest Book of all that I started to read and really started to live. Yes, even here in my present situation, I think I am happier than I have ever been before. My cell no longer seems dull and empty but in my quiet moments I feel that God is with me and as I read my Bible I find him ever near ... I would like to take this opportunity to thank you for your visit which was basic to my new found faith and conversion ... I am working hard to pass on God's message to other inmates of this institution and in some cases I have met with success. Already I have managed to bring one of my workmates to God.

It is often said in here that prison is the breeding ground of crime but from my own experience I know that it can be also the birthplace of Christians.

One of those he brought to Christ was Dennis Lockwood whose family are still close to the Lord today. Another had been divorced by his wife following his conviction for robbery with assault. From prison, he first led his ex-mother-in-law to Christ through his letters and her visits, and later his ex-wife also found Christ through his witness. After his release, it was a joy to learn that he and his ex-wife were reunited. One day he wrote and told me that they were going to remarry. He wrote: 'Is it all right for me to live with my wife until we are married?' That was in the days before society recognised the common law wife, and he was concerned to know that by taking this step he would not be committing a sin. I replied with 'What God hath joined, let no man put asunder,' and explained that in the eyes of God they were still married.

As news got around about the prison ministry, enquiries started to come in from the Army, the Royal Navy and the Royal Air Force. They too felt that they had an indigenous population which needed the gospel. We were asked if we could extend the ministry to include the military also. We felt that this was appropriate and, although it meant even more absences from home, I was asked to include this extra brief. Often it was possible to combine the two: prisons mostly wanted a film in the afternoon; for the military it was more convenient in the evening. Thus we were able to maximise our time and effort.

It was during this period that I first met Billy Strachan. He was at RAF Stafford where, through the ministry of the chaplain, the Reverend Keith Ensor, he had been brought to Christ from a truly pagan background. At the time of his call he had been camp comedian, so his conversion to Christ was noticed by all – especially as one of his duties included serving in the bar of the officers' mess.

The film *Souls in Conflict* meant a lot to Billy, and consolidated a concern he had to get involved in Christian work. A year later, Keith Ensor invited me back to Stafford, both to show films and to conduct a series of evangelistic meetings. On my arrival he said that one of the young airmen would like to carry my bag during the visit. This turned out to be Billy Strachan.

During that visit we had many talks together, and he shared with me his desire to get trained to enter the Christian ministry.

But academically he was unqualified to enter any training college in the UK. I said that I thought I could get him a scholarship or bursary at my old college at Northwestern Schools in Minneapolis.

I wrote to George Wilson, and the long and short of it was that Billy Strachan went to Northwestern; he returned to work with the Torchbearer Fellowship, and was ultimately to become principal of the Winter Bible School at Capernwray Hall and a much sought-after speaker around the world, including at the Keswick Convention. If Billy Graham had never invited me to attend Northwestern, that option for Billy Strachan might never have happened. God has His own way of putting the right people, with the right experiences, in the right places at the right time.

                    ✳   ✳   ✳

The Chaplain General to the Forces approached us, and asked if we would take the films to show to Army and Air Force establishments in Germany. The British Army of the Rhine (BAOR) maintained a presence right across Western Germany, and in Berlin, and the chaplains were struggling both to minister and to keep up morale. BAOR undertook to plan a trip for us and to cover all the expenses. Over the next five years we were to visit BAOR on three occasions, each one meticulously planned to give us three days of film shows; a day off and travel to the next area; three more days and so on for a three to four week period.

On each trip I took a colleague to help carry my bag and to provide company for the journey. We had many adventures together. We were made honorary colonels for the period of our visit, and we lived in the officers' mess at each location. Henry Hole was the first companion I took. He and I were accommodated in the main visiting officers' mess at Munchen Gladbach. The food there was atrocious – and Henry complained about it. One day, we came home to lunch and on the sideboard were two magnificent plates of hors d'oeuvres. Henry commented that they had taken note of our complaint, and had provided us with superior fare. He brought the two plates to our table, and we had just consumed – and enjoyed – them when the steward came in. When he saw his two plates missing, he

looked at our table and blanched, guessing immediately
what had happened. It turned out that the plates of hors
d'oeuvres had been specially provided for an inspecting
brigadier who was expected for lunch! We considered we had
had enough to eat, and promptly disappeared from the dining
room, leaving the steward to cope with his problem.

While Henry was with me, he and I had one of the days
off thoughtfully planned by the chaplains' department. We
took off into the hills in bleak and stormy weather. High up
in the least likely place, Henry got hungry and suggested we
should find somewhere to eat. There was neither a hotel nor
a restaurant within miles, and I protested that we would have
to wait. Henry would have none of it, and directed me to stop
outside an unlikely looking tiny mountain farm while he went
in to talk to the lady of the house.

To this day, Henry claims he was guided! Not only did she
welcome us with open arms, but she had a freezer packed
with luscious steaks, and she cooked us a meal which will
always remain in our memory. Superbly cooked and served,
the meal was rounded off at her insistence with a tiny glass
of honey liqueur. It would have been ungracious to refuse and
we tasted the most delectable beverage that we had ever found.
Thereafter, Henry tried (and has tried in the forty years since)
to rediscover this particular beverage – but without success.

Another companion I had was Jim Sargeant. He was taking
leave from his work as a civil servant and was good company.
But, whenever we ate, I had to decide for him what he would eat.
Like a good civil servant, he found it hard to take a decision.

Trevor Brient came with me on one occasion. On our rest
day we were accommodated at the Park Hotel in Düsseldorf.
Our rooms were on the top – fifth – floor. Trevor's room was
along the passage from mine, and the next morning I called
him on the housephone to ask if he was ready for breakfast.
He said he was, and would come along to my room. I awaited
his knock on the door – but it never came; instead, there was a
knock on the window. Trevor had climbed out of his window
and walked along a five-inch-wide parapet (five storeys up) from
his room to mine! My knees went weak as I thought of all that
might have happened had he fallen.

An old colleague, Peter Bond, came on one trip. He had
not had a lot of experience of travelling abroad and was not

entirely clued up about exchange rates. Our first day – en route to BAOR – was spent in Brussels, and he managed to spend all the currency he had brought with him. He had to telephone his wife, back home in England, to ask her to send him some more. Thereafter, I took charge of his money, and issued him his daily allowance.

He was not one of those who completely understood what I was trying to do in these evangelistic film shows. He was puzzled because some of the chaplains we met seemed to be talking the same language while others tended to hold me at arm's length. I tried to explain to Peter that not all the chaplains were involved in evangelism – indeed, to some of them it would be entirely strange. He asked me if I kept a little black book in which I put the names of those chaplains who were all right! After that, Peter would sidle up to me after we had first met a new chaplain and would whisper in my ear: 'Is he in the black book?'

It was while Peter was with me that one of the chaplains took us to the German pub at which the zither man (famous for the theme of *The Third Man*) played. At the time I had just discovered that I had contracted German measles on the trip, so I was not entirely thrilled with the idea of a long drive to the smoky atmosphere. Peter did not realise that German beer was infinitely stronger than British beer and both he and the chaplain had rather more than they should. On the hair-raising journey back to our Army base, the chaplain suggested a stop at another pub. I protested vehemently, and in the end told Peter that if he aided and abetted the chaplain, I would put him on the train back to London the next day. Peter persuaded the chaplain to go straight back – but things were not helped when we went to turn in. Peter was OK: I discovered, however, that under the cover my bed was unmade. Feeling rotten, I slept on the bare mattress with just the cover over me, determined that the next morning Peter was going home. But I relented – and he didn't. In fact, he turned out to be an enormous help for the remainder of the trip.

In between these adventures, we had the film shows. They were wonderful occasions. We gave mostly one, sometimes two or even three a day; always in packed Army cinemas, and always with a vociferous and responsive audience. But best of all was the appeal which I made after every showing. Never was there an occasion when men failed to respond, and all who responded were counselled. I am still in touch with many of them today. Some have travelled with their families to live in faraway places, but they still keep in contact. Those precious days were an extension of the ministry of Billy Graham from the Harringay Arena, and it was a privilege to have a part in them.

Of course every film we showed was a Billy Graham film. Thus the Billy Graham Evangelistic Association was deeply interested in this ministry and from time to time I reported to them, as well as to my own EA Council. The BGEA responded by making more and more films available to us. I was conscious of the fact that through this film ministry I was maintaining my contacts with Billy Graham and his team, and I felt content that, at the time, I appeared to be in the centre of God's will.

In addition to this film work, George Wilson tended to keep me fairly well occupied – with the support of the Evangelical Alliance – in numerous ways. For example, he told me about Kenneth S. Keyes – a wealthy professional man from Florida – who would be visiting Britain to deliver a series of lectures entitled 'In Partnership with God'. Basically these were messages on the Christian responsibility of giving, and his meetings changed the giving habits of countless people who heard him. George Wilson invited me to handle the details of his visit, and to take him around.

In appreciation of the time we spent with him and his wife, Ken Keyes took Marilyn and me out to dinner at the Savoy Hotel. It was a magnificent dinner, but I was a little shocked when I saw that the tip he was leaving was twenty pounds – a lot of money in those days. If that was 10 per cent of the bill, I shuddered to think what the total must have been! As we left the hotel, Ken put his arm around my shoulder and said, in all sincerity, 'You know, Maureece, the thing that Polly and I like about the Savoy is that it's so *reasonable*!' I suppose it is all a question of relativity!

Some time in 1959 I received a visit from Stanley High. At the time he was a senior editor for *Reader's Digest*. He had come to England, he told me, to do a survey on the results of the Harringay crusade of 1954. He told me that he was a sceptic, and that his expectations were low. From me he wanted as many contacts as I could give him.

Three months later he was back. 'I don't want to believe what I've got to believe,' he said. 'I have discovered that at least 72 per cent of those who responded at the Harringay crusade are still involved in religion.' I told him that most of them would not confess to being involved in 'religion': rather they would tell him that they were still involved with Christ as their Saviour and Lord. He was obviously shaken by his discoveries, and later wrote a very fair report in the magazine. Later still, his position had so changed that he became a member of the committee organising Billy Graham's subsequent crusade in New York.

Then, out of the blue, in May 1961 I received a telephone call from George Wilson who was now running the Minneapolis office of the Billy Graham Evangelistic Association. He asked me if I would have lunch with him as he was passing through London on his way back to America after the 1961 Manchester crusade. I met him for lunch in London and he asked me what I was currently doing. I explained about the continuing ministry of films in prisons and among the military. I told him that the EA was beginning to run out of funds for this film ministry and that they might be closing it down. He asked what I would then be doing. I replied that there was to be a bible exhibition in the early autumn in which I was involved. 'And then?' he persisted. I replied that I did not know what would happen after that.

'Then that's the date you start with us at the London office of the Billy Graham Evangelistic Association,' he said. I could scarcely believe my ears. I had never dreamt that I would be invited to join such a ministry. At first, my reaction was one of doubt – but George went on to reassure me. They were planning an expansion of the London office. Possibly London might become the office from which all international arrangements (especially in Europe) would be made. He added that one of the American team members was being seconded to London to run this office, and I was to be his assistant.

It took me so much by surprise that I could not give an immediate answer. I said that I must talk it over with Marilyn, and that I must pray about it. One of the biggest obstacles was my involvement with the EA. What would Sir Arthur Smith say about this after all I had said to him? I decided to talk it over with Gilbert Kirby, my present EA boss, and seek his counsel.

When I got home, Marilyn was thrilled with the invitation and said: 'Of course you must accept it.' The next day I saw Gilbert, and shared with him the invitation that George Wilson had given to me. Gilbert replied: 'Well! This is truly remarkable. Just yesterday I was talking with Sir Arthur Smith, and I said to him, "I can't think what in the world we're going to do with Maurice. The EA ministry is altering so much. We are moving into the world of relationships and diplomacy: not really his forte. He's a project man."' He went on to indicate that both he and Sir Arthur would lay no obstacle in my path if I decided to move over to the BGEA. He also made it clear that there would still be a place for me at the EA if I felt that it was not right to move. 'We'll find some development in which you can be used,' he said.

Sir Arthur Smith wrote to me in his own distinctive handwriting:

> If you feel it is 'of the Lord' there is no more to be said, for we *all* want God's will to be done. Nevertheless the EA will miss you, though I am sure there will be many opportunities for you in the Dr Billy Graham Organisation in Great Britain. Thank you for all you have done for EA, and may God bless you in your future responsibilities.

Once again, I felt that God's guidance was abundantly clear. I had felt that I was getting stale in the film ministry; finance to support it was beginning to run out; there was no immediate future activity for me in the EA; Sir Arthur was aware of this, and was ready to release me; Gilbert was happy for me to accept; Marilyn felt that it was of the Lord. So my guidance circle was complete and I joyfully told George Wilson that I wished to accept. I was appointed to start in September 1961. The thin gold line was continuing!

Above:
Harringay 1954.
The view from the
platform.

Right:
Cliff Barrows and
the choir.

Below:
Wembley 1955.

Left:
Billy Graham on
the platform at
Harringay.

Above:
Spre-e 73.
Dave Foster
interviews
Cliff Richard and
Billy Graham.

Above:
Billy Graham with Bishop
Goodwin and Mrs Hudson.

Right:
Cherylyn Rowlandson after
receiving the Duke of
Edinburgh's Gold Award.

4

Creating a London Base

'Thy hand, O Lord, has guided': looking back on the years from 1946 to 1961, there was a quiet consciousness of the presence of God in all of my life. To those who truly believe in His omnipotence, then there is comfort in allowing Him to have His way in our lives.

To me this has meant that whether the sun is shining, or there is a violent storm, He is in control and the end result will be for His glory. Not always is it what I would want it to be; Marilyn and I were to learn all about that as the years went by. But we need to wait upon Him. The prophet Isaiah said: 'Those who hope in the Lord will renew their strength. They will soar on wings like eagles; they will run and not grow weary; they will walk and not be faint' (Isaiah 40:31). My prayer has always been: 'Teach me, Lord, to hope.'

Sometimes His demands are enormous – but He helps us to be ready for them. So it was not altogether an impossible demand that George Wilson put upon me when he said: 'In the Billy Graham Evangelistic Association, we employ you for 365 days a year and for twenty-four hours a day: any time left over is your own!' That is commitment: that is what having a vocation is all about. Sadly, there is a denigration of both commitment and vocation today. The question more often asked is, 'What is in it for me?'

In later years when interviewing a personal assistant for a job I learned that if their first question was, 'What will my hours be?' then they were probably not suited for the job. The most dedicated PAs that I have had have been those who made their job their life – and loved it!

What George Wilson's statement really meant was that when you were needed, you should be available. And so it has been over thirty years – and still is, even though I am retired. Sometimes the telephone would ring in the early hours because one of my colleagues in the USA had forgotten the time difference. It is a struggle to wake up sufficiently in an instant to be bright and positive on the telephone, but after years of coping with it I would not have it any differently.

There was one occasion (after a hectic period of preparation for a crusade) when my colleague Dr Walter Smyth telephoned me from California at around 3 a.m. Marilyn and I had a flat in Frinton where we had gone for the week, but I had had to return to my home in London mid-week for a special meeting of the committee the next day. At the last minute, Marilyn had decided to come up to London with me. When the phone rang Dr Smyth said: 'I hope I didn't wake you up!' On occasions like that, a little white lie is probably permitted, so that you don't make the other person feel too bad. 'No,' I responded and we discussed our business. His last question was: 'How's Marilyn?' I replied, still a bit woolly from waking up: 'She's fine – she's down at Frinton.' Marilyn turned over in bed and said to me: 'Who do you think you're in bed with?' Afterwards, she said that she'd missed her cue – she should have said, in a dreamy voice unlike her own: 'Honey, who's that on the telephone?'

Walter Smyth had asked me to plan a press conference aboard the *Queen Mary* in May 1961, when Billy Graham arrived at Southampton on his way to the crusade in Manchester. This was to be on the Bank Holiday Monday, May 22nd, and two of my colleagues from the Evangelical Alliance went down with me to Southampton. It was an emotive day for me, because over the weekend there had been three or four false alarms concerning the arrival of our fourth child. Marilyn had gone into hospital and had been sent home. 'She's a fraud,' the matron had said. I left her at home while I went to Southampton for the press conference.

After the press conference I was asked to take Billy Graham to visit Mr and Mrs John Cordle at their home. This detour delayed me somewhat and put me at the back of the home-going Bank Holiday traffic. It had been an excellent and hot day, so there was a lot of it. It was close to midnight by the time I reached Edgware, and I thought it worth driving by the small nursing home to see if there was a light on in the room which I knew Marilyn would be using. It was dark, so I went on home. Marilyn's mother was with us from America, and for the last two nights, Marilyn had slept in a spare bed in her mother's room because she was uncomfortable in ours. I peeped in the room as I reached home and both she and her mother appeared to be in bed. Ten minutes after I had gone to bed, the telephone rang. It was Matron. 'Mr Rowlandson, you've got a daughter,' she said. I replied: 'I can't have; my wife's asleep in the next room!' What foolish things we say. Of course, in the dark it was the pillows on the bed that I had seen, and Jacqueline Mary Rowlandson was born in the early hours of May 23rd.

The first London office of the Billy Graham Evangelistic Association was opened by George Wilson in 1955, so I was not in at the very beginning. He had invited the Reverend (later Bishop) A. W. Goodwin Hudson to set up the necessary legal arrangements, and an office was opened at 9 John Street, WC1. That was Goodwin Hudson's office when he worked with the South American Missionary Society. A year or so later, he acquired the lease of 54a Tottenham Court Road, which then became the London office of the BGEA until 1961. Around 1959, Goodwin Hudson (or 'Huddy' as he was lovingly and universally known) invited a young girl from the former church of his friend the Reverend Harry Sutton in Blackpool, Jean Wilson, to come and run the office. Like me, she is still associated with the Billy Graham Evangelistic Association today. Jean was a tall, competent, exceptional person, and if God had designed someone specially for this task with the BGEA, then she was the exact person. She had an interesting background, coming from a non-Christian family (her mother was a Tiller Girl, and Jean had inherited her long legs!).

Until 1961, 54a Tottenham Court Road had served the BGEA well and Jean Wilson had set up an excellent base under the guidance of Huddy. But in 1961, a new project was on the horizon. It was possible that London would become the new headquarters for the overseas ministry of Billy Graham. The headquarters of the Billy Graham Evangelistic Association was, and would remain, in Minneapolis; but it was decided that much money could be saved by locating the organisation of Billy Graham's international ministry in London.

I was told that 54a did not have the right image for this new and important role. I was asked to look around for more suitable premises. I found several, but the one which attracted us the most was Bush House, in Aldwych. The second floor of the north-east wing was available at an acceptable rent, and I was instructed to negotiate for these premises.

All of this happened before I took up my full-time appointment on September 1st, 1961, the day on which I officially became a member of the staff of the Billy Graham Evangelistic Association. A great many friends sent their good wishes to me at that time – but the message which meant most came from my friend and former employer, Tom Rees. He wrote on a card from New York: 'May God's richest blessing be on you both in your new sphere of service. Yours, 'til the devil joins the PBs, TOM.'

In early September 1961, George Wilson asked me to travel to Minneapolis for training and orientation in the work of the association. Marilyn was to come with me and on September 13th, 1961, the night before we left, we were packing our bags. There came a ring at the front door, and there was Tom Rees who had driven all the way up from Hildenborough Hall in Kent. He told us he had come to pray with us before we left for America. We felt that that was a wonderful thing for him to have done. It was so typical of his caring interest.

For the three weeks after our arrival I was put through an intensive period of training. George arranged for me to spend a day in each department and I was able to sit down and learn the procedures. I was taught everything from card-punching for the computer to mail-opening and reading the thousands of letters which arrived every day. George wanted me to install in London as many as possible of the systems and routines which were used in Minneapolis. There was much to learn, and we spent long hours going over a myriad of details.

While I was busy at the office, Marilyn was able to see her family. For her a visit to Minneapolis was a visit home. Her father and mother and one of her two brothers (as well as dozens of aunts, uncles and cousins) still lived in the twin cities of Minneapolis and St Paul, on either side of the Mississippi River, and she was able to spend time with them. It was our first visit since 1955. God takes care of the little things too! How remarkable it was that Marilyn's family home should be in the same city as the headquarters of the Billy Graham Evangelistic

Association. Over the next thirty years there were to be many times when a visit to headquarters was necessary or possible.

The lease of Bush House was finalised during my time in Minneapolis, and Jean Wilson supervised the move from 54a Tottenham Court Road to the new offices. They were very grand after the warehouse-type premises at 54a. So when I came back from America and joined the London office on October 9th, 1961 Jean Wilson was already there. It says volumes for her grace and stature that she should so willingly accept a newcomer imposed upon her in this way. She and I immediately went into consultation about the plans for London.

Most important and urgent of these was the impending publication of the British edition of the magazine, *Decision*. We negotiated with numerous printers, and Mr Philips of Waterlow's was successful in gaining the contract. From America we received silverprints of the magazine, together with a set of positives. From these the magazine would be printed. But before that could happen, we needed to anglicise and sub-edit all the articles. Publication in London meant that we could inject British spelling, British news and British articles. Waterlow's would take note of these changes and alter the positives. When necessary new positives would be made.

We started off by sending a copy of the magazine free to everyone on our mailing list. That was some 230,000 in all. An invitation to subscribe was enclosed, and about 25,000 formed our initial subscription list. After the first year, we sent the magazine only to our subscribers.

We were up against deadlines from the start. Often the positives were delayed; sometimes the delay was editorial, and sometimes it was the air mail – but most often it was a delay at Customs and Excise. Many a month, Jean Wilson would dash out to London Airport at the eleventh hour to rescue overdue positives which had been rushed through all the formalities by our excellent agents, Messrs Schenkers Ltd, and we delivered them to the printer in the nick of time. It was knife-edge timing, and mostly we were on the right side. Jean Wilson loved the drama of those airport trips, but it put years on the rest of us.

Another big activity during the first few months at Bush House was our negotiations with the firm of Messrs Marshall, Morgan and Scott, the evangelical publishers. They were on the brink of closing down their weekly newspaper, the *Christian*. When Billy Graham heard about this, he urged that they should allow the association to purchase the paper and publish it. The negotiations were successful and we took it over – editor, staff and all. We were to publish it for the next seven years with varying degrees of difficulty. The story will emerge in later pages.

On the morning of November 19th, 1962 I received two items of news. First I learned that my colleague from the team who had been working with me in London would be returning to America for good. Secondly I learned that I was invited to attend the team meeting, starting the next day, in America. It was quite unexpected and I was surprised to receive the invitation. I was told that my air tickets would be waiting for me at London Airport. This was to be the first of many conferences which, year by year, were highlights of my life.

That first team meeting at Airlie House in West Virginia was a precious experience because it was so new. There was an atmosphere of unity and love such as I had never known before. I counted myself fortunate to have been invited. Many of those present I knew from the crusades in London. Most of them were old and trusted friends.

I still have two vivid memories of incidents at that team meeting. First was the strange accommodation. My room had a private bathroom – or so I thought. But there was a door the other side of the bath which I discovered led into the room of another member of the team, Frank Jacobson, and his young daughter. My private bathroom was also *their* private bathroom! So we had to devise a scheme of knocking on the door first before entering. The second memory was of the enormous red apple which was left outside my bedroom door each morning. Without exaggerating, it was the size of an ogen melon. I had never before – and have never since – seen such enormous apples.

Those 'rose-coloured spectacles' through which I was often accused of looking at Billy Graham and his team were working overtime at Airlie House. If I am insufficiently critical for some of my readers, I can only reply that I have recorded things as I found them. I am able to tell only of my own personal experiences over thirty years. In all that time I cannot recall a harsh word; there was justified criticism often, but always given constructively and with grace. I cannot recall the insidious 'have you heard about . . . ' syndrome, when one company member talks about another. If the team members did talk about each other, it was either jokingly, or in support or concern: never in a scandalous manner. When we joined hands around the room (some 185 of us) at the end of the conference and sang 'Blest be the tie that binds our hearts in Christian love', it was real as well as experiential. I left the team meeting uplifted, inspired and blessed. How could God be so good as to have allowed me to be part of this remarkable movement? It is small wonder that in the 1990s, the essential team on the platform, in the offices and close to Billy Graham comprises the same personnel as were with him in similar capacities in the 1950s.

I returned to a strange office in London. At Airlie House, Billy Graham himself had asked me to carry on running things in the absence of my former team colleague. He said that in all probability someone else would come from America to take over the leadership of the office. Indeed, during the next few months a number of American friends came with this project in mind; the last was a Dr James Jauncey.

George Wilson had asked me to meet him at the airport, show him the ropes and introduce him to the office. He was to be there three or four days, at the end of which time he would decide whether or not to come to London to run things. He was a delightful person and I would have had no difficulty in working with him. He went into great detail about the office procedure and ministry. At the end, as I took him back to the airport, he said: 'I don't know why Billy wants someone to come and take over this office. Seems to me he's already got the best person to lead it in you. I shall tell him so.' I think he must have done so, because no one else ever came and a few months later the British board appointed me as the London director – an appointment I held until the London office closed in September 1987.

So now it was a matter of getting down to business. I con-centrated on increasing the subscriptions to *Decision* magazine. After negotiations with the *Kent and Sussex Courier*, we were able to put a free copy of the magazine into every edition of their paper, a remarkable opportunity.

Decision was essentially evangelistic. One day a man walked into my office. He had the air of a bank manager – and such he had been. He was smart and well dressed. He told me that twelve months before he had been a tramp on the streets of London. A few years before that he had been manager of a branch of one of the big five banks, and then the demon drink had changed his life. His wife had left him; his children were estranged. He had no income other than that which he received from begging in the streets. His clothes were in tatters and, in common with other such vagrants, he slept rough and searched the waste bins on London's lampposts for scraps of food and occasional treasure. One day, he pulled out a copy of the magazine *Decision* which someone had thrown away. He took it out; attracted to the cover and the title of the cover story, he sat and read it right through. My visitor told me that this was his own story. The message of the gospel had brought him back to his senses. He had been reconciled to his wife and family, and he was back at the bank as a cashier, working his way up the ladder once again. His drink problem was behind him, as Christ had brought a new perspective to his life.

When George Wilson heard that story, he claimed that we should put a copy of *Decision* magazine in every lamppost bin in London!

Over the years, there has often been considerable hilarity generated by letters we have received. This letter about a sub-scription to *Decision* magazine needs to be read aloud to get the full impact:

Dear Sir

I enclose a cheque for .75p for twelve monthly issues of *Decision*. I sent you one pound some many months back for *Decision* as I did not know what the cost of it was – this was sent to London. Ever since I have been receiving *two* copies of *Decision* instead of one; one addressed to Miss B. Evans and the other to Miss E. Evans. I wrote to explain this to London and I still keep getting two copies of the same edition each month.

May I explain that Miss E. Evans and Miss B. Evans is the *same* person: when I sign a cheque I put my signature on it as E. Evans, but for everything else I put B. Evans as I am known as *Bessie* Evans. My sister is Miss R. Evans of the same address and she also gets *Decision* magazine. But I am the one who is getting two copies of *Decision*. So please send me one copy in future to Miss B. Evans, although the cheque will be signed E. Evans.

I hope this is clear now. If it will be easier for you to send
all communications to me as Miss E. Evans, let me know,
and I will always sign myself E. Evans.

Yours sincerely

B. Evans

Occasionally people have expressed themselves in a way which
is clear to them but open to misunderstanding when we receive
it, like this letter: 'I apologise for the delay in returning the
enclosed list of names but the advent of a baby and the fact
that I had mislaid the same has been responsible for this. I
send you my prayerful regards.' The list . . . or the baby? The
following letter also left us perplexed:

Would you please correct your mailing list. For some years
you have sent literature to us as Mr & Mrs Jones – and we
have just received the latest letter from you.

However, I have to tell you that Mrs Jones has been
'called home'. I have just become the second Mrs Jones
and I would be grateful if you would amend your mailing
list to take care of this.

What were we to do? Then sometimes people give us something
of a surprise. This happened just after we had circulated one of
Mr Graham's prayer letters. A lady wrote: 'In the letter you wrote
recently, you enclosed an envelope for me to send back with a
gift. I'm sorry to say that I sent the envelope back to you, but
without the gift I intended to put in it. Please send me another
envelope, and I'll send you the gift.' Couldn't she have put the
gift into the envelope which contained her letter to us?

We had a visit regularly from a dear old Chelsea Pensioner.
He would come in to leave a gift 'for Billy' he said. He told us
that the gift he was giving us was the tithe of 10 per cent of
his winnings on the football pools! He must have done fairly
well, because sometimes his gifts were not insignificant. We
deliberated whether or not to accept this tainted money. Then
someone remembered that one of the team had commented at
the time of Harringay, 'The money's all the Lord's: we've just
got to get it back from the wrong hands!'

Through all of this time the *Christian* was a great problem
to us. As newspaper journalists, the editorial team insisted on

the freedom of the press. We did not always share the views of
the editor, and one day when George Wilson was in London he
drew attention to severely critical articles about evangelism in
general and Billy Graham in particular. 'How can they write
things like that?' he asked. He called for the editor to come
and see him and he made this statement: 'Before the Lord, you
must either be loyal to Billy Graham or tomorrow morning I will
have your pay cheque ready and we can part company.' It was a
bold and challenging step to take – but it was right. He gave the
editor overnight to think about it. The next morning, the editor
returned to say that the principle of loyalty was unacceptable,
and George Wilson handed over the pay cheque.

Finding a replacement was not easy. We interviewed many
potential editors. One of them presented a list of twelve conditions to be accepted by the BGEA before he would commit
himself. Mostly they were totally unacceptable to us. Then, one
day, Billy Graham telephoned to say that he had spoken with
the Reverend Tom Allan, minister at St George's Tron church
in Glasgow and a great supporter of Billy Graham. He was also
a capable writer. Tom had said that he would accept the post
of editor if, with it, came the direction of the London office of
the association. Billy Graham asked me what I felt about this.

I said that if Tom Allan would work with us in this way, I would
be delighted to work under him. I felt that if this was the answer
that the Lord had to our prayers for an editor, then I would be
both happy and content to follow His will.

An invitation was then formally extended to Tom Allan, and
he accepted. He came to London for consultation, and he and
I hit it off. The chemistry was right, and I looked forward to the
years ahead with much anticipation. He made an immediate
impact on the newspaper, and it became a very positive and
meaningful publication under his editorship.

He quickly grasped many of the intricacies of the London office, and determined that he could leave the day-to-day running
to me. So he did not plan to move immediately to London but to
direct the office by remote control from Glasgow. Those days of
working with Tom Allan were happy days; he gave a sense of
confidence and purpose to everything that we did.

The 1963 team meeting was to be held at the Biltmore
Terrace Hotel on Miami Beach. This time, both Marilyn and
I were invited and I looked forward to her participation in this

highlight event. We travelled over to America on December
2nd, 1963. At the opening meeting on December 3rd, Billy
Graham announced that on the way over on the airplane,
Tom Allan had had a heart attack from which he never recovered. It was desperately sad, and we felt we had lost a real
friend. As far as the *Christian* was concerned, we were back
to square one. The search was on again and this time, after
a great many interviews, a Scottish author and journalist was
invited by Billy Graham to assume the editorship. He was Jim
Douglas, who was to remain with the *Christian* until it closed in
May 1969.

✳   ✳   ✳

Earlier in 1963, Marilyn and I had received an invitation to
the wedding of Billy Graham's daughter, Gigi. It was to be
held in Montreux, Switzerland. We felt honoured and privileged to be invited, and we were able to go. On April 30th,
1963, I received a telephone call from George Wilson, who
was already in Paris. He was on his way to the wedding and
was finding it lonely on his own in Paris. He told me to drop
everything and to come over and join him. I had not been
to Paris since I was a boy of twelve, so it was a wonderful
invitation.

I expected him to mean that I should come over the next
day . . . but no! He told me I was to come that very afternoon:
take a plane and a taxi downtown and join him at his hotel.
It was a rush. Not only did I have to go home and pack, but
I had to make arrangements for Marilyn to come over a few
days later to join me for the wedding.

I arrived in Paris around 9.30 p.m. When I got to the hotel
there was no answer to George Wilson's phone. I tried again
at 10 and 10.30. At 11 p.m. I had had enough and decided
to go to bed. I determined I would call him in the morning.
Around 1.30 a.m. my telephone rang. It was George: 'What
are you doing, Maurice?' I told him I was in bed. 'In bed?'
he exclaimed incredulously. 'This is Paris, man! Get yourself
up. George Clark from our Paris office is with me and we're
going out to eat!' So at 2 a.m. we sat down to a hearty meal, and
afterwards he gave us a guided tour through the fruit markets.
Quite an introduction to Paris for a first adult visit.

The next morning we went to the Paris office of the BGEA, and George Wilson and I spent most of the afternoon visiting the Palace of Versailles. That evening he took George Clark and his wife and me out to a meal at the Mouton de la Panurge, a slightly off-beat Paris restaurant, very French and somewhat unusual. In later years I heard that George had got himself into trouble for taking us there! Apparently George Clark had had something to say about it.

From Paris we flew to Geneva. George had other engagements, and left me to stay in Geneva overnight to await Marilyn's arrival. I went out to the airport to meet her but she was not on the plane! I telephoned London to find she was in tears because she had misplaced her passport and missed the plane. She had prayed that God would show her where the passport was, and she found it at once hidden under some clothes in the wardrobe, where she would not normally look. Happily there was another plane late that night, and she arrived in Geneva in the early hours of the morning.

The next day we drove in a hired car to Montreux and attended the beautiful wedding in a chapel beside Lake Geneva. Later the same night we returned to London.

Soon afterwards Billy Graham held a crusade in Paris, France. On May 14th, 1963 I flew to Paris to join in the meetings which were held in a tent erected on the Place de Clignancourt. This was the first occasion I ever flew in a jet plane, and I still vividly remember the 'kick in the back' which I felt as we took off and climbed so steeply into the skies.

If ever clear evidence was required that emotionalism was not a part of the reason for the response to Mr Graham's invitation to accept Christ, you had it in Paris. First, the audience sat on benches without back-rests. Just sitting on such a seat is not conducive to emotionalism! At the end of an hour and a half, the seat is both hard and back-breaking. On top of that, the tent leaked – profusely. Large numbers of the audience were sitting under constant drips of water. But to top it all off, the marquee had been erected on the site of a former fruit and vegetable market and was infested by rats. Throughout the meeting, and especially during the invitation, rats were running hither and thither, in and out between the feet of the audience, and around those who had responded. My colleague Joyce Manning said to me:

'You have never seen so many unconcerned people,' and indeed they totally ignored the pests and concentrated on the meeting.

It was to the Paris crusade that we first took the office staff to a crusade location for the weekend. It seemed to us unfair that they were deeply involved in the ministry of Billy Graham, yet they rarely saw a crusade in action. With Mr Graham's approval, and with the help of George Wilson, we booked space on the London to Paris flight, secured economical hotel accommodation in Paris, and gave each of the staff the opportunity to share in the thrill of seeing people come to Christ at a crusade. It was appreciated by them all, and was something that we repeated at Dortmund, Copenhagen, Gothenburg and Stockholm. We also organised a tour group for members of the public to the crusade in New York.

On that tour we invited one member of our staff to come as our guest – selection to be determined by the achievement of securing the largest number of new subscriptions to *Decision* magazine. Competition ran high and it was eventually won by my secretary, Dawn Chandler, who had the foresight to keep quite a number of her subscriptions under her hat until the last minute. So while others thought they had a good chance of winning, Dawn pipped them at the post with some twenty last minute subscriptions.

※   ※   ※

Still the letters kept coming into the office – and still they sometimes raised a smile. It was difficult to decide how best we could respond to this money-saving idea which came from one of our contributors: 'It would save the cost of postage if you do not bother to send me a receipt. I don't need a receipt and paper is very expensive these days as well as postage. If you would just write me a brief letter to set my mind at rest that you have received the gift safely, that's all I need to know.' Our accountants told us around that time that – including letter heading, envelope, postage, time for dictating and for typing plus a contribution towards overheads – every letter we wrote cost us five pounds. A receipt needed neither dictation nor typing; probably it cost little more than the price of the envelope and postage. It might have been cheaper to send her the receipt – but it would have been difficult to explain that to her!

Often our correspondents would write their names indistinctly. One such person wrote, after we had tried to decipher their writing, as follows: 'I would like to point out that one mistake often happens in the letters you write me. You spell my name wrongly and I would like you to know that it was no fault of yours. I write very badly and I want your typist to know that it was a very nice joke. But do not tell her off because it was not so bad after all.' The main problem with that letter was that the writer did not sign it!

Billy Graham himself wrote a letter which gave us a smile on one occasion. It appeared to give conflicting advice, but conceded that there was a reason why. The letter was written to Dr Sherwood Eliot Wirt, editor of *Decision* magazine at the time:

> The Board had quite a discussion about your request for permission for one of your photographers to travel. In an organisation like ours, far too many people are travelling – and too few are staying home! The Executive Committee is making new rules. The financial burden is growing by leaps and bounds and I am amazed that in all of Great Britain there is not a photographer who could be used. I'm sure Maurice could dig up some excellent ones. Europe has an abundance of photographers. However, I agree that your man is better than any of them – therefore, approval granted! You see, you have a tremendous influence with me!

Following a crusade or mission and after we had showed one of the films, it was the practice of the association to send letters to local counsellors when spiritual help was needed. After one of the film shows in London we sent such a letter to one of the local ministers. He responded: 'Thank you for forwarding the names of those who require counselling locally. I am returning two of the cards to you as the people who are named on the cards are not known to me and they do not come to my church. Indeed, we do not understand how they even came to be at the showing of the film. The other names are our own people and we are dealing with them.' Maybe a lesson in marketing would have helped him to understand that evangelism is the way to make your church grow!

At times we were amazed at the incredible deciphering which went on at the Post Office. Our office in Minneapolis returned an envelope to us (which had reached them). It was addressed: 'Billy Graham Evangelistic Association, Many Applause, Many Souls, England'.

The lighter moments did not come from letters alone: the telephone also provided its share of surprises. You never knew what questions might arise when you answered the telephone. You always had to be prepared for any eventuality. One day, a caller asked if I could tell him which church Billy Graham attended.

I replied that, as far as I was aware, he was in membership at the First Baptist Church in Dallas, Texas, but was rarely able to worship there.

The caller then asked what 'First Baptist Church' meant. I explained that, in a large city like Dallas, there were many Baptist churches. In order to distinguish them, they gave them each a number in this way.

He then asked me what an Anglican church was. This turn of the conversation had me somewhat puzzled – but before I could reply he told me that he had been converted at Billy Graham's West Ham Mission in 1989. He said he was shortly going to the United States and would like to visit the church that Billy Graham attended.

He returned to the topic of the Anglican Church. I explained that it was the established Church of England: in America, I told him, similar churches were called Episcopalian.

He told me that he had attended an Elim church since his conversion and one of the speakers there had said that the world would end in five years. This presented him with some difficulty, because he was thinking of building an extension to his home. 'If the world is going to end in five years,' he said, 'I don't see the point of doing it. What does Billy Graham think?' he asked. I told him that Billy Graham would never commit himself to something as specific as this.

Then another thought occurred to him: 'What will happen if the world doesn't end in five years?' I said that the speaker at the Elim church would then have to admit that he had got it wrong.

He grunted, and then said: 'I think it is worthwhile to go ahead and build the extension. If the world does end in five years . . . so what! If it doesn't end in five years, I won't have wasted those five years waiting!'

※   ※   ※

I returned to London immediately the Paris crusade had finished. Billy Graham and his wife, Ruth, followed with T. W. Wilson a few days later. On June 27th, 1963 I went to London Airport to meet them. That turned out to be a significant date, for it was on the ride into London that Billy Graham had a conversation with me which ultimately led to the 1966 crusade at Earls Court.

He is always a delight to have in the car. His first concern is always for news of the family – he asks about each person by name. Then he will share with you some of the thrilling stories of the most recent crusade, for which he gives all the glory to God. Then, without warning, he will come out with some earth-shattering idea or proposal which he asks you to think about. He always gives the impression that it is your opinion which matters most to him.

Often he will ask if you mind if he exercises his voice. He then proceeds with a series of earth-shattering and explosive yeses – 'YES . . . YES . . . YES . . . YES' – several times over, as loudly as he possibly can. T. W. Wilson stops his ears with his fingers, and if Ruth Graham is in the back of the car, she responds with a quiet 'No . . . no . . . no!' But it works! On occasions when I have had to do a lot of public speaking, I often used to find my voice tired. I tried Billy Graham's remedy, and I never found it a problem to talk loudly for a long period afterwards.

On this occasion he told me of a meeting he had had in Paris with the television personality, David Frost. Billy Graham and David Frost had been friends for a number of years and each respected the other. On this occasion, Billy Graham said, David Frost had asked him why he had not stayed in Britain after the Wembley crusade in 1955. David Frost said that, in his opinion, Britain was on the verge of a breakthrough leading to a spiritual revival at that time, and he regarded it as tragic that Billy Graham had not stayed on. Billy Graham told him that the advice of the Archbishop of Canterbury had been to let the churches consolidate what had been started, and that he had felt it would have been inappropriate to stay any longer. 'So when,' David Frost asked, 'are you coming back again?' Billy Graham told him that he would come when he was invited.

David Frost asked who would give such an invitation, and Billy Graham said that he had no idea at the present time. Whereupon David Frost had said: 'Well then, I will invite you, here and now!' Billy Graham gave his inimitable chuckle which says (without so many words): 'I hear what you say.'

Now, in the car en route to London, Billy Graham asked me: 'Maurice, do you think the Evangelical Alliance would invite us back to London?'

Strangely enough, the subject had come up at a meeting of the Evangelical Alliance Council (of which I was a member) just two or three weeks previously. There was a voluble response against such an invitation. Major-General Wilson-Haffenden had asked me to sound out the EA Council and I had been left in little doubt that their support would not be forthcoming. So, in the car, I was able to share that response with Billy Graham. He pondered this situation for a few minutes: he surmised that it would be unlikely that the bishops or the non-conformist churches would invite him. He had been deeply moved by David Frost's insistence that he should come and he recalled that David was a layman. 'Do you think there would be a group of laymen who might give me an invitation?' he asked. I assured him that it was quite possible and could easily take place.

Just about that same time, there was a pacifist and anti-nuclear lobby known as 'the Committee of 100'. This prompted me to suggest: 'How about an evangelical "Committee of 100"?' The idea immediately caught on, and Billy Graham asked me to make some suggestions. First and foremost I recommended the involvement of Tom Allan (who had just become director of the BGEA in London). This would give a clerical leadership to a layman's committee. Billy Graham felt this to be a good idea, and he asked me to draw up some names for him to consider during his brief stay in London.

The next night, Billy and Ruth Graham accepted our invitation to dine at our favourite Chinese restaurant, the Kwan Yin (now the Good Earth) in Mill Hill, North London. Ruth had been born and brought up in China, so it was always a pleasure and an education to eat a Chinese meal in her presence. The proprietor, Mr Cheng, was delighted to have Billy and Ruth Graham in his restaurant and exclaimed, as he looked at Ruth Graham: 'But she's so *young*!' That meal gave us an opportunity to have a relaxed talk about the proposed 'Committee of 100' and Billy made many suggestions.

The difficulty was not in finding the names: rather, with the limitation in numbers, it was hard to decide who to leave out. A week later, Billy Graham attended a meeting of the London board of the BGEA and he was much encouraged by their response to the whole idea. I gave him the first list of a hundred names which he approved, and the matter was now left with me to discuss with Tom Allan.

In due course a luncheon was held in London under Tom Allan's chairmanship, and an invitation on parchment was signed by those of the hundred who were present, and by proxy for those few who were unable to come but were clearly in sympathy with us.

Thus the 1966 crusade which was to be held at Earls Court was germinated in thought, covered in prayer, and put into motion immediately. An executive committee was formed under the chairmanship again of Major-General D. J. Wilson-Haffenden; Bill Brown came from the United States as a member of the team to lead the administration under the general watchful eye of Dr Walter H. Smyth. It was Walter who took me for a walk near the Natural History Museum one day and asked: 'Maurice, what do you think about bringing Harvey Thomas in to help Bill Brown?' Harvey had worked with the team radio station in Hawaii for some time, and Walter was anxious to bring him back into crusade preparation. Walter felt that Harvey had great potential. As will be revealed later, he was right in that assessment.

Shortly after the 'Committee of 100' had met for their lunch, and had sent the invitation to Billy Graham, I had a telephone call from Gilbert Kirby, asking me to come and see him at the Evangelical Alliance offices. A day or so later I went to his office and he was obviously distressed that the invitation had gone to Billy Graham without their involvement.

I referred back to the meeting held only a few months before, when the Evangelical Alliance Council had been so against any invitation to Billy Graham. Gilbert understood that under those circumstances I honestly did not think they would wish to be involved. He and I talked for a long time and, in the end, we agreed to put forward our recommendation that there should be retrospective involvement of the Evangelical Alliance. We both accepted that, had the approach been made to them, it is likely they would have accepted it.

With Haffy's agreement, the minutes were rewritten to appoint the Evangelical Alliance retrospectively as sponsors of the crusade – and the mental agility of the 'Committee of 100' in accepting this spoke volumes for the executive committee when they next met. In his inimitable way, Haffy explained all that had happened and sought the approval of the committee for this change. They gave it unanimously. This was surely one of the best examples of the evangelical diplomacy for which both Gilbert Kirby and Major-General Wilson-Haffenden were famed!

Earls Court was significantly bigger than the Harringay Arena – but it was still not big enough in its main arena. Some 20,000 could be accommodated with all the seats in place. We equipped the two wings outside the main arena with closed circuit television screens each to accommodate an additional 5,000 people. Even that was insufficient on two or three occasions.

The first thing I did was to get the old team of stewards together. Henry Hole agreed to head up the planning once more, and he recruited a new member to the team, Peter Worthen, at the time a court clerk at Wells Street Magistrates' Court and later a vicar in the Church of England. Peter became the link on radio between each of the team members, and together the fellows involved handled innumerable problems which arose daily.

In soliciting help for the crusade, I wrote to one man among the many who had found a wife or a husband while working with the Harringay crusade in 1954. So many people were involved in the counselling classes, the choir or with the stewards that it was inevitable there should be a number who formed lasting relationships. In reply to my letter, seeking his help once again, he said: 'I met my wife during a coach trip which I had organised to Harringay in 1954. In spite of this, I will still be glad to give whatever assistance I can at Earls Court in June!'

Like Harringay, the story of the 1966 crusade and the subsequent 1967 closed circuit television crusade (to twenty-five other cities throughout the UK by coaxial cable link) has been told in other books, so the full story need not be repeated here. There are, however, several stories which can bear repetition.

One of the earlier members of the team to arrive at London Airport was Dr Robert Ferm. He had come as a special assistant to the team in London. Marilyn and I went out to the airport to meet him. While we were waiting in arrivals I suddenly heard my name on the public address system: 'If Maurice Rowlandson, waiting to meet Dr Ferm, is in the terminal, would he please go through Customs and Excise to Immigration.' I'd never done anything like that before (apart from my special pass from years gone by) and there was a sense of power and destiny as I boldly strode through Customs and Excise – in the wrong direction – to Immigration. I was met by a brittle immigration officer who asked me to vouch for the gentleman he had with him. He wanted to know how Dr Ferm was to be paid while he was working here: did he have a work permit? (he didn't need one). Numerous other, rather belligerent questions were directed at me. I explained that Dr Ferm was a member of the American team, whose salary was paid in the United States, and that his stay in the UK would be limited to the period of the crusade. The immigration officer then declared that he was sorry that he would have to let him in. 'You people are anathema to me,' he said. 'I wish that there was some regulation through which I could exclude you – but I can't. I've got no time for you religious fanatics.' He stamped Bob Ferm's passport, and Bob was through.

I had never had an experience like it, and remained astounded that a British official should be so rude and discourteous to a foreign national arriving at the airport. Bob Ferm shook his hand, and invited him to the crusade! It was an invitation which Bob followed up and which, it is only fair to say, was accepted by the gentleman concerned and they became quite close friends. I only wish it were possible to add that he had gone forward in response to the invitation – but he did not, as far as I am aware.

At one meeting a man responded to Mr Graham's appeal and Bob Ferm counselled him. It turned out that he was a smuggler of drugs. The message of the gospel had really penetrated his mind, and he understood what sin and salvation were all about. He committed his life to Christ that night in 1966. A year later he turned up at another crusade and asked if Bob Ferm was around. We went and found Bob, who recognised our ex-smuggler friend. He simply wanted to tell Bob how good the Lord had been to him in the past year. He finished up: 'Oh, by the way, I've given up smuggling ... I'm a croupier now!' At least it was a step in the right direction.

Shortly before the crusade in 1966 I received a cable from Atlanta, Georgia in the USA. The cable came from the then press officer for Mr Graham, Gil Stricklin. In those days, the cable office would telephone me as soon as the cable arrived and give me the message. It would then be followed up with a copy in the mail. This cablegram read: 'Walter Smyth recommends contacting Graham at his hotel in Stockholm, Sweden, concerning statement for press about the end of the world.' The cable operator read out the cable to me and there was a pregnant pause. 'That's made my day,' she said, and hung up.

✳   ✳   ✳

Wanda Mercer, who was Billy Graham's secretary in 1966, came to London. She was a very big, broad-shouldered woman with a commanding voice. Some of the younger girls were terrified of her.

One day she telephoned to invite Marilyn and me to the performance of an opera at Covent Garden. We had never been there, and we counted it a privilege to be able to accept.

On the day in question there was a breakdown on the Underground and Marilyn was delayed on her journey from home. I was already in London, so I was on time. Covent Garden does not look kindly upon late arrivals, and when Marilyn eventually arrived, she had to wait outside the Opera House until the first interval; then they let her in.

She found us and was warmly greeted by Wanda who wanted to hear all about the delay. It was not a short story and the last two sentences were spoken after the lights had gone out and the curtain was raised. The lady in front of Wanda turned round to protest about the whispering in the row behind her. She reached over and tapped Wanda firmly on the knee and said: 'Shush!' Wanda drew herself up to full height and, in a voice that could be heard above the music of the opera, said: 'Madam, please don't do that – in fact, don't you *ever* touch me again!' The poor lady in front cowered down in her seat. I am sure that, had she looked at Wanda in the seat behind her, she would never have risked a confrontation in the first place.

It was during 1966 that Cliff Richard first made his public declaration of faith. It was a moving experience and I admired his courage in nailing his colours to the mast so openly. Because of his involvement, World Wide Pictures decided to make a feature film in which he would play the leading role.

The director of the film approached me one day and told me that he wanted me to play the part of the platform steward who would try to prevent Cliff Richard (Jamie in the story) from going on to the platform. The first part of that scene (which included a speaking part) was filmed in 1966, but they had to complete the filming a year later. I was told by Jim Collier, the director, that I could not wear that suit or tie again until 1967, because they couldn't risk the suit being damaged and consequently the need to film that part all over again. They also told me not to gain weight, so I could still manage to get into the suit.

When the filming was all over in 1967, Frank Jacobson of World Wide Pictures came to me and said: 'Maurice, by rights everyone who has a speaking part should appear in the credits of the film. But you don't have an Equity card, so we can't do that. But don't worry, we've taken care of it in another way.' He wouldn't tell me what he meant.

Later in the autumn we held the première of the film *Two a Penny* at the Prince Charles Theatre in London's West End. Cliff Richard and other stars in the film came to see it, together with many VIPs, many friends of the BGEA, and a host of our personal friends. The film included a scene in a hat shop. The lady being served by a nervous salesgirl was getting more and more frustrated. Eventually, she pompously got up, shook her finger at the salesgirl and said: 'I shall certainly complain to the managing director about you. Mr Rowlandson is a good friend of mine, and he will hear all about you!' The theatre exploded! Most of those there knew me, and it took a long time to live down that sort of acknowledgment.

The reception afterwards was almost a disaster. My colleagues from America had taken advice about the right way to launch a film into the cinema circuits, and had been advised that this reception was a must. Ken Bliss of World Wide Pictures, who was in charge, had left the arrangements to the agencies.

I went out shortly before the film ended, to check that everything was ready. To my horror, I found tables stacked high with hard spirits – whisky, rum, vodka, etc. It was obviously intended to be a drinking occasion! Rapidly I issued orders and when the film finished a few minutes later, there was not an alcoholic drink to be seen anywhere in the room. I believe the stars were aghast. But that was the way we wanted it – especially as we had so many of our friends from the evangelical world as our guests.

At the time of the 1966 crusade I was the secretary of a trust and the trustees suggested that a diorama of Earls Court should be made using one of Russ Busby's photographs as the background. In particular they wished to feature the appearance of Cliff Richard on the platform when he first gave his testimony.

In due course, the diorama was made and delivered, in a beautiful glass case. There was the Earls Court arena all over again, with actual model participants on the platform: Billy Graham, Cliff Barrows and Cliff Richard along with other platform guests the same day. It was a unique item which is now in the Billy Graham Archives, in the Billy Graham Center, Wheaton, Illinois.

Among the many stories arising from the 1966 crusade is one of the most dramatic of all. It was the visit of Billy Graham to Soho when, from the roof of a car, he had the opportunity to preach the gospel. It had been made clear that Mr Graham would not be going to Soho to condemn, but to show his concern for all people and to extend a personal invitation for them to attend the crusade meetings at Earls Court.

A crowd quickly assembled outside a sordid Compton Street cinema showing the movie *Orgy at Lil's Place* and Mr Graham arrived. He climbed on to the roof of a car and as he got to the middle of his talk his friends and aides surrounding the car became aware of a scuffle nearby. We had been warned by the chaplain to Soho that there was a plot afoot to discredit Billy Graham. So we had been watchful. However we were hardly expecting it when a scantily clad stripper from one of the night-clubs pushed her way to the front of the crowd. She was wearing a very short skirt and she tried to scramble up on to the roof of the car and stand alongside Billy Graham. 'Hey, Billy,' she yelled, 'what do you think of my skirt?' Billy Graham ignored her and went on preaching. The police moved in and lifted the girl down from the car. One of the police officers said to Mr Graham, 'Please get out of this area as quickly as possible. It has become rather dangerous.' Billy Graham climbed down from the car and was quickly whisked away to his hotel room. It was probably the closest he ever came to being compromised: the help of the police and the quickness of his colleagues had prevented any compromising pictures that the press had hoped to take. Later we discovered that it was they who had found the young girl, and had persuaded her to attempt this confrontation. Happily they were thwarted in their plans.

After the 1966 crusade we decided that a new approach to the advertising was necessary for the 1967 crusade. Alan Whitaker was on our committee, and he was a partner in a graphics design firm. We left the ideas to him. It would be an understatement to say that when the committee received his suggestions, they were somewhat startled. He showed us a black and purple portrait of the *back* of Billy Graham, with the slogan 'Billy's Back' written across it. It was different and dramatic. It was accepted by the committee and became one of the most unusual publicity campaigns mounted in preparation for a Billy Graham crusade. Later it received an award.

There were several bomb scares during the week in 1967. One night, the police discovered a brown paper package in one of the galleries which had wires coming from it – but it was a sick hoax. In fact it was simply a brick. On the advice of the police, we never evacuated the hall as they felt that the warnings they had received came from practical jokers who thought this might be an excellent way of breaking up the meetings. Certainly God protected us from anything serious.

During that week at Earls Court, two Elim pastors volunteered their services (and cars) to drive Mr Graham around while he was here. One of them was assigned to Mr Graham, the other to Cliff Barrows. They were a wonderful asset to us and the generous sacrifice of their time was deeply appreciated.

One of them cultivated strawberries. He turned up in the platform room one night with a wooden box. It was for Mr Graham, he said. When it was opened there were some twenty-four magnificent strawberries, each about the size of a small peach. They were obviously delicious and Mr Graham handed the box around to those in the platform room, including me. Our impressions were confirmed: the strawberries were perfectly ripe, sweet and tasty.

There were about four of us in the platform room when Mr Graham picked up the box and said: 'What in the world am I going to do with these?' He indicated the twelve or fifteen straw-berries left in the box, each in its own little crinkled paper cup. Then, as if inspired, he looked at me and said: 'Maurice, you take them home to Marilyn and the family.' A few minutes later, all of us left the room and accompanied Mr Graham to the platform.

There were many administrative duties to be done during the process of a meeting, so we were accustomed to leaving the platform about the time of the offering, and returning during Mr Graham's address. On this occasion, a little earlier than usual, I suddenly thought of those strawberries. Oh the temptation of the devil!

I left the platform, made my way to the platform room, collected the box containing the remaining strawberries, and took it out to my car in the car park. As I came back into the building I spotted Dr Walter Smyth and T. W. Wilson strid-ing purposefully to the platform room. They emerged seconds later looking puzzled. Soon they spied me, and they called me across. 'Maurice,' said Dr Smyth, 'do you know what has happened to those strawberries?' I had beaten them by just seconds. They forgave me when they heard what I had done, and although I offered to go out and get them from the car they told me not to bother. Marilyn and the family really en-joyed them when I got home!

During the same 1967 Earls Court crusade the organising committee took the unusual step of holding a meeting on the Sunday. It had not been done before for fear of giving offence. But it was pointed out that it was the Lord's Day – and what better day to be about the Lord's business! This decision provoked numerous letters, some commending the decision, others objecting to it. One man wrote: 'I think it is a great pity that Dr Billy Graham is not given a day off for a Sabbath rest on Sunday 25th June. I am also concerned that the staff of Earls Court must be employed. Could we not staff Earls Court with Christians for the day, and let another preacher take the platform that night? Then I would feel happier.'

We also had an impassioned plea from one gentleman: 'Please do not send your magazine to me any more. I went to the crusade at Earls Court in 1967, and greatly enjoyed it. But I have now gone back to my own religion in the Salvation Army.' And all the time, we thought we were preaching the same message as the Salvation Army!

Our final departure from Earls Court in 1967 was marked by the team of chief stewards, and myself, being called to the office of Major-General Ritchie, the chairman of Earls Court Limited. He thanked us all for the part that we had played over the two years, and told us that they had been memorable to him. He said he would never forget us. Then he presented each of us with an Earls Court tie. 'You'll never have difficulty in getting in to any event if you wear this tie,' he said and he was absolutely right. Actually, of course, we knew the secret way in to Earls Court in any case – but the tie was useful and treasured by us all.

In preparation for the 1966 crusade, there were innumerable opportunities for Billy Graham to appear on television programmes. One of these was a panel programme on which, among the participants, was David MacLagan. The briefing before that programme did nothing to prepare Billy Graham for the outrageous attack made upon him by each of the panellists. Mr Graham handled it well, but he had been led to believe it would be something quite different. In the event, it was objectionable television, and the BBC received many complaints about the programme. Interestingly enough, David MacLagan was so impressed by the way that Billy Graham handled the vicious questioning that he himself did a rethink, and was to become one of the warmest supporters we had in Scotland. Later he was to attend a team meeting in America where his address on 'The Unconscious Influence' became a contribution which remained in the memories of the team for many years to come.

Another person who was impressed by the way in which Billy Graham handled hostile questions on television was the motor racing driver, Graham Hill. After watching one such programme, he telephoned the crusade office, and asked for tickets to the meeting. Later he came with his whole family.

There were many perpetual critics. One persistent critic never missed an opportunity to take a dig at Billy Graham. One night at Earls Court, Marilyn was serving on the bookstall when she says she experienced a strange feeling that there was something evil behind her. She turned around, and there was that very person. Several years later, in connection with my association with Trans World Radio, we had been to the studios in Monte Carlo and were returning to England via the airport at Nice. We were sitting in the waiting room when Marilyn suddenly turned to me and said: 'That's strange ... I've got the shivers.' She went on to say that it was just as if something evil had come near to her and changed the atmosphere. She turned around in her seat, just in time to see the same person coming into the waiting room. Maybe it's a woman's intuition: it was strange it should have happened twice (and only twice) and both times with the same person involved.

Shortly after the 1967 crusade was over, Scripture Union published a report from the Evangelical Alliance entitled *On the Other Side*. It was a critical examination of mass evangelism, and was especially critical of much that had happened at Earls Court. It is the considered opinion of many (which I subscribe to) that the publication of that book put back the clock on evangelism for at least the next ten years. The sad thing was that, in many places, the author based his premise on irrelevant or unrelated facts. For instance, as an example of decreasing interest in mass evangelism, he refers on p.93 to a church which, in 1966, sent more than eight 'trains' to the crusade, while in 1967 the same church sent only one. No mention was made that the 1966 crusade lasted eight weeks, while the 1967 crusade was for one week only. By my reckoning it leaves the percentage of interest precisely the same.

It saddened me that about eight of my friends each sent me a copy of the book, asking if I had seen it. From their letters there was almost a gloating over what had been written. It was deeply hurtful to those of us who had been so intimately involved in the crusade, and I know that one of those most hurt was the chairman, our beloved Haffy.

In the middle of 1967 we received news that our rent at Bush House was to be trebled. It became imperative for us to move, for we could not justify so big an increase. Bishop Goodwin Hudson and I spent many hours looking at likely buildings. He found one and I went to see it; I found one and he came to look at it. Neither was suitable. We looked at many properties before we realised that we had not prayed and asked for God's guidance. So we paused and prayed. The very next day, Huddy excitedly telephoned me. 'Maurice, I've found just the place,' he said, and within the hour I met him at 27 Camden Road where the whole of the second floor was available at an unbelievably low rental. It was a brand new building and the floor was totally devoid of any obstructions.

George Wilson was informed, and he supported our negotiations for a lease which would take us through to 1995. He also told us that America would pay for the fixtures and fittings which would be needed and this included all-over carpeting. When it was all ready for us to occupy, it was a really lovely office and we moved in on February 8th, 1968. Jean Wilson was able to include adequate space for the ministry in which she was specially interested – Gospel Light Sunday School materials. This helped her a great deal, and we were glad to have the Gospel Light ministry associated with us in our new offices.

We were very busy. Public relations is a complex exercise. We tried to keep our many friends happy. We held open days for ministers and clergy when we invited them to our offices and gave them lunch. We told them all about the ministry of Billy Graham, and we showed them our latest film. It was all worthwhile and helped to engender good relations with the churches. This was one of many other activities, the stories of which are covered in later chapters.

5

Spre-e '73

Being attentive to the will of God – and listening to 'the voice behind' – often leads us in directions we do not anticipate. Sometimes He uses strange means to influence our lives and to guide us into the direction of His choosing. In the case of Spre-e '73, it was an advertisement in the magazine *Christianity Today* which He used as the catalyst to bring about a series of activities which was to stretch over a period of several years.

Billy Graham was behind the founding of the magazine. He was, and still is, on the board. He has always had a great concern for its ministry, and he had shared his vision with his contemporaries. As a result, the magazine had taken the lead in many areas of evangelical life both in the USA and overseas.

A full page advertisement was carried late in 1971, and was repeated on a number of occasions early in 1972. It described an evangelistic and teaching programme planned for June 1972. One of the later announcements was that Billy Graham would have a major role in this Dallas, Texas event. Immediately I was alerted and felt a strange compulsion to be involved in the plans. As a result, I wrote both to George Wilson in Minneapolis, and to Billy Graham at his home, to ask if they would give me authority to attend Explo '72.

Billy Graham called me on the telephone; he was both enthusiastic and insistent that I should be there, and shortly afterwards the authority to go came through from George Wilson. The event was timed to take place in the middle of June and I made arrangements to travel to Dallas. On June 7th – the day before I was due to leave – my elder son, Gary, announced

that he also wanted to attend Explo '72. Helped by his mother
and me, he managed to scrape together the fare and made his
booking to follow me over in a few days. I flew over to New York
(where, immediately after I arrived, I had my travellers' cheques
pickpocketed in the hotel lift) and went on to Dallas.

Explo '72 was a remarkable event. It was essentially a resi-
dential youth training event, although I was by no means the
only older person there. It was run by Bill Bright's Campus
Crusade for Christ – the first time I had ever come across the
organisation. It was also the first time I encountered the booklet
'The Four Spiritual Laws', and the first time anyone had ever
spent time teaching me how to initiate a conversation with a
stranger with a view to bringing him or her to Christ.

For many years I had been trained as a personal worker in
the Tom Rees campaigns. I had been through the counsellor
training classes for the Billy Graham crusades. All of these had
taught me how to talk to a person *after* the evangelist had done
his job. None of them had taught me how to do the work of
the evangelist also. Now, I was not only being shown how to
work a conversation around to talk about Christ, but I was also
being sent out on the streets to put it into practice. At first
it was terrifying; it soon became exciting. I was shown how to
share Christ in the power of the Holy Spirit, and to leave the
results to God. Using 'The Four Spiritual Laws' I learned how
to take a contact step by step through the truth of the gospel.
I saw people respond, and I was excited by the whole project.

Gary arrived from England on the day that Explo '72 started.
Each age group was segregated so we hardly saw each other at
all during the whole period. Both he and I had volunteered
as stewards at the huge evening stadium meetings (to which
almost 80,000 people had come). He was assigned to one side
of the stadium and I to the other, diametrically opposite to
him. Just once during the week, we met in the stadium when
he walked around to my side and spent about five minutes
chatting with me. Six months or so later, when the Explo '72
film was released, the cameras zoomed in at one point to two
people talking amid the enormous crowd – and it was us! It
was remarkable that it happened to be just at that moment
that the cameras were whirring.

I came back to England starry-eyed. There were so many
stories to tell, and I had many slides with which to illustrate

them. I also had carried my tape recorder everywhere, so I had the sounds as well. Once again I put together slides and tape and made another soundstrip. It became important to show these pictures wherever and whenever the opportunity arose. I found that the story of Explo '72 on slides and tape captured the imagination of those who saw it. Time and time again, people said to me: 'We need something like that over here.'

One such occasion was at the Keswick Convention that year. I rented a room at the Keswick Hotel, and gave out invitations to everybody I could find. The film strip programme was shown to them one afternoon and it received an enthusiastic response. Among the audience was a couple unknown to me at the time. They were Victor and Charitie Pippett, son and daughter-in-law of a former secretary of the Keswick Convention. They now lived in Australia, but were visiting the UK and had planned to include the Keswick Convention in their programme. Unbeknown to me, they had also been at Explo '72, and were deeply involved in the ministry of Campus Crusade. They felt that the soundstrip story had captured the atmosphere of Explo '72 and made an excellent documentary. I told them that, time and time again, people had said to me that we needed something like that over here. Victor and Charitie echoed that sentiment and encouraged me to believe that this was something I could do. Eventually the message got through. Towards the end of July I began to ask myself the question: 'Why not?' I felt that we should import the whole of Explo '72 lock, stock and barrel, making as few changes as possible.

If Billy Graham had made a major contribution to Explo '72 then it was vital that he should make a similar contribution to the event in Britain. We began to speak about the event as Reachout '73. On July 27th, 1972 I wrote to Mr Graham to tell him about my burden, and to ask him if he would commit himself to a similar event in London. On August 15th, 1972 (my birthday!) a letter came from him, accepting the invitation:

I think there ought to be an 'Explo-style' gathering in Britain. I think it could possibly be sponsored jointly by the BGEA and other youth organisations like Campus Crusade, Inter-varsity and the Evangelical Alliance. It would be great if we could mobilise all the Christian forces of Britain for one great out-pouring ... Unless the Christian forces of

Britain rise up to do something dramatic like this, I am informed on the highest levels that Britain is in deep and dire
and desperate difficulty. It seems to me that this ought to
be organised and planned for next August . . . Naturally, I
would be delighted to participate as one of the speakers . . .
anything you like. Perhaps you could bring young people
from all over Britain for this great Christian happening.
You might want to get a different name from Explo.

When that letter arrived I was on holiday, but from then on I
could think about nothing else. I made countless telephone calls
and sought advice from every available quarter. Much as I loved
Haffy, I did not believe he was the right person to be chairman
of a youth event of this nature. From my many enquiries, one
name emerged above all others, and I invited David Pickford
to be chairman of a committee to plan Reachout '73.

Shortly before the first committee meeting in September,
Bishop Goodwin Hudson came into my office one morning.
'Maurice!' he said. 'I don't like that name, Reachout. There's
got to be something better.'

For half an hour we talked about possibilities. In the end,
in his effusive and explosive manner he said: 'What we want
is something like "Jamboree". We can't use that of course . . .
but something like it.' He urged me to get out my thesaurus
and see what might be suitable.

The next day, when he was in the office, he and Jean Wilson
stood in my office while I read out the alternatives
to jamboree from the thesaurus. 'Liaison; libertinism; lubricity;
revelry; riot; spree. What a pity we can't use spree,' I said. 'Spree
'73 has the right ring about it.' Jean Wilson immediately responded with: 'Why not? SPR for Spiritual, RE for Renewal,' she
said. We saw the opportunities of this immediately, and Spre-e
'73 it became – always with the hyphen to point out the difference between the dictionary spree (which meant a drunken
frolic) and *our* use of the word to mean spiritual renewal.

So we had a new name to present to the committee when
they met on Monday, September 4th – a day I will never forget
as long as I live! Sunday, the day before, all the family had gone
to Trafalgar Square to join in one of the Festival of Light rallies.
It was a great occasion; a spiritual high. Songs and hymns and
spiritual songs, with testimonies, shouts of 'Give me a J . . . give

me an E,' etc. As we left Trafalgar Square, I turned to my
thirteen-year-old son Julian and said: 'That was a mountain-top
experience. Now be ready for the valley.' I explained to him
that so often when God allows us to catch a glimpse of heaven,
the devil has a shock around the corner for us.

On Monday at lunch-time we met in committee in the board
room at 27 Camden Road, the offices of the Billy Graham
Evangelistic Association. There was a hundred per cent turnout:
such was the interest in the proposed programme. Dr Walter
Smyth had come over from America to meet the committee, and
to be able to take a first-hand account back to Billy Graham. We
had a good meeting, and the plans were beginning to fall into
place. Then there was a knock at the door and my secretary,
Dawn Chandler, came in. Coming straight up to me she asked
me to come out of the committee to see someone. I told her
that we were nearly through, and that she could ask the person
to wait. 'I think you'd better come straight away,' she said.

Puzzled, I followed her out of the office and found Marilyn
waiting for me in my office. Gently, she told me that the police
had been on the telephone earlier that morning to say that our
dear daughter Cherylyn had met with a car accident, just outside
Colchester, on her way back to Frinton. She had died immediately from her injuries. Without stopping to think, I went straight
back to the committee and asked them to pause and pray for me
and for my family. I told them what had happened.

What a mixture of emotions and feelings follow! At first there
is the inevitable reaction: 'It can't be true. They must have
made a mistake – maybe it's mistaken identity.' But gradually,
the recognition that it is true sinks home, and you realise the
delicate thread upon which all of us live and move and have
our being. The one true comfort we had was that Cherylyn had
a deep and real faith in the Lord Jesus Christ as her Saviour and
Lord. So for us, we knew that she was now in His presence and
more alive than she had ever been on earth. Human sorrow is
real, but spiritual joy can enable us to cope at a time of loss. It
is then that you realise that all you have said you believed over
many years is true. God is the God of all comfort, and He does
sustain in time of need. It was the reality of that experience
which enabled us to live through those early days.

Shortly afterwards, Walter Smyth came out of the committee
to express his sorrow and condolences. I told him that, for me,

Spre-e '73 would become a memorial event for my daughter and that I couldn't think of anything better that she would have wished for. There was great sorrow in the office. They were all so supportive and kind. The family rallied round too. Gary, our elder son, volunteered to take from my shoulders the burden of going to Colchester to identify Cherylyn, and he was a tower of strength through that and the following days.

I went up Haverstock Hill to meet Julian as he came out of school. It had been his first day at his new school, and I had been worried for him, because he had a radiant faith for which he had suffered in his old school. But I needn't have worried: when I picked him up after school, I saw that his school case was covered with Jesus stickers – so he had nailed his colours to the mast that first day. As I met him, I had the task of telling him what had happened to his sister. He replied: 'Dad, I didn't know the valley would be that deep!'

The first visitor we had when we got home was my old Crusader leader, Fred Cursons. He came to pray with us and comfort us, and others quickly followed in his trail. Marilyn's parents made the sad journey from Minneapolis to be with us in our time of sorrow, and they got here before the funeral.

Ruth Graham had made a detour to be in London for the funeral, and her participation as representative of all our colleagues and friends on the Billy Graham team was deeply appreciated by all of us. The funeral itself was a triumphant occasion as we gave thanks to God for the life of our beloved Cherylyn. She was now with the Lord she had served so faithfully, and we were sustained by the large number of friends who came to share the service with us. The church was packed to capacity. As we reached the last hymn, 'Thine be the glory, risen conquering Son', the whole congregation was uplifted. We left the church to the strains of Widor's *Toccata* – a favourite piece of Cherylyn's. Afterwards we heard that a number of her friends from St Paul and St Mary College in Cheltenham had come to know the Lord as their Saviour as a result of her testimony and life. Later, we held a thanksgiving service in the chapel of the college, and that too was filled to capacity. It was a moving experience to know that there were so many who had counted it a privilege to have known her.

Two years later at school, our other daughter, Jacky, was given an assignment in the Religious Education class. The subject was 'Death'. She wrote:

When my sister died two years ago
It was at first an awful blow.
But as time passes I remember
What it was like to go to her for help.
What fun it was to go out with her –
On holiday or anywhere.
What fun it was at Christmas and birthdays
And Easter and every day of her life.

I also remember sadder bits of how my mother
Would sit and weep.
I also know how hard it is to get to sleep.
And as for me I could go to the funeral.
I also knew that I loved her very much.
And even with us now although she is no longer.
I know how it feels to be the last to see her –
As indeed I was the last in the family.

Now quite often I go to the cemetery
To see the grave
And how so nice it feels to put flowers in a bowl.

And when my grandpa died in March
My dad had said how he would be able to hear
Just what my sister said to him:
And this is it.
When the rollcall is called, Cherry would walk up to
Him and say, 'Hiya! Gramps. How are you today?'

For us, as a family, it was a time of picking up the pieces. For a long time there was something missing – a sentiment expressed so vividly in an article that Marilyn wrote for *Decision* magazine (see Appendix A). Subsequently that article was reprinted in numerous other periodicals, and was translated into more than eight languages world-wide. We still use it to help comfort those who have been through the same experience as us. It seems that God guided Marilyn's pen in a special way as she put those thoughts together.

From all the multitude of letters which arrived, there were two which expressed our needs so well. The chairman of my local Magistrates' Bench wrote: 'The wound will heal, but the scar will always remain.' It was a comfort to know the former; our experience is still the latter. Bishop Goodwin Hudson wrote: 'All life is long enough if we find Christ – for then life becomes eternal.' We later repeated that comment upon the memorial stone which stood at her grave.

As far as our own Christian faith was concerned, I was to come across a passage years later which exactly expressed how we felt at the time:

> Our [Christian experience] is not a painkiller, no analgesic, no patent medicine. It is not there to make tolerable the intolerable suffering that, at one time or another, we all undergo in this world. It is not to be abandoned because we are in pain. The Cross was suffered without an anaesthetic and so have our several, and lesser, Calvaries. Christianity does not cure the toothache or alleviate sea-sickness. It did not prevent the cry of dereliction from the Cross. Why then, should it reduce the pain of bereavement?
>
> Lord Hailsham, *A Sparrow's Flight*

Although our friends were able to express their identification with us in sorrow in their letters, it was quite a different experience when we met them. It was almost as though we had become outcasts! At church, people avoided us; our friends seemed embarrassed to be with us. It took time and understanding to realise that people, by and large, did not know how to deal with death. They did not know how to speak to a person who has suffered loss – so they avoided them, or tried to move away. From this experience we learned the need for love and fellowship at a time like that, more than any other. Death is a natural experience; we are all going to 'pass through the valley of the. shadow of death'. Unless Christ returns in His glory, none of us will escape. So, if it is a natural experience, we need to treat it naturally. Talk about it: tears may flow, but they are a natural expression also. Those who have lost a dear one need to talk about it more than ever. They *want* to talk about the one who has moved on to the presence of the Master.

In later years, when I was asked: 'How many children do you have?' I always replied: 'Four: three on earth and one in heaven.' And if that sometimes puts a stop to the conversation, I try to handle it head on, and ask why that has been embarrassing. Strangely, we find that it is more often among our Christian friends and contacts that this problem arises. It is far less prevalent among those we meet who have no faith.

So, Spre-e '73 was born in sorrow and anguish – but the work of God remains, and there was much to be done.

It quickly became clear that there was more than I could handle on my own. Furthermore, there were political matters which needed someone with closer team experience than I had. For example, the committee (comprising mostly under-thirties) felt that it would be inappropriate for Cliff Barrows to be included in the participants; likewise Bev Shea. For me, I could not comprehend any Billy Graham event without our dear friends, nor did I believe that it would be easy for Billy Graham without them. I did not feel that I had the right to express the committee's view to my colleagues. It needed someone with far more team experience than I had.

Accordingly, I telephoned Billy Graham and asked him if there was anyone on the team who could be seconded to London for the period of Spre-e '73. He promised to have a look at commitments and see who could be spared. George Wilson called me a few days later to say that John Dillon would be coming from Minneapolis to fill this slot. I cannot think of anyone else who could have done it better. John commended himself to everybody, from the moment of his arrival. He was a dear soul, and exactly right for our needs.

Soon after he arrived, in February 1973, we tried to find him a suitable place to live. It seemed sensible for him and Louise to live fairly close to us, so we looked in the Stanmore area. The house agent gave us a long list of rentable properties and we set out to look at them. Eventually we found one which was exactly right ... except that when we went into the lounge and the dining room, each of the rooms was like a picture gallery, only every one of the pictures was of an unclothed lady! There was no way we could see John and Louise living there – although John did suggest that he might go around and turn all the pictures to face the wall.

The thing that did surprise us was the squalor in which so many people (in nice houses) lived. House after house was dirty and the kitchens unbelievable. How decent people can live like that we will never know. Eventually, we found a lovely ground floor flat which was just what they wanted. They took it for the duration of their stay and were very happy there.

One of the first decisions John Dillon had to take related to the promotion of the event. We had a visit one day from three men – Geoff Shearn, David Payne and Pete Meadows. They were associated together in an organisation called Musical Gospel Outreach. They had examined the initial publicity which we had distributed (based almost exactly on that used for Explo '72) and told us that it would never 'reach' today's youth. In their opinion, they said, we would miss the boat altogether. As an alternative, they offered their services in putting together a package which they felt would successfully attract the crowds we wanted.

John felt that they had much to offer, and contracted with them to give us the advice which they felt we needed. At that time, we were not aware that they would be charging us for this advice and, through this misunderstanding, that amount was never added to our budget. As a result, at the end of Spre-e '73 we were short by almost exactly the amount that their services cost us. Generously, the office in Minneapolis met our shortfall and saved us from financial embarrassment.

We shall never know if their approach was more successful than our original approach would have been. It went directly against my initial conception that we should model our event exactly upon the successful Explo '72.

In the end, they mustered some 15,000 or more participants, all of whom were either resident nearby, or whom we accommodated in church halls, local hotels and other venues. My own vision had been for at least double that number, but those who came were greatly blessed. Indeed, almost twenty years after the event, one is constantly running into effective ministers – both male and female – who declare: 'It was at Spre-e '73 . . . ', and that experience is world-wide. Just recently, I discovered Jerry Pereira, the pastor of a church in a small town in the southern states of the USA, who said: 'Spre-e '73 shaped my ministry and set me alight!' In Belgium, Switzerland, Spain, Holland, France, Italy and many other European countries, there are those who testify to what Spre-e '73 meant in their lives. So we thank God for the 15,000 and more who came.

We had problems to contend with too! On three occasions, Billy Graham began to wonder if he had made the right decision to come to Spre-e '73. We simply received a message to question whether it was right to come. On one occasion we received an outright cancellation – which prompted John immediately to call Billy Graham in the USA, and to say how impossible it would be at this stage for him to withdraw. 'You cannot close the acorn once the oak begins to grow'.* Happily these traumas were put behind us, and we were assured that he would come.

We had a large mailing list at the office, much of it compiled and updated ever since the Harringay crusade of 1954. Many of those on the list of over 230,000 had never responded in any way and in 1972 we had weeded them out, reducing the mailing list to a responsive 27,500. None the less, when we came to Spre-e '73 I urged that we should send a sample mailing to some of the weeded-out names, and we selected 3,000 at random. We must have been guided in our selection! You can imagine our surprise when on January 10th, 1973 we opened one letter (of a very limited response) and found inside a cheque for ten thousand pounds. We were tempted to repeat the experiment, but because the remainder of the replies brought in less than a hundred pounds between them, wiser counsels prevailed. But we were grateful to the Lord – and to that donor – for that magnificent contribution to the cost of the event.

In the office John Dillon kept us all amused. The pressures of Spre-e '73 were immense, and we were all working long hours. Committee followed committee: finance, music, programme, counselling, seminars, exhibition and many more. We had to attend them all as we were the connecting link between each facet of the organisation. At one meeting, the chairman turned to John Dillon and said: 'John! Will you close in prayer?' John prayed fervently that the Lord would bless the work we were doing. He reached the end, and closed: 'So we thank you,

---

* Children of Eden

Lord, for your presence with us. Yours sincerely, John Dillon.' He has never lived that down!

On another occasion, when Walter Smyth was in town, we took John Dillon and Louise, his wife, together with Walter Smyth and a few other guests, to dinner at the Grimsdyke Hotel in Stanmore. Grimsdyke was formerly the home of W. S. Gilbert (of Gilbert and Sullivan fame). Once a week they have a special dinner when 'Mr Gilbert' himself, with some of his guests, joins the diners for dinner and, with his friends, entertains them by singing some of the songs from the operettas. At the end of the dinner, the singers finished up by singing 'Dance the Cachucca' from *The Gondoliers* by Gilbert and Sullivan. They concluded by taking a dance around the floor. Then each of them turned to a guest at the tables and asked them for a dance. Anne James, one of the most attractive of the singers, turned to John Dillon and invited him. John was covered with embarrassment. He hummed and ha'd; Walter Smyth meanwhile was egging him on. 'Go on, John,' he said, 'you can't keep a young lady waiting.' John did not move and Walter got more and more insistent. This prompted Louise to turn to Walter and say: 'Walter, don't make him: he wouldn't know what to do with his hands!' Poor Anne was turned down by one after another at our table, but by then the music was over.

Relationships are important: sometimes they are engendered by the most unexpected of events. One day, I was terribly busy and inadvertently sat down on the edge of my office chair. In that position it became unstable; it capsized, and catapulted me under the desk. John Dillon, sitting at his desk opposite mine, saw me suddenly disappear! His immediate concern was that I was not hurt – but when he found I was all right he dissolved into laughter. But this small event, in some way, cemented our friendship. Now, many years later, he still refers to it and we remember – through it – the happy times, the heartaches and the ministry which God had given us together.

He could never understand some of the English idiom. We were discussing two alternative programmes which would shape some of the overall decisions. Thinking out aloud, I said: 'If we do one and not the other, we will be in danger of falling between two stools.' John collapsed into gales of laughter. He asked me to repeat what I had just said – and could not believe his ears. That phrase has a somewhat unpleasant meaning in the USA.

How do you explain the English sense of it to an American? I told him that it was like trying to sit on one of two bar stools in the pub. You can't make up your mind which one to sit on, so in the end you fall 'in between two stools'. Years later he still laughs when he thinks about it.

Gradually the planning of Spre-e '73 took place. Each day would comprise morning training seminars, afternoons witnessing on assigned streets, and evenings filled with a musical concert and an evangelistic message. We ran into problems with the seminar teachers. I had wanted to use the Campus Crusade teachers who had done such a fantastic job in Dallas. The training committee were insistent that the teachers should all be British. In the end we compromised with some of each – and those participants who were assigned to the American-led seminars were the most appreciative of the training. Our American colleagues had, after all, had years of experience in this particular ministry; those in Britain had to follow a pattern which was often strange to them – or they adapted their own ministry to try and fit in.

I woke up one Monday morning, to realise that the handbook for Spre-e '73 would never be published unless I sat down and wrote it. The whole job was done in one day, using as the basic pattern the handbook from Dallas. We received a lot of warm comments about that handbook – and some people still use it as a reference book today. Preparing it was a marathon job, and when the writing was all complete, there was still the artwork to be done. By the end of the week, the whole job was in the printer's hands.

Dave Foster of Eurovangelism was in charge of the arrangements for the evening concerts. He supervised the production of a film to publicise the event. At the time we thought it was a masterly production. Looking back on it today, Dave would agree with me that it was quite ghastly! In it, he reiterated: 'Spre-e '73 is not a Billy Graham crusade: it's something totally different.'

For the evening events he found a superb choir from Sweden – Choralerna. They were, without a doubt, a highlight of the musical programme each night. Their music was totally acceptable, and technically excellent. They fitted in with most of the other musical talent. On the final night, there was a major concert by Cliff Richard, which was very well received. The same night, Mr A. Lindsay Glegg – a veteran British evangelist then over ninety years of age, made one of his last appearances on a platform when he was interviewed by Phil Herbert, our master of ceremonies. In his inimitable way, Lindsay shared with his young audience some of the wealth of experience he had gained over many years. 'Mr Glegg,' asked Phil, 'you are always so well dressed. I've never seen you without very smart clothes.' Lindsay replied: 'When I was a boy, I told my father that my ambition was to be a managing director. My father said, "Very well, son, always dress like one!" '

Lindsay Glegg had had a somewhat unusual ministry, in the course of his life as an evangelist. He had a great talent for spotting young preachers and he never failed to bring them forward. It was not unusual for him to accept a preaching engagement, and to turn up with a young man in tow. In his slightly husky and high voice he would say: 'I've brought this young man with me tonight and I'd like you to hear him.' Often, that sermon was enough, and Lindsay Glegg would simply close the meeting. Occasionally he needed to bring a closing message afterwards. But, by this simple act, he introduced to the evangelical world such men as Alan Redpath, Tom Rees, Stephen Olford and many others (including my own son, Gary, who later entered the ordained ministry after a number of years at Lindsay Glegg's Down Lodge Hall in Wandsworth).

There is no one today who is fulfilling that function. Young men are not being brought forward in the way that Lindsay Glegg did. We are poorer for this missing emphasis of his ministry. It was entirely appropriate that a ninety-year-old veteran should be honoured and introduced at what was essentially a young people's event. Billy Graham joined enthusiastically in the applause which greeted his appearance.

In the afternoon the witnessing on the streets was a new experience for many. One young and rather inexperienced woman was assigned Park Lane in London's West End. In this smartest of streets, she went into the famous Dorchester Hotel, where she saw a man sitting by himself. She asked if she might talk to him, and he invited her to have tea with him. As they sat, she shared 'The Four Spiritual Laws' with him, and then invited him to the evening meeting. He came to Earls Court and met her, and stayed through it all – but he went away without responding. The next night he was back on his own – and the next, and on the third night he responded to Billy Graham's invitation to accept Christ.

It was a traumatic experience for him because he later disclosed that he was a high official in the Mafia! It so happened that he was counselled by a lawyer, who immediately realised the hot potato he was holding. In order to protect this gentleman after his spiritual experience, arrangements were made for him to go and stay at the country home of a friend of the lawyer. In the months that followed, his spiritual decision was reinforced: he spent some time at L'Abri, and ultimately went to live in the USA, where he sought to serve the Lord. He had no idea of the name of the young lady who first confronted him; indeed they did not meet after the first evening that he came to Earls Court. It may be that, if she reads this book, she will learn for the first time of the end result of her witnessing.

On the last night at Earls Court, it was learned that the arena management would charge three thousand pounds to clear the floor of the hall of chairs. As the evening concert and meeting ended Henry Hole, the chief steward, came to the microphone. He had every participant stand up, turn around, pick up their chair, and walk to the side of Earls Court where other stewards were ready to stack them. Thus, in about five minutes, we saved three thousand pounds of the funds! Later, all the chairs were sold to churches up and down the country where they are still in good use today. John Dillon had selected the type of chair we would use by a unique test. He had all the suppliers send a sample chair to our office at Camden Road. Then, one night after everybody had gone home, one by one he dropped the chairs out of the second floor window. Only the chair we selected, made by Remploy, survived this stringent test and we ordered some 20,000 of them. The entire cost was covered (with some left over) by selling them off at the end of the event.

On the final afternoon at Spre-e '73 we moved location from Earls Court to the Wembley Stadium. Johnny Cash with June Carter Cash and his team had promised to be with us at the stadium for the final meeting. It was an excellent conclusion, although the numbers who came fell far below expectation. Billy Graham gave the closing address and there was a remarkable response – not least from the occupants of the royal box (no royalty were present), many of whom were household names in the show-business, political and industrial realms. It was a great conclusion to an effective week.

That it had been effective was clear from the testimonies of so many who came. Almost ten years later a letter came from the Reverend Bill Alston, then minister of the North Kelvinside Church in Glasgow. He wrote:

> David Coomes's book *Spre-e '73* closes with these words, 'Time alone will reveal which stories of real significance have come about as a result of Spre-e '73.'
>
> For me, Spre-e '73 marked a new liberty in personal witness, especially through the Four Spiritual Laws. This gave me a spur to service as it did to my colleague Alex Gordon who worked with Luis Palau in Aberdeen in 1979.
>
> I have had over three years of tough, hard organising as Chairman of Field Work for the Luis Palau Scottish Crusade but I would like to pay tribute to you for the way in which you organised Spre-e '73 – despite some criticism you received both then, and since.
>
> I know you can't tell a certain gentleman across the water about this, but please feel encouraged that your labour was very far from being in vain. The toughening I learned at Spre-e '73 has helped me very much. Thank you most sincerely for conceiving the idea, and for all you did to bring it to fruition.

David Coomes tells the complete story in his excellent book so there is no need to repeat it here. One thing is clear: from Spre-e came other similar events inspired, as Spre-e had been by Explo, by the event itself.

Among those who came to Spre-e '73 was a large contingent from Germany. One such group who returned were so inspired by events that Christoval '76 in Essen, Germany was the result. Following a very similar pattern to both Explo and Spre-e, the German event drew participants from all over Europe. The sessions were in a multitude of languages, all of which were translated into English (or, where the speaker was English, into many other tongues). Billy Graham was also a speaker in Essen along with Luis Palau, Bishop Festo Kivengere and many other evangelical leaders.

Spre-e '73 inspired the Belgians and the Dutch to another Europe-wide event in Brussels in 1975. Known as Eurofest '75, the event was largely organised by a team from the Billy Graham

Evangelistic Association. In numbers it greatly exceeded both
the British and the German events, and got much closer to the
numbers involved in Explo '72. Once more, Billy Graham and
the team were involved and the event included an evangelistic
crusade-type meeting in a nearby stadium.

The entire Palais de Beaulieu close to Brussels was booked
for the event. Six or seven major exhibition halls comprise the
complex, and the entire area was reserved for Eurofest '75. One
hall was used entirely for a girls' dormitory and, at the other
end of the site, a similar hall was used as a men's dormitory.
Another hall was reserved for meals and yet another for a
massive exhibition area. One was used as the administration
building, and one was used as the medical centre. In spite of
the enormity of the dormitory accommodation for each sex,
there was still insufficient room for all the participants, and
several fields close by were taken over as campsites for those
who brought their own tents.

The largest hall was reserved for both the plenary and the
seminar sessions. A remarkable public address system, conceived by David Rennie, was installed which meant that each
of eight or nine language groups heard the messages simultaneously in their own tongue. Instead of pointing outwards,
all the loudspeakers pointed directly downwards. This had the
effect of limiting the coverage from each loudspeaker. The
various language areas were not marked within the hall: rather,
as you entered, you walked around until you found an area
where you understood the language. The effect upon entering
the hall was a living example of the Tower of Babel. All one
could hear upon entering was *noise*. But as you walked around,
gradually other sounds disappeared and your own language
came through loud and clear.

After Eurofest '75 and Christoval '76 it seemed as though
this type of event had played itself out. During the four-year
period, tens of thousands of young people had been set on
fire for God, and eternity alone will reveal the lasting effect.
These events were symptomatic of the needs of young people
at the time, and they were effective in meeting those needs. It
was a remarkable example of the way in which Billy Graham
was inspired, ready and willing to try different methods. It is
significant that they did not, in the end, change the well-tried
crusade and mission approach. For the four years that youth

came to the fore, there were no major crusades in Europe. Subsequently – and after many traumas and much heart-searching – crusades returned with as great effectiveness as ever before. Billy Graham's contribution during these intervening years was of inestimable value, and many young people have cause for thanksgiving for Explo, Spre-e, Eurofest and Christoval.

6

The Years Between

Evangelism has always been at the centre of my thinking. I remembered that it was Christ Himself who said: 'Go into all the world and preach the Gospel.' I was thankful therefore that the Lord had led me into the orbit of Billy Graham, and that I had had the privilege of association with him, at Harringay, Wembley and Earls Court.

I had found the critique on mass evangelism *On the Other Side*, edited by my friend Morgan Derham, very hard both to understand and to accept. My human reaction was one of bitterness, but I asked the Lord to take that spirit away, and to replace it with one of understanding and love.

The last crusade meetings in Britain were held in 1967. When Billy Graham was next to come for a series of evangelistic meetings it would be 1984 – and they would then be called 'missions'. The Lord showed me that there were other ways of doing evangelism which might be appropriate for the years in between.

I did not, of course, know in 1967 that it would be 1984 before Billy Graham would return, but in the meantime I saw my brief as two-fold: first to provide opportunities for evangelism on a smaller scale and second to keep the name of Billy Graham, and his commitment to evangelism, before the British public. The latter was never a problem in the USA because Christian radio opportunities allowed the radio programme *The Hour of Decision* to be broadcast weekly. In addition there were several 'Television Specials' which were televised several times a year. So the American public were always kept informed. Not so the British, to whom regular Billy Graham

broadcasts were denied. There was, of course, the service provided by Trans World Radio from Monte Carlo. *The Hour of
Decision* was carried twice every Sunday but reached only a
limited audience because of the difficulty of tuning in to the
station.

One regular source of evangelism was the release of new films.
World Wide Pictures produced a new evangelistic feature film
almost every eighteen months. In Britain, we organised a press
and VIP preview for whatever new film arrived from the USA,
and then sought to release it as widely as possible across the
country.

This programme culminated in three major film releases: *The
Hiding Place*, the story of Dutch patriot Corrie Ten Boom, who
had helped Jewish people to escape from German persecution
in the Second World War; *The Prodigal*, a family story dealing
with many of today's family problems; and *Joni*, the story of
Joni Eareckson, who had been rendered quadriplegic following
a swimming accident as a teenager. All three of these films
we succeeded in getting into the normal cinemas on general
release and at least two of them were highly successful. We
were particularly pleased when we heard that Jeanette Clift,
who played Corrie in *The Hiding Place*, had been nominated for
a British Academy Award. I received an unexpected invitation
from GTO films, our distributor, to attend the award-giving
ceremony at the Wembley Conference Centre. I was devastated
to find that the date clashed with the date on which I was to
meet Her Majesty the Queen.

As part of the Silver Jubilee celebrations, a small group of
magistrates had been invited to attend a reception at St James's
Palace where the Queen and Prince Philip would be present. I
was fortunate to have been one of those selected to attend. It was
a grand occasion and one that I would not have missed for the
world. Yet I also wanted to be at the Academy Awards. The
problem was how to do both.

The reception at St James's Palace was in lounge suits, but
for the British Academy Award event, the dress was to be
dinner jackets. The reception was due to finish at 7.30 p.m. and
Wembley was due to commence at 8 p.m., with a forty-minute
drive between the two. I also had to change clothes midstream.
In the event, I found a dark tree and a big bush in St James's
Park, just outside the Palace gates. There I furtively did my quick

change. Happily no one spotted me and my fears of arrest by the police were never realised.

At the reception, Her Majesty the Queen spoke to everybody: with some she had a long conversation, with others there was simply a greeting. At the time, I was sitting on the Harrow and Hendon Bench in the Gore Division of Middlesex. I had hoped that the Queen would have a longer conversation with me: 'What work do you do in real life?' and I would have been able to talk to her about Billy Graham. But it was not to be. She simply asked: 'And which division do you serve?' to which I replied: 'Gore, ma'am' – which is all I said to the Queen until some years later. But that's another story, which appears in chapter 10.

Wembley was a grand occasion too. We had the awards first and then a superb dinner to which Bill Gavin of GTO entertained us. Our disappointment was that Jeanette missed the award, but she was in the final three places. Had she won, it would have fallen to my lot to receive it on her behalf – but it wasn't until afterwards that Bill Gavin told me that I would have had to make an acceptance speech. I didn't even have the thought in mind, so it is perhaps as well that she didn't win first prize.

A later release, *Caught,* together with *Joni* and *The Hiding Place* was sent to Buckingham Palace for inclusion in the royal library of videos.

One of the first events to be planned, following the end of the 1967 Greater London crusade, was the première of the film *Two a Penny.* Reference has already been made to the near-disaster which accompanied the première. It was, none the less, a glittering occasion with Cliff Richard and some forty other stars of stage, screen, television and radio present. Above all, it gave an opportunity to present the gospel and, during the three-week run of the film in central London's Prince Charles Theatre, many thousands saw it and hundreds of response cards were returned to the office. All of them were followed up in exactly the same way as were those who responded at the Earls Court crusade.

Much of the work of counselling was undertaken in a voluntary capacity by a London minister, the Reverend C. Alan Stephens. For almost thirty years he gave dedicated service to handling the London office counselling, writing to many hundreds of enquirers from both the film shows and other events.

Like most of the film premières of those days, the opening night was an evening dress occasion. It added something to the event, and showed that the gospel was equally relevant to the up-and-outer as to all other strata of society. The fact that the star of the film, Cliff Richard, had given such a clear testimony himself meant that his peers were prepared to listen. As a result there is today a strong representative group of committed Christians in the show-business world. God has used Cliff's clear testimony, and Cliff has been faithful to the Lord through all of these years.

Apart from the film ministry, we planned many other events, some of them rather unusual. In November 1968, we heard that Dr Sherwood Eliot Wirt, the first editor of *Decision* magazine, was to be in London for an extended stay. Jean Wilson suggested to me that we should put on a special event to recognise his visit.

We booked the assembly hall at Church House, Westminster for the event, and then planned the programme. From the outset, we were determined to make it something different and evangelistic and we invited Alan Stephens to write a script for a dramatic sketch to tell the story of printing the magazine in England. He wrote something super-dramatic! He planned a programme which would use an overhead projector, a slide projector, film, a tape recording, lights and live action. As in so many things we did, we were ploughing a new furrow. Today multi-media presentations are run-of-the-mill; in those days they were unheard of.

The narration was done by Peter Bond, a BBC announcer and presenter, who was a long-standing friend of mine through the Venturers Cruise. It was an exciting concept simply because it was new, and had never been done before. The programme took the audience through the London production of the magazine, the dramatic highlight of which was a faithfully reproduced crisis when the positives (from which the magazine was printed) were held up in Customs at London Airport. In this reconstruction we were at the printers awaiting the delayed positives. Jean Wilson came running in (as from the airport) and, waving the roll of positives in the air, declared: 'I've got them, I've got them!' The audience had by then been raised to such a fever pitch that they stood and cheered her as she arrived.

But drama of itself was nothing without evangelism. First there was a question and answer session with a panel to provide the answers. The last question – with somebody prepared in advance to ask it – was 'What does *Decision* magazine aim at?' It was a question which led naturally into an evangelistic address from Sherwood Wirt. There were counsellors there afterwards, and they were well used. It had been an effective event.

For the staff, these were busy and happy days. We tried to create an atmosphere which focussed upon our spiritual ministry. So each day commenced with a brief devotional time together. At that time, once a week, we were privileged to have special speakers, each a leader in the Christian world. One such was Corrie ten Boom. Her book *The Hiding Place* told the story of her valour in the face of Nazi Germany when the Jews in Holland were persecuted. It cost her her freedom and she, with her sister Betsie, was incarcerated in the infamous Ravensbrück concentration camp. Her sister died there, but, through an administrative error, Corrie found herself released and she spent the rest of her life tirelessly telling about Christ and His love.

Her story from the book was made into a film by World Wide Pictures. This meant that we were deeply involved in the production, as the set for the concentration camp was an old army camp near Aldershot in the south of England.

Twice, during the filming, we took members of the staff down to Hobbs Barracks (and once to the Bray Studios near Windsor, where there were ten 'sets' for the film). They were able to watch the filming. They stood amazed on a hot June summer's day as they watched the filming of a snow scene! Snow lay thick on the ground, and almost blizzard conditions existed as enormous fans blew tons of plastic 'snow' to create the desired effect.

They were taken into the dormitory area, where there had been a reconstruction of the overcrowded sleeping arrangements. They watched as – almost in reality – the actresses fought with each other, and Corrie (Jeanette Clift) sought to restore some sort of order. "Cut" called the director, and we all relaxed as we realised it was not 'for real'.

The atmosphere in the concentration camp did seem to be very real, however. Not only had the technicians converted the barracks, but they had encouraged the film 'extras' to live the parts they were playing. Even off the set they seemed to live as inmates of the concentration camp. We saw them sitting around, still in their concentration camp clothes, filling in the waiting time by working on handicrafts. They looked so real that we instinctively felt sorry for them – and when they all banged on their food bowls with their spoons, and held them out to us, one of the staff dropped in some sweets she was carrying! The look of gratitude on the face of the actress almost led us to believe that she was not playing a part.

Then, around the corner, came a bunch of jackbooted camp soldiers and the camp commandant. Instinctively we recoiled: it was all so very lifelike.

Filming started at 6.30 a.m. and did not stop until 10.00 p.m. at night, so it was hard work. I had been involved before the production started, with instructions from my colleagues in America to recruit some 250 'skinny women' who would be used as 'extras' for the film. The advertisement read: 'gaunt and thin women required for a film' and over 500 turned up to be interviewed! Also the search was on for World War II vintage clothing which would lend to the authenticity of the film.

Some of the filming also took place in Haarlem, Holland where the ten Boom clock shop still existed. Then the film was finally edited and assembled at the World Wide Pictures studios in Burbank, Hollywood.

Corrie had come to Britain to watch some of the filming. She acted as an advisor both in Holland and at Hobbs Barracks to help make every detail of the film authentic. It was during her time here that she was able to come and speak to the staff during their devotional time.

She said:

Watching the film of *The Hiding Place* being made has sometimes been hard on me. To relive the difficult life during the war and to see father (played by Arthur O'Connell who is so much like my father) suffer, has moved my heart. The day we were arrested was the darkest moment of my life and now I saw this again before me. The film is being made so realistically, and the dedicated people are portraying my family so well. Once there came self-pity in my heart as I watched them. But then I realised that the film will bring the message of Jesus's victory to millions in many countries, through the Billy Graham Evangelistic Association.

As I realised what Jesus could do, that took away my

self-pity because I knew that He could see the part of life we cannot see. He knows what we do not know. He knows everything and His negative answer is part of His plan for our lives.

She showed the staff the tapestry she had made and demonstrated how the tangle of threads on the reverse bore no relation to the order and beauty of the picture on the other side. She recited a poem to us:

> My life is but a weaving, between my God and me.
> I do not choose the colours, He worketh steadily.
> Oft times He weaveth sorrow, and I in foolish pride
> Forget He sees the upper, and I the underside.
> Not till the loom is silent and the shuttles cease to fly,
> Will God unroll the canvas and explain the reason why.
> The dark threads are as needful in the skilful Weaver's hand,
> As the threads of gold and silver in the pattern He has planned.

Her visit to us was a moving occasion and one never to be forgotten!

Quite often I was asked to speak to various groups about the work of the Billy Graham Evangelistic Association. One of the most difficult of these talks in 1969 was to the Central London Mensa Group. This club for the highly intelligent had invited me, and I gave a lot of thought and prayer to my address. It was clear that it had to be on a far more intellectual level than the talks I normally gave.

I spoke to them for about half an hour and then allowed time for questions. During my address, I referred to the fact that rarely did I speak on this topic without someone in the audience declaring that they had been converted to Christ through the ministry of Billy Graham. I implied that I knew I could scarcely expect this to be the case with so highly intelligent a group as Mensa. I was encouraged, therefore, when we came to the questions, to have a man stand up and say: 'Mr Rowlandson can know that his record is untarnished. I came to Christ during the Harringay crusade in 1954.'

In 1969 Billy Graham was to conduct a crusade in New York. It occurred to us that this would be a wonderful opportunity to become involved. 'If the hill will not come to Mahomet – then Mahomet will go to the hill!' If there was no way to bring Billy Graham to Britain, then Britain would provide a way to go and hear Billy Graham.

Through the team travel agents in Chicago, we got a special rate for travel and accommodation which would be attractive to our potential travellers. We publicised the event through *Decision* magazine, and advertised it in the Christian press. Because we wanted to keep the party compact, we were limited to one coachload of fifty-five people, and fifty-four places filled up very quickly. The last place was won by my secretary, Dawn Chandler, as mentioned previously.

We had a great time. The team in New York (where Bill Brown was responsible for setting up) welcomed us warmly. They made sure we had good seats in the Madison Square Gardens, and they organised all sorts of extra activities for us. In those days, there was still a restriction on the amount a British visitor could take overseas: twenty-five pounds was the maximum in cash and travellers' cheques. So everything we did had to be on a shoestring: we included visits to free museums; open air free entertainments and a visit to a TV game show with free tickets. *The Match Game* was a simple show, and as we went in, each of us was given a cloakroom ticket with a number on it. I stuck mine in the side of my shoe and forgot about it. As the show started, they called out – at random – some numbers from the cloakroom tickets. Idly I reached into my shoe to retrieve mine and, to my utter surprise, found that one of the numbers called was mine. I was chosen to be a contestant on the show!

Contestants were asked to write down a missing word from a sentence; another person (in my case, at the other end of a telephone) was also asked to supply a missing word. If it matched the one I had given, then we were both winners. 'The (blank) is so sharp' was my sentence. I wrote down 'knife'. The telephone caller also said 'knife' – and we had a match! I had won three hundred dollars and a set of Tourister suitcases. They told me to bring my wife and come to collect my cheque and luggage; but Marilyn was at a luncheon with Ruth Graham at the time and had not come with us. So the game show host told me to grab a blonde and 'come on down' anyway. It was certainly one of the most embarrassing moments of the trip. Not only was I ribbed by members of my party, but several of my team colleagues had seen the show in Minneapolis. It took me a long time to live that one down! But with so small a cash allowance from England, the three hundred dollars provided a bonus for the party. Sometimes the Lord provides in strange ways.

A day or so later, George Wilson came into our hotel clutching an airline ticket. 'Where's Marilyn?' he asked. She was found, and he gave her the ticket to fly to Minneapolis and see her parents. It was totally unexpected and another example of the thoughtfulness and love of the team – a wonderfully generous gesture.

The crusade meetings were inspiring. It was great to see people responding to the invitation. Billy Graham was preaching with great power and our hearts thrilled to see the response. After the crusade was over, we took our party on a brief tour through the northern part of New York State, planning to include a visit to the Niagara Falls. But when we got there, there was not a drop of water flowing over them! Due to some incredible engineering works, the flow of the river had been temporarily diverted, and we must be one of the few tour groups to see a dry Niagara. But those brief days were full of fellowship and fun, and lasting friendships arose from them.

One of the party celebrated her twenty-first birthday while she was with us. We later discovered that, by profession, she was a go-go dancer, yet a Christian! She knew how to witness, and she amazed us with her Christian testimony – but she was clearly also a member of her profession. A couple of years later, she came with us on our tour to Israel. We had to carry shawls and skirts with us to cover up her bare arms and mini-skirted legs at all the holy sites. And again, when we took a tour group to Stockholm to attend the Billy Graham crusade there, she was once more in the party and it was an education to see her at 2 a.m. in the local café, with her bible open, talking about Christ to the young drug addicts and drop-outs. We were worried as to her whereabouts at that hour of the morning, when she had not come back to our hotel. Marilyn and I found her in that café and were reminded that it was Christ who said to his parents: 'Do you not know that I must be about my Father's business?' We felt that that was Tracy's forte, and we would not have had the same rapport with those local youngsters that she had.

In 1970 there was a celebration for the 350th anniversary of the sailing of the Pilgrim Fathers to America. As we thought about it, it seemed to be an occasion which we too should use to the glory of God. Tentatively, we thought about the type of event we might plan, and then we extended an invitation to Billy Graham to have a part in it. To our joy, he accepted and we moved into high gear.

We planned an event with three elements, partly celebration, partly evangelism and partly outreach. For it, we booked the Royal Albert Hall on Monday, November 23rd, 1970. We called the event 'Freedom and Faith' and printed a luxury commemorative programme on parchment paper.

For the celebration aspect, we invited the band of the Grenadier Guards to play from 7 to 7.30 p.m., culminating in a full-scale rendering of the National Anthems of the United States and Great Britain. For the benefit of the British, we printed the words of both National Anthems so that everyone could join in the singing.

Henry Hole, who had produced many pageants for the Covenantors Union bible classes at the Royal Albert Hall, was invited to devise and produce a pageant suitable for the occasion. Alan Stephens again wrote the script and the narrator was the head of the dental department of the National Health Service, John B. Woodward, who had the right sort of Dimbleby-style ceremonial voice.

It was during the planning of this event that John Woodward and a number of us working together went up to the Norfolk Broads for a weekend's rest. John Woodward came with us to dinner. The restaurant we had selected was blasting out juke box music throughout our meal. Eventually, John could take it no more. Calling to a waiter he asked: 'How much does it cost to buy a song on that juke box?' The waiter told him ten pence. Digging into his pocket, John brought out four ten-pence pieces. Giving them to the waiter he said, in his commanding voice: 'Will you *please* buy us forty-pence worth of *silence*!'

The pageant was in four parts: first, 'The plea for freedom'; second, 'Seeking for freedom'; third, 'Permissive freedom' and finally, 'Disciplined freedom'. Many hundreds took part from Boys' Brigade units all over the London area, supported by students from the London Bible College and Billy Graham staff members. It was a moving pageant which was exactly right for the occasion.

The BBC reported on the event the next day:

6,500 people joined in singing the Battle Hymn of the Republic while cymbals clashed, drums rolled and spotlights played on the Union Jack and the Stars and Stripes . . . the pageant told the story of the Pilgrim Fathers with their faith pointed out by a strident ballet number, all flashing lights and a puff of smoke, with an illuminated cross shining out above the stage. Billy Graham said that it was clear that if we didn't put our faith in the same God as the Pilgrim Fathers did, and discipline ourselves as they did, we shall take the slippery slope which could lead us to the ash heaps of history.

Admiral Sir Horace Law introduced the American ambassador (Walter H. Annenberg, a friend of Billy Graham's), and he handed to Billy Graham a special message from the then President Nixon.

Billy Graham gave an address which concluded with an act of rededication, and provided an opportunity for those who wished to make a full commitment to Christ. A great many responded, including some of the Grenadier Guardsmen. After the benediction by Bishop Goodwin Hudson, the band of the Grenadier Guards played us out with *A Musical Ritornelle* and our friend Gordon Brattle continued with music from the great organ. It was a moving, emotional and impressive occasion.

The third part of our planning – the outreach – was to be a dinner at the Hyde Park Hotel. We invited some 200 VIPs from all walks of life to meet Billy Graham at dinner. Most of those who came were from government, industry, commerce and the professional fields. Only a few of them were known to be committed Christians. As always on these occasions, Billy Graham was at his best, and he presented a powerful evangelistic address.

Almost exactly a year later, in November 1971, came the opportunity for Billy Graham to address the National Institute of Directors. The invitation had come to him from one of those who had been present at the dinner a year before. Once more he returned to the Royal Albert Hall, in which a most influential audience had gathered for the occasion. His address was not without interruption: one of the audience took objection to the powerful message which Billy Graham gave, and expressed his displeasure by heckling. But Billy Graham continued to his final exhortation to his audience to seek a living and vibrant faith and in this, he concluded: 'I say to you never give up! Never! Never! Never!'

In the autumn of 1971 the Reverend David MacLagan of East Kilbride, Scotland, asked Billy Graham if he would consent to Bev Shea and Cliff Barrows coming from America to assist him in a televised broadcast of a BBC *Songs of Praise* programme from his church. Billy Graham readily agreed and on January 30th, 1972 the programme was televised. It was an unusual format for *Songs of Praise*, as the songs were led by Cliff Barrows in his typical style, and Bev Shea sang a couple of solos during the programme, which were well received.

On March 17th, 1972 I had a telephone call from Billy Graham. He told me that the needs of Northern Ireland had been on his heart and, in the midst of the current turmoil, he wondered if there was any possibility of holding a crusade. He asked me to assemble a group of people who would go to Ireland and make an assessment of the situation.

Accordingly I invited a team of four – the Hon. Crispin Joynson-Hicks (now Lord Brentford), Sir Eric Richardson, Neville Knox and an American, David Enghauser – to travel with me to Belfast to meet with some of the Irish leaders and to ask appropriate questions. We went over on March 23rd, 1972 and met first with Basil McIvor and the Speaker of the Stormont assembly (on the day on which it was to be disbanded). We then saw a number of evangelical leaders in the city before taking the train on to Dublin.

The next day we met with a representative group of clergy and ministers in the home of Miss Margaret Hamilton Reid. Having assembled our information from both cities, we returned to London by air that evening. We went straight to my office where we remained until 10.30 p.m., compiling our report. Briefly we concluded that there was no evidence to suggest that a crusade in Northern Ireland at this juncture would be either acceptable or possible. On the other hand, there was strong evidence that a crusade would be welcomed in Dublin. Politics, however, decreed that you could not go to Dublin without going also to Belfast, and as it would not be possible to conduct a crusade in Belfast, Dublin was also ruled out.

In May 1972 we planned to celebrate the eighteenth anniversary of the Harringay crusade with a gathering at London's

Grosvenor House Hotel. We called it 'It Happened Once' and while we tried to avoid too much nostalgia, we tried at the same time to express our thankfulness to God for all that had been achieved in the intervening years.

We enrolled the help of the Regent Hall Salvation Army band, and they played crusade hymn tunes while our guests arrived for a time of fellowship over coffee. Then, as the meeting started, Dr Robert Ferm (a member of the Billy Graham team) invited those in the audience who had found Christ through the Harringay crusade to stand up. There was a rustle among the audience, as many hundreds stood in testimony to what the crusade had meant in their lives.

There were three other special items on the programme: first, we showed the film *Souls in Conflict*. Made during the 1954 crusade at Harringay, it was still regarded by many as the best film that World Wide Pictures ever produced. It proved to be as relevant and topical as when it was first released.

There followed a series of brief testimonies from those who had committed their lives to Christ at the time of the Harringay crusade. Foremost among these was Ernest Shippam, whose radiant testimony over many years had been used by God to bring his family and many of his associates to the same decision. Another was Major Richard Carr-Gomm whose work through the Abbeyfield Society, and later the Carr-Gomm Society, was directly inspired by his conversion to Christ at the crusade. But perhaps the most poignant of all was a sequence of five testimonies. The first of these people had gone to the front when Billy Graham gave his invitation to accept Christ at the Harringay Arena. The second was someone who had been led to Christ by the first. The third, by the second and the fourth by the third, leading to a young teenager who had been brought to commitment to Christ by the fourth. Thus we were able to trace five spiritual generations to the present time – a direct result of the ministry at Harringay eighteen years previously.

Finally, we were linked by telephone to Birmingham, Alabama, where Billy Graham was in the middle of his second 1972 crusade. The call was amplified to all the audience and Bishop Goodwin Hudson had a conversation with Billy Graham. This concluded with a brief evangelistic message and a direct appeal to the audience to rededicate themselves to Christ.

Later in 1972 came the experience of Explo '72 in Dallas. On my return from it, God gave me the idea and vision of a similar event to be held in Britain. From that early inspiration grew the planning and execution of Spre-e '73, the story of which has already been told.

An important event, to which Billy Graham was invited, took place in July 1975. It was the centenary gathering of the Keswick Convention. From early in the year, I was involved in the planning and I went to Keswick in April to meet their committee.

They had decided that, in addition to the special centenary celebration in the large Keswick tent, they would like to have an open-air evangelistic rally – an optimistic venture, bearing in mind the Keswick weather! Crow Park, beside Lake Derwent-water, was selected as the venue and I was given the responsibility of organising that special meeting.

A graphic designer from Windermere designed a superb platform which was to be built upon a large farm waggon, loaned to us by one of the local farmers. I had visited many farms before locating one where they had a suitable waggon.

Canon Tim Houghton, then chairman of the Keswick Convention, had insisted that Billy Graham should stay with the speakers' house party at Underscar Hotel while he was in Keswick. I pointed out to him that this plan was fraught with problems, because it was the natural place for the press and television representatives to look for him. As a result they would have little peace. None the less, Canon Houghton said: 'Please let him stay with us.' So we did – and the media found him. They were camped outside the doors of the speakers' hotel from early in the morning until late at night. There was little or no peace. Finally, Canon Houghton came to me and said: 'Maurice, we were wrong and you were right. Could you possibly find somewhere else for Mr Graham to move to?' In the event, Mr Graham decided to go straight on to Manchester after the meeting, so the question of moving him did not arise.

Mr Graham travelled by train from London to Keswick, and we met him at Penrith Station. He shared with us, on arrival, a story of a conversation he had had on the train. It appeared that he and T. W. Wilson had gone to the restaurant car for a meal. Someone had told him that it was all right for Christians to drink cider, so he had ordered a glass of cider with his meal.

Part way through the meal, the waitress in the restaurant car came and said to him: 'You know, you look awfully like that American preacher, Billy Graham ... but you can't be, or you wouldn't be drinking cider!' To which Billy Graham gave his standard reply: 'Oh, my!'

On the day in question, the police suddenly got cold feet. They realised that the only approach road to Crow Park would be thronged with people and the security risk would be too great for them to bring Mr Graham by that route. In consultation with them, we negotiated with the boatyard at Portinscale for us to use one of their launches, and for them to bring Mr Graham by boat across the lake.

Crow Park lies to the north of Lake Derwentwater, the beautiful lake which forms one of the delights of the town of Keswick. Some 15,000 people had gathered on the lake shore, and for many the event evoked a picture of that scene in faraway Galilee where Jesus taught the multitude by the lake shore. The fact that Mr Graham arrived by boat made the bible narrative even more realistic although it was not planned because of this.

A full crusade-type programme was planned, with Wanda Adams of Trans World Radio singing the solo immediately before Mr Graham's address. The rainy morning had cleared by lunchtime and although the clouds hung low over the hills, the sun broke through and blessed us with superb weather. Mr Graham brought a powerful evangelistic address at the conclusion of which he invited enquirers to come forward to the front of the platform. Many hundreds responded and they were counselled by a team of Keswick participants who had gone through a crash course in counsellor training, led by Billy Graham team member Norman Sanders.

Stephen Olford was one of the speakers at Keswick that year, and he counselled one young man well known in the pop music world as Jethro Tull, who had been among those who responded to the invitation. While the counselling was going on, Billy Graham returned to the boat and was taken back to the waiting cars at Portinscale.

We left Portinscale for Manchester. My wife, Marilyn, had taken another car with Rosemary Wheeler (my PA) and our daughter Jacky. Earlier in the day they had collected all the luggage of the party, and the idea was that they would wait in a layby just outside Keswick in order to fall into convoy behind us on our arrival from Portinscale with Mr Graham and Grady Wilson (who was with him). I gave Marilyn my walkie-talkie radio unit so that, as we approached the layby, I could call her and she would be ready to change cars to ride with us, while Rosemary and Jacky would follow on in the other car.

As we approached the layby, Marilyn was out and ready to join us in our car and we set off, in convoy, for Manchester. We left the walkie-talkie with Rosemary in her car because we wanted to call her from time to time. She had a reputation for falling asleep whenever she was in a car – and we wanted to make sure she stayed awake while she was driving!

Billy Graham heard me speaking on the walkie-talkie and asked me who was in the other car. When he heard that Jacky (then thirteen years old) was there with Rosemary, he picked up the walkie-talkie. 'Calling Jacky, calling Jacky, this is Billy Graham,' he said. A surprised Jacky responded from the other car and she and Billy Graham had quite a long conversation. On and off on the journey to Manchester, he would pick up the instrument and have a chat with Jacky. It was a lovely unsophisticated involvement which meant a lot to a young teenager.

✳   ✳   ✳

Also in 1975, the very first moves were made to open the way for an invitation to be extended to Billy Graham to re-turn to London for a crusade. The full story of that, and the consequences, will be told in a later chapter. But a meeting on February 12th, 1976 produced three major results which, ultimately, contributed to the mission to be held in 1984.

The meeting had taken place in the Friends' Meeting House in London, under the chairmanship of the Reverend Gilbert W. Kirby. It was attended by many Christian leaders from all over the British Isles. There was full, frank and free discussion. Significantly, one of the most pressing points was that, if Mr Graham were to return to Britain, we should not consider a crusade held in London alone, but that he should visit, say, six centres around Britain. Gilbert Kirby expressed his view that while this was an excellent idea, we could hardly expect Mr Graham to commit himself to such a heavy programme. Eight years later, of course, this was exactly what Billy Graham did.

Another question was raised about the effectiveness of his ministry among young people and students. Questions were asked as to whether an elderly evangelist had any relevance for modern-day young people. The view was expressed that a good testing ground for this would be to hold university missions at both Oxford and Cambridge. Once more, the reaction was that this was something very unlikely to happen. But in 1980, there were indeed missions at both of the senior universities. They were highly effective and provided many opportunities, including an address to each of the Oxford and Cambridge Unions.

The third suggestion – which found little sympathy from the organisers – was that Mr Graham should be invited back for a mini-crusade to test out whether or not he was still able to draw a crowd in the UK. That this should even be in question spoke volumes about the influence that the book *On the Other Side* had had upon evangelical leaders since the Earls Court crusade of 1967. That such an event would be quite impossible was the consensus of opinion. You could never expect Billy Graham to come on those terms – yet again, that is exactly what happened in 1982 when, at the invitation of Jean Wilson, he attended the Christian Booksellers' Convention in Blackpool as the featured speaker. Billy – and Ruth – Graham would always do anything to help Jean Wilson. She had a warm place in their hearts and still does. Not without cause either: she would put herself out to help them in countless ways.

So when she wrote and asked if Billy Graham would come to Blackpool, he readily accepted. Later the folk in Blackpool (which had been Jean's home town) heard about the visit, and quickly responded by asking Mr Graham if he would consent to conduct a one-night crusade-type meeting in the Winter Gardens in Blackpool on the night following his address to the Christian Booksellers' Convention. He accepted. As soon as that meeting was made known, and tickets became available, they were entirely taken up within the first day or two. So the committee in Blackpool came back, figuratively with their cap in their hand, to say: 'Please would you do a second night?' Once again he agreed to this – with the proviso that he could not do any more because of other commitments.

While these events were going on in Blackpool, another drama was being played out on another stage. We were down in Bath, visiting our son Julian at Monkton Combe School, when

I received an urgent message to telephone London. It transpired that a message had been received from Uganda, to say that Bishop Festo Kivengere had escaped from the clutches of the dictator Idi Amin and was desperately seeking help to get out of the country. I called Billy Graham in America; within hours a ticket was on its way to the bishop and he was safely extricated. So I was able to return my thoughts to the events in Blackpool.

Mr Dickinson, a member of the Blackpool Crusade Committee and a well-known local surgeon, was deeply involved in the preparations. Shortly before the meetings started he invited all the team to an open house at his lovely and extensive home.

Afterwards he wrote to me with an assessment of those who came:

Dr Smyth – he's a wise sage
Dr Wilson [T.W.] – is a lovable and jolly man. He says he will let me do his next operation!
Cliff Barrows – who could have a better Master of Ceremonies?
Russ Busby [photographer] – a quiet man who gets on with the job
Blair Carlson – a hundred per cent American efficiency; he frightens me as we surgeons are often out 1 cm or 2 cm!
Yourself – like the others . . . wonderful!
Your wives – are all lovely
Thank you, thank you, thank you all for coming.
PS The next operation is a gall bladder: she is a cook!

In the event, the two nights were so over-subscribed that the committee reserved four additional auditoria in Blackpool and relayed the meetings to each of those halls. During the meetings, I took Billy Graham by car from one hall to another as necessary, walking through from hall to hall whenever possible. He appeared in each of the four halls and brought a brief greeting. The meetings were relayed directly from the Winter Gardens to the other locations.

It was clear that the popularity of Billy Graham and his ability to draw crowds were in no way diminished with the passing years. These various events all played their part in ultimately persuading him to return to England for a crusade

– then to be called a 'mission' – in 1984: but more of that anon.

There was a significance about the Blackpool crusade which none of those who were there could have been aware of. The visit took place at the precise time when Billy Graham had received an invitation to speak at a peace conference in Russia. He was in two minds whether or not to accept. Throughout the Blackpool crusade he privately struggled to reach his decision.

He was staying in a hotel seven miles south of Blackpool, and it was my privilege to travel there and collect him for each of his engagements. On the journey in, with T. W. Wilson in the car, Billy Graham rehearsed with us all of the pros and cons of the invitation. If he went, there would be some politicians in the United States who would criticise him. If he didn't go, he would miss an opportunity – one which, incidentally, might open other doors for ministry in the Soviet Union. Throughout the journey into Blackpool we went over and over the arguments on both sides.

We arrived at the Winter Gardens and I was inevitably thinking to myself: 'How in the world can this man be effective in his preaching when he has so much on his mind?' But when he arrived on the platform he was a different man. All of the uncertainties of the Russian invitation were put behind him for the certainties of the message of the gospel. He preached with power and authority, and he gave a strong appeal to accept Christ at the end. Many responded: but as always he returned to the car doubtful that he had been faithful to his calling. We encouraged him and told him how effective his preaching had been.

No sooner were we back in the car, than we returned to the old arguments about the Russian invitation. All the way back to his hotel we rehearsed new and different angles that had come to him during the meeting. There is a feeling of utter helplessness as you seek to advise and counsel him in these matters. It must be between him and God – and that is what we told him. In the end, a few days later, he decided to accept the invitation and I was commissioned to write the letter of acceptance.

On Saturday afternoon, Dr Walter Smyth and Dr Alexander Haraszti (a Hungarian who spoke Russian, and who was the negotiator between Billy Graham and the Russian authorities) came with me to our offices at Camden Road. Dr Haraszti dictated the letter of acceptance as I typed it out on the word processor. Then he and Dr Smyth examined the draft; altered it; I retyped it; it was altered again and retyped again and again and again! Eventually they signalled their final acceptance of what was written. The letter was signed and despatched and, in due course, Billy Graham went to Russia with dramatic results. Not only was he invited back on several occasions, but he was instrumental in helping towards the release of the Siberian Seven (a group of charismatics who were unable to leave the embassy compound in Russia). Nearly ten years later, he was able to organise in the heart of Moscow a School of Evangelism for all of the Christian leaders in the Soviet Union, to which many thousands came. His decision, taken in the car between the Winter Gardens and his hotel in Blackpool, had been significant and right!

Another event which was concurrent in planning with the crusade in Blackpool was the first International Congress for Evangelists. Dr Walter Smyth carried most of the responsibility for the initial planning of this event, and one of the factors which had occupied his mind for many months was where the congress should be held. He had visited many European cities: Rome, Stockholm, Paris, Copenhagen and Amsterdam. Each city had some benefit over another, and in the end it was narrowed down to either Rome or Amsterdam.

As Blackpool started, the news reached us that a decision had finally been taken and that the Rai Centre in Amsterdam had been booked – but Billy Graham had some reservations. One morning, on our way back from the Christian Booksellers' Convention to his hotel, Billy Graham started talking about the decision to go to Amsterdam. There were, he said, at least four reasons why he felt it was not correct. First there was the problem of high profile. Amsterdam is a notorious city, and known to be expensive. He feared that the media would latch on to the cost of the event. Secondly, he feared for those Third World preachers who might try to preach on the streets of Amsterdam. They would find it hard to cope with the reactions of the Dutch. Thirdly, he was worried about the fact that Amsterdam was the drug capital of Europe. 'Is it right,' he asked, 'to bring these folk into that sort of atmosphere?'

Finally, he was worried about the Amsterdam red light district. He wondered if it was right for him to bring the evangelists – mostly men – into a city where this feature is not only very public, but a tourist attraction as well.

As we drove along, he commented upon the many hotels on the seafront in Blackpool. 'Why,' he exclaimed, 'this would be just the place to hold that congress.' He felt that it answered all four of his concerns – not least because hotel accommodation in Blackpool would be only a fraction of the cost of hotel rooms in Amsterdam.

Just at that moment, we were passing the Imperial Hotel. 'Let's stop here for lunch,' he said, and I swung off the road into the driveway of the hotel. As we went through the door he said to me: 'Maurice, give Walter a call and tell him to come and join us.'

I telephoned the Norbreck Castle Hotel (where Walter was staying with the other CBC delegates) and asked him to drive to the Imperial Hotel. Ten minutes later he arrived, and as he came through the door, Billy Graham greeted him: 'Walter! Maurice has been suggesting that here in Blackpool would be the ideal place for that Congress!' I looked rapidly at Walter (who gave me a cut-throat sign across his throat), and said: 'Please, Walter, not me! It was Billy's idea!' Dr Walter Smyth has a very keen sense of humour, and he pulled my leg about Billy's suggestion for a long time to come. 'Was that your idea, Maurice . . . or Billy's?' he would ask, with his tongue in his cheek. (In the end, the first International Congress of Itinerant Evangelists, described in Chapter 11, took place as planned in Amsterdam.)

※   ※   ※

During the years between the crusades and the missions there were numerous small events. Each of them was important in its own way, and together they continued to keep the Billy Graham Evangelistic Association and the ministry of Billy Graham him-self in focus.

One of these was a memorial service which we organised on June 22nd, 1983 following the death of Corrie Ten Boom. Corrie's nephew, Peter Van Woerden, came from Holland to be with us and to bring the Memorial Message. We showed the film *Jesus is Victor*, which had been made by Corrie shortly before her death.

She had come to prominence following the publication of her book *The Hiding Place*. Her story, although virtually unknown until the book's appearance, was one of courage, intrigue and imprisonment in a Nazi concentration camp. Her ultimate release was the result of an administrative error. World Wide Pictures in America had filmed her story in Haarlem and other Dutch locations, and partly in the United Kingdom.

When the film was made, we negotiated with GTO films for its release through the normal commercial cinemas. Bill Gavin (the person responsible at GTO) and I held many planning sessions. We in the BGEA agreed to do whatever we could to help make the film widely known in the churches.

Bill Gavin would give me a list of the places where the film was to be released, and I would organise a meeting for clergy and ministers in that town. We showed them part of the film, gave them details about the release and encouraged them to make the film widely known among their people. We hoped that, by these means, there would be capacity audiences at most of the cinemas. In this way, during the many months of the release, I travelled the length and breadth of the land and met hundreds of clergy and ministers. That in itself was good PR for the BGEA and for Mr Graham.

In many places the film was an outstanding success; in other places it flopped. I found it interesting to assess why. In each city I always asked a local church leader to organise the planning meeting for me. I asked for it to be done 'nicely' and the interpretation of that word was very much in line with the local church leader's views. Some meetings were held in a meeting room at the Grand Hotel; others took place in a room at the back of Joe's Café! In those places where the planning meeting had been held in a Grand Hotel atmosphere, there was a Grand Hotel-type showing: totally successful, and with big crowds turning up. Those that went for the Joe's Café-type meeting ended up with a Joe's Café-type showing to which few people came, and the local cinema was not enamoured. I think that 1 Corinthians 14:40 has something to say about this: 'But everything should be done in a fitting and orderly way.' It reminded me of a Children's Special Service Mission (CSSM) chorus which we used to sing when I was a boy at the Crusader class in Mill Hill:

The best for God, the best for God
I want to be my very best for God
It's the only life worth living
It's the only thing worth being
So I'll live it . . . and I'll be it!
The best for God!

So *The Hiding Place* had a great ministry throughout the British Isles and, coupled with the many books that flowed from Corrie's pen, it affected the lives of many people. Thus when she died, it was not a time of sorrow, but a time of rejoicing for her memory, now that she was in the presence of her Saviour. She was ready to die, for as she said in one of her books, she had asked her father about death when she was just a young girl. 'When we go to Paris,' he had replied, 'when do I give you the ticket?'

'When we get on the train and are ready for the journey,' Corrie had replied.

'So it is with death,' said Papa. 'God will give you the ticket when you are ready for the journey.'

There were also many continuing activities which kept us busy throughout the years between. Already we have told how Trans World Radio, broadcasting to Britain from studios in Monte Carlo, carried the weekly programme *The Hour of Decision* and hundreds of letters a month were received in our office – many of them seeking spiritual counselling. This was a task also faithfully undertaken by our good friend Alan Stephens. He was assisted by an elderly gentleman, a volunteer who worked exceedingly hard for us. He spent most of his time going through the bible study replies which had come in from the enquirers. Frank Churcher was a dear man who faithfully used his time and talents in this service for his Master. He passed into the presence of the Saviour whom he loved and served, while still active in this ministry.

Then there was the ministry of *Decision* magazine, published on a monthly basis from 1961, and still going strong in 1992. In association with the magazine, we also organised a series of tours to Israel, inviting readers of the magazine to join us. Six of these tours took place, each with a complement of around fifty people. Some of the tours had with them (to give the spiritual leadership) a member of the Billy Graham team, most notably (on our first tour) John Corts. His bible expositions were often referred to in later days. He was, eventually, to succeed George Wilson as the executive chief of the Billy Graham Evangelistic Association. On other tours, we had the ministry of various friends of the association.

During the organisation of these tours, we sometimes received letters which amused us. Before we left on one tour we had such a letter from a young engaged couple who were coming with us. They wrote a note about the accommodation they wanted on the trip: 'When my fiancée and I join your tour group to Israel would you please note that we would prefer not to share a room.' He *meant* to say that each of them wanted a single room.

Not everyone who came on the tours was already a committed Christian. When Billy Strachan of Capernwray Hall was our spiritual leader, a young lady named Nicky Fletcher from the village of Henlow in Bedfordshire was on the tour. It was clear to us in the early days that she had never committed her life to Christ. Then, on the final day in Jerusalem, Billy Strachan had just conducted a communion service for our group in the beautiful garden adjacent to the Garden Tomb. As we left the area where the service was held, we looked back, and there was Nicky with an open bible on her knees. I looked at Billy and said: 'I think it's a case of "Understandest thou what thou readest?".' Billy suggested that we should ask Fiona, our son Julian's wife who was on the tour, to go back and speak to her. She did so and she led her to the Lord right there in the garden. A few days later she gave her testimony to the group, and a real inspiration she was to us all. So the tours were not just holidays; they were also holydays!

✳   ✳   ✳

One morning I had a call from the BBC. They said that they were preparing the obituary notice and programme for Mr Graham. Startled, and thinking they must know something that I didn't know, I asked for more information. 'Oh, don't be alarmed,' they said. 'It's just that we like to have it all ready for use whenever it may be required.' That was in 1978 and at the end of 1991 it was still in the archives.

The years between culminated in an invitation extended to Billy Graham from the newly appointed Archbishop of Canterbury, Dr Robert Runcie. Dr Runcie personally asked

Mr Graham if he would accept an invitation to Canterbury Cathedral on the occasion of the enthronement. Mr Graham felt that this was a great honour and he was happy to accept.

During the university mission at Cambridge, Dr Runcie's son James had been one of those who had called to see Billy Graham at his hotel. He had given James a good slice of time; he had impressed the young intellectual with his direct and lucid presentation of the gospel, and Dr Runcie had expressed his gratitude to Billy Graham.

T. W. Wilson rode with Billy and Ruth Graham and me on our way from London to Canterbury. They wanted to stay overnight in the Canterbury area in order to be fresh for the service the next day. We chose a lovely little secluded hotel in a village just outside Canterbury. Ruth loved it, and the food was outstanding. Eleven years later when the new Archbishop, Dr George Carey, also invited Billy Graham to his enthronement, Ruth asked to stay in the same hotel again. We booked the rooms; then some instinct told me to go and check it out. I said to Marilyn that we would drive down to Canterbury during the next weekend and see that everything was OK.

How glad we were that we did so! The hotel had been taken over some years earlier by one of the hotel groups. They had not kept it up, and it was considerably dilapidated; worse still was the fact that there were extensive roadworks going on outside which would have prevented the Grahams from having a quiet evening. We also discovered that the menu had deteriorated. I proved once again the truth of the adage that Major-General D. J. Wilson-Haffenden had given me many years before: 'Time spent in reconnaissance is rarely wasted!' We were able to find a beautiful hotel in another village close to Canterbury. In the event, Ruth never came to the enthronement of George Carey as she had to spend a short time in hospital just then.

The film ministry also kept us busy during these years. New films were constantly being released, and for each one we organised a central London première. Mostly they were oc-casions when we asked our guests to wear tuxedos or evening dress, and often we would follow the première with a dinner when we could have fellowship together. These occasions were important for building up, and maintaining, an interest in the association's ministry and in Billy Graham's crusade work. The ties and fellowship established have stood the test of time, and the many friends of Billy Graham have maintained their prayers and interest over the years.

Many of the première showings in those days were held in the University of London's Collegiate Theatre. It was a convenient and comfortable venue, and we enjoyed using it for this purpose. Mostly we sold tickets for the film shows but occasionally, when there were some left over, we would send the staff out on the streets to give the unsold tickets away free. Going out into the highways and byways in this type of evangelism appealed to them.

One young lady who was given such a free ticket was a young hospital auxiliary from Scandinavia. She came to see the film, and it awakened in her an interest in spiritual things. She decided to take out her bible: not knowing where best to start, she took pot-luck and began reading Leviticus! Years later she told us that she owed her conversion to that unlikely book of the bible. As she read it, and as she discovered the laws of hygiene that God had given to His people, she realised that these expressed exactly what she had learned in her training. She rationalised the position to herself: 'If this God of whom the bible speaks had these laws right from the very start, then He must be a God worth knowing.' Not really understanding what she was doing at the time, she committed her life to God – later coming to realise exactly what this meant in the light of Christ's sacrifice on the Cross.

She spent many hours in our home in the months ahead, and often came away with us to various places. I think she was trying to learn as much as she could of what it meant to be a Christian. Eventually, she married a Britisher who was himself deeply involved in Christian work, and together they set up a Christian home. It was all a direct result of the outreach of that film ministry.

We maintained our intimate involvement in the film ministry until 1978, when we reached a working agreement with International Films, under the direction of Nigel Cooke, to take over this ministry and to secure it for the foreseeable future. During the years of the film ministry we knew of many thousands who committed their lives to Christ as a result of seeing one or another of the films. Although Billy Graham could not be there in person, he was able to communicate the gospel by this medium.

So the years between were full and active. There was never a dull moment, and at all times we kept our eyes on two targets. First, we made sure that we never lost sight of 1 Corinthians 2:2: 'For I resolved to know nothing while I was with you except Jesus Christ and Him crucified.' Secondly, and on the human level, we set out to keep before the praying public, the ministry of a man so signally chosen and used by God in evangelism.

7

The Home Team

'An excellent wife is the crown of her husband,' says King
Solomon in Proverbs 12:4 (NKJV). So if there is any credit
due to me, it can be directly traced back to the excellence
of my wife. Indeed, any full-time Christian worker may count
himself fortunate to have the love and support of his wife. Since
Marilyn and I met and were married in 1949, I have worn a
crown! So she may be understood to be 'an excellent wife'.
She has fulfilled everything that could have been wished for in
a helpmeet sent by the Lord.

Not always has it been easy, for there have been times when
I have been away for long periods. I have already recounted
the debt of gratitude that the children and I owe to her. There
have been, too, times of anxiety, even of sorrow, but we have
been able to stand together in facing whatever God gave us to
experience. Then, too, there have been times of intense activity
when there has been little leisure to think about family matters.
But God has made up to us for those times.

To have that type of support at home is invaluable. But in
the area of work too, good support is vital. Not only does
it give confidence on a day-to-day basis, but it also frees the
full-time Christian worker to concentrate more upon his family
and their needs. It also means that the work burden can be
gratefully shared. Next to an excellent wife and a supportive
family, dedicated secretaries and personal assistants are worth
their weight in gold!

I have been fortunate in this area. Every one of those who
has been associated with me has been dedicated to the Lord's

work, and has been enthusiastic also about supporting the work
of Billy Graham. So there has been a oneness of mind in what
we have been doing. That has often meant that they have given
sacrificial service, often working long hours without additional
pay.

I hesitate to name any of the secretarial team as it is impossible to mention them all – and those left out would be
hurt to have been omitted. But there are a few who must be
named for a variety of reasons.

First and foremost among those is the indefatigable and
indestructible Jean Wilson. She was there when I first came
to the Billy Graham office in the Bush House days. She ran the
London base for the Billy Graham Evangelistic Association with
supreme efficiency and, for the improvement of that side alone,
my arrival was unnecessary. Alongside her work for the BGEA,
she was also deeply involved in the Sunday school materials
ministry of Gospel Light. This American programme was new
to the British Isles, and it was hard and grinding work to get
it off the ground. Jean was about the only person who could
have done it. Ever since I was invited to join Jean in running
the London office, her gracious acceptance and ready welcome
have never wavered. She has been through some traumatic
times, but she has always come through with colours flying,
and eager for the next challenge.

In more recent years she has added a great many other
activities to her work. She founded The Office London, an
administrative base which could be used by any Christian worker
passing through the capital. She became the British representative for African Enterprise which has occupied a great deal of
her time. She imported greeting cards and Regal Books and
became the secretarial base for a number of ministries such
as Family Radio. Most recently she has added the work of
Samaritans Purse, a Christian relief agency founded by Franklin
Graham, Billy Graham's eldest son.

Since the London office of the BGEA closed, she has handled
the nitty-gritty of everyday work which still remained to be
done. While she has dealt with the unglamorous side, I have
been privileged to handle the more glamorous aspects involving the team and Mr Graham.

Her other big activity in recent years has been as secretary
and organiser of the annual Christian Booksellers' Convention,

a highly successful enterprise which has earned her the respect and admiration of a great many people.

She was not, in any way, my secretary, nor my personal assistant. She was far more my associate in everything that we did. I leant upon her heavily for advice and guidance and she never failed to give wise counsel. To keep her humble I regularly gave her notice to quit – at least once every three months! But it was always rescinded before we went home that night. We have been associated since 1961, and we are still closely involved thirty years later. If something needed to be done, you could count upon Jean both to be able to do it, and to carry it out without counting the cost. She was invaluable in many ways.

Quite often she got herself into amusing situations. The one delight was that she could see the funny side as well as we could. On one occasion, World Wide Pictures had asked her to meet one of their technicians coming to London from Paris. He had telephoned her to say when he would arrive at London Airport and he told her that she would recognise him easily. 'I will be wearing Red Indian shoes and I will carry a copy of *Decision* magazine,' he said.

Jean went to the airport and stood among the large crowd awaiting arrivals. She looked for Red Indian shoes; two people went by wearing them, but neither was carrying a magazine.

All of a sudden a strange man spoke to her. 'Are you Jean Wilson from the London office?' he asked. Jean replied, 'Yes. But what happened to the Red Indian shoes and the magazine – and how in the world did you recognise me?'

The visitor replied: 'I'm sorry! I changed my shoes and forgot and packed the magazine in my suitcase – but it was easy to find you. I just looked for someone who was staring at people's shoes, and not their faces!'

There came a time when the team wanted Jean to have a new car. She and I went to the motor show to see what we could find. She already had a Vauxhall, but it was now appropriate to replace it. My instructions from America were to get her a good quality car. This was an occasion when those long legs of hers got her into trouble. We found a nice Toyota, but when she came to sit in it, she just did not fit! So we moved on to the Rover stand. We told the salesman the difficulty we had had with Toyota, and he said: 'There'll be no problem with a Rover.'

His face was a picture when Jean sat in the car. Again she just did not fit. He couldn't believe it. But it was the same story again and again at every car manufacturer we visited. We left behind us a long line of red-faced salesmen. In the end, the only cars in which Jean felt comfortable were either a Rolls Royce (and I thought that was going a bit far) or a Vauxhall. So that's where she ended up, and she stayed with Vauxhalls for many years until other manufacturers started taking extra-long-legged people into consideration.

Around 1977 came the big cutback in the work of the London office. Bishop Goodwin Hudson was called to New York for a consultation, and returned with the news that our staff was to be cut from twenty-eight to four. We never did manage to reduce ourselves to four but we did achieve five as our minimum. Quite obviously there was insufficient room for two top executives, and either Jean or I had to move aside. In the end, in her generous way, she accepted that it made sense for her to concentrate fully upon the Gospel Light work and her other activities, leaving me to focus on the work of Billy Graham (to which, a couple of years later, I added the secretaryship of the Keswick Convention).

The change did not make a great deal of difference to Jean. She still worked very closely with us, and continues to do so. She is an exceptional person, and those who have worked with her soon learn to appreciate her talents and her ability. Ruth Graham regards her a companion whenever she is in the United Kingdom. Jean writes off the whole time Ruth is here, and devotes herself to looking after her and taking her around.

Of all the home team, Jean was the tops. We could be frank with each other – and there were times we did not agree. But so long as she was handling the business affairs of the BGEA, I felt confident and content. She was an associate whom I was fortunate to have alongside me.

As for my own secretarial help – a long line of excellent colleagues – most of them left me to get married. That is a hazard of using younger secretaries. When I tumbled to that I said that, in future, I would have secretaries who were already married. But then they left me to have babies! Ultimately I discovered that even mature ladies are inclined to leave you to look after the grandchildren – so you are in a no-win situation.

Dawn Chandler was one of the best secretaries I ever had. I hesitated to offer the job to her, because she was the daughter of family friends of ours who lived very close to us at Frinton. The Dudley Brients were a very integrated family, who shared most things with each other. Dudley Brient had two sons, Trevor and Alan; his wife had died some years before and he had married Norry Chandler who had two delightful daughters. Thus Trevor and Alan had two ready-made sisters a little younger than them and it was hard in later years not to think of them all as one family. Dawn was one of Norry's daughters. When she came to me I expressed concern that the affairs of my office would get back to the Brient family. I told Dawn that, the first time I discovered such a lapse in confidence, it would be the end of a beautiful friendship.

Her sister, Heather, had recently married a senior army officer who had responsibility for the deployment of units of the British Army overseas. His work was highly secret, and neither he nor his wife could talk about it.

One Sunday morning Dudley Brient, founder of a large firm of stationers, invited us to his home after church. 'Maurice,' he said, 'I've got a problem. I can't talk to Heather about Colin's work because she says it's very confidential. Now I ask Dawn what's going on in Billy's world and she says, "Pop, don't ask me. Maurice's work is confidential and I can't tell you!" Maurice,' he exclaimed, 'you've put me out of communication with the only one of my daughters I could talk to about her work!'

Dawn was my secretary at the time of the closure of the *Christian* newspaper in 1969. It was a hard time for her and she was under intolerable pressure. Yet she remained supportive throughout.

When she left me to get married she invited me to her wedding at St Paul's Church, Robert Adam Street. Because her husband-to-be was in the Army, it was a military wedding, and she asked me if I would be able to attend in my Royal Naval Reserve uniform (complete with sword) to help form part of the guard of honour. To do this, I had to get permission from the Admiral Commanding Reserves, and he readily gave his agreement. After the wedding and reception, her bridegroom took her away on the top of a number 13 bus!

She was succeeded by Rosemary Wheeler who became my first secretary/PA, and she set a standard which was hard for others to follow. I learned from her what a PA needed to know in order to do her job properly and well. She also drew my attention to one of the dangers of a secretary's role. She told me that the words I dictated came in through her ears and flowed out through her fingers to the typewriter, so that at times she felt little more than a machine! I learned how important it was to involve my colleagues in the work I was doing. It was important to let them feel that they had more than a mechanical interest; they had a real part to play.

I had been protective in many areas of my work. Rosemary taught me that she could take them over and do them just as well. As a result the office became more efficient and I appreciated her approach to her work and her commitment to it.

It was towards the end of her time with me that she came into my office clutching a catalogue. She tried to show me the description of a new kind of typewriter on which the letters appeared on a television screen as they were typed. I dismissed the whole idea as a seven-day wonder – and probably too expensive to boot! Rosemary was disappointed. She left me to get married. She invited us to her wedding in Bristol, and we were able to go. At the reception the baser side of my nature came to the fore. There were two wedding receptions going on at the same time, and the guests for both of them were mingling in the same hallway. Another of Rosemary's guests, whom we knew, dared me to get into both lines and kiss both brides. I am sure that the other bride must have thought I was one of her new husband's friends.

Shortly after Rosemary was married, Marilyn and I went to the United States and visited the Billy Graham Evangelistic Association headquarters in Minneapolis. There they showed me a bank of some twelve Wang word processors, operated by just two girls. These machines turned out work at a fantastic speed and, as I watched them, I immediately knew that we needed similar machines in London. I talked to Don Bailey, who was then responsible for the office operation in Minneapolis. He told me: 'Not the Wang, Maurice. Go for the Lanier – it's simpler and far better.'

I returned to the UK where I made enquiries. The Lanier was named the AES in the UK, and I ordered our first machine in 1978. Later we had no fewer than seven AES machines in the office. Today we could not imagine life without them. Don Bailey was right: the AES was exactly what we needed. Most girls could learn how to operate it within half an hour, although to realise the machine's full potential, you would always be learning. Rosemary was vindicated. Her vision was amply rewarded in the years that followed, although her immediate successor was not enamoured with these new-fangled machines and eventually found other employment to avoid using them. For me, however, the opportunity to discuss with my colleagues in the USA the value and use of modern office equipment was always an advantage, and there were many areas where their expertise helped to keep me up to date.

It would become tiresome to list all the attributes of a whole team who followed Rosemary: Jane, Leslie, Linda, Pat, Enid, Wendy, Desiree and Corinne, most of whom after several years of excellent service left me to get married. But there came a day when I could not find a replacement secretary. I wrote in desperation to my American colleague, George Wilson, to ask if there happened to be a secretary/PA in the Minneapolis office who might be seconded to London.

This resulted in the arrival of Wendy Mitchell, grand-daughter of Ralph Mitchell, who had been very involved with Youth for Christ in the north of England. He had been responsible for the visits of Billy Graham to the north-east many years before. Some years later he and his family had emigrated to the USA. Wendy was able to come without the elusive work permit, because, as the grand-daughter of British nationals, she had a Certificate of Patriality. This gave her the right to live and work in the UK, although she herself was an American citizen.

Wendy came for two years. On the day she arrived we met her at London Airport and took her straight to St James's Park and to the Horseguards' Parade to watch the Trooping of the Colour. Not every American visitor could have timed their arrival so well. An incorrigible Anglophile and a great admirer of the royal family, Wendy was thrilled to see the Queen on her very first day in Britain.

She was quite the most unusual secretary I had ever had. She spoke her mind; if she didn't approve of something I had done, she made it very clear. On February 8th, 1979 I had dictated a letter to my colleague Jeanette Hoivik at the Minneapolis office. I cannot remember what the letter said, but as Wendy listened to it on the dictation tape, she refused to type it! I told her that it had to be written; she again refused and when I went on to insist, she stamped her foot and said, 'I will not write it' – and she didn't. That foot-stamping episode became famous in the office – but she was probably right. On reflection it was not a letter I would have wished to have had kept on file. Wendy and I got on well together in spite of her eccentricities.

On my birthday in August I had invited her to come sailing at Frinton in response to an invitation I, in turn, had had from my good friend Norman Farrar. Many of my colleagues had accepted earlier invitations to join Norman. He, in his generous way, had always been happy to welcome my guests. On the appropriate day, Wendy travelled down to Frinton and we joined Norman on his Royal Harwich One Design sailing ship *June*. On her return to London, Wendy wrote a description of the day:

I remember Norman Farrar. He was a photographer, but in real life, he was a sailor. He came from a fine sailing family. His brother was a sail-maker; in fact, his brother made the sails used by the British Olympic sailing team. Norman Farrar was a proper old man with not much white hair. And when I sailed with him, I remember that he arrived at the marina in a dark suit, white shirt, tie, and right there he changed into rubber-soled shoes and then snapped a huge plastic raincoat over himself.

Tradition has it that on Maurice Rowlandson's birthday, Maurice takes his secretary sailing. Maurice *would* take his wife, but Marilyn is not a good sailor and, quite happily, remains home annually for the occasion. Maurice, like Norman, is another sailor. Since I was Maurice's secretary, it was my duty to sail with Maurice on August 15th, and this year we were sailing with Norman Farrar in Norman's boat. The day was a fine one, and Norman and Maurice thought we might sail to Harwich Harbour; what did I think? Of course, I had no preference, that was fine with me. I was along for the lunch – a fine selection of apple and marmalade sandwiches, cheese and date sandwiches, peanut butter and bacon sandwiches (Maurice believes that all sandwiches should have *two* fillings!). And there was cake too – there's always cake when Maurice plans a picnic! So we set off and we sailed and eventually I could see the harbour off in the distance.

And then the wind came up. I mean the wind came up! Maurice says it increased from about a force 3 to a force

5. And there were waves! Norman and Maurice quickly decided that a trip into the harbour was not such a good idea after all, and this time they didn't ask my opinion. The sailing was rough. The wind blew and the sea was wild and swirled and the water came sloshing over the sides of the boat and sprayed everywhere, and the boat rocked a lot too. It was kind of scary I guess. But I watched Norman. Norman sat in the back of the boat, his hand on the tiller, and directed Maurice. Maurice was tacking. 'Come about,' Norman would say, and Maurice would scramble, making the sail do what it was supposed to do. The wind was blowing and the water splashing and I was sitting near the front, getting wet, hanging on, and watching Norman. Norman sat on his throne in that raincoat. He would turn his head slowly as though he were beholding all creation – and he did seem to be taking it all in – and at the very right moment he would call out the command in his old-man voice, 'Come about.' Maurice would fly from his rest position and wrestle with the ropes and the canvas. I remember his skinny white legs. I still don't think I was afraid. I knew that Norman, in all his years, had never gone down. Never. And I was perfectly confident that Norman, with Maurice, would get me back to land. I was kind of cold and wet, but still, I had no fear.

Sometimes I think I'm still in that boat, only it isn't Norman sitting back there. It's God. Life is fine and we sail along. Sometimes there isn't much wind and living's a little dull, and then of course, there are good, enjoyable, happy times in the boat, and exciting, adventurous sails too. And then sometimes storms blow up and life is so crazy and all I can do is hang on. Oh, for sure I get wet, maybe cold, pretty uncomfortable, but Maurice followed Norman's directions. He never paused or argued; he never even offered alternatives (which is pretty unusual for Maurice!), and we came through.

Unfortunately, I have a tendency to jump out of the boat. I've told God, time and time again it seems, that my destination would be so much better than His, or that I know the best way to get there; and silly old God doesn't even seem to listen! So I plunge out – and talk about wet and cold and uncomfortable! Sometimes it takes a while, but it's always awful in the end. I shamefacedly swim back to the boat; or to be more honest, I'm usually rescued at sea. Thank God, and oh, the Lord Jesus always welcomes me back and it's so wonderful to be on board again.

You see, I'm learning what I already know. I know that God will not fail me. I have His Word. 'I have been young, and now am old; yet have I not seen the righteous forsaken, nor his seed begging bread' (Psalm 37:25). Two sailors took me for a sail I shall not forget: and I can only hope I remember the lesson they provided.

'They that go down to the sea in ships, that do business in great waters; these see the works of the Lord, and His wonders in the deep. For He commandeth, and raiseth the stormy wind, which lifteth up the waves thereof. They mount up to the heaven, they go down again to the depths: their soul is melted because of trouble . . . and are at their wit's end. Then they cry unto the Lord in their trouble, and He bringeth them out of their distresses. He maketh the storm a calm, so that the waves thereof are still. Then are they glad because they be quiet; so He bringeth them unto their desired haven' (Psalm 107:23-30, KJV).

After Wendy returned to the United States there was a lengthy period with some more difficult and not entirely suitable secretaries. This was in spite of careful briefing, instructions and training which I gave to each of them. I was conscious of my belief that a good teacher should so instruct his students, that they turn out to be better than he is. After all, they are mostly younger: the teacher is imparting to them as much as he can of what he already knows. The student should be able to input his own expertise and ideas, and thus improve upon what he has been taught. Sometimes my PA was able to exceed my own capabilities and I stood back in amazement that a situation had been thought through so thoroughly and handled so carefully and with such competence.

Sometimes I got into trouble. I always believed and practised the adage that 'The more intelligent people know, the more intelligently they can behave.' I therefore tended to share confidences with my colleagues because, in the course of their work, they might need to know what I knew. In the Royal Naval Reserve there is a degree of secrecy known as Cosmictopsecret. That is, it is shared with no one. The next degree is that of Need to Know: such information should be shared only with those who really need to know. All other information is shared on the basis of an intelligent understanding of a situation. In the office, to enable my PAs to act more intelligently in any situation which might arise, I often shared things with them which others regarded as confidential. Yet there were many occasions when, having shared in this way, a major catastrophe was averted.

My former boss, Prebendary Colin C. Kerr (who founded the Campaigner uniformed youth movement), once told me: 'Maurice, if I tell you something terribly secret that I don't want you to tell to anybody else, I do so because I thoroughly trust you and believe that you will respect my secret. But, in so doing, I must recognise that you too have someone you thoroughly trust and that you believe that they will respect the secret you share with them! They too will have someone . . . ' He concluded that the only way to preserve something as Cosmictopsecret was to keep it completely to himself.

It was always important for me to choose a colleague who filled the bill. During this interim period I made some bad judgments which resulted in the wrong people coming to work with me. One turned out to be a very bad lot. She stole from people in the office, and later we discovered that she had a record of convictions related to drugs. None of this came out in the interviews, nor in the application forms she completed. It all came to light when she accidentally left a letter on the word processor which she had written to one of her friends. The index on the disc displayed a name I could not identify, and when I recalled the letter in question, all her misdemeanours were laid out in front of me:

> Becoming a responsible member of society hasn't been the traumatic experience I expected it to be though I must admit I can't wait to get out of my posh frocks and into my pseudo-hippy gear in the evenings . . . Being pleasant on the telephone is quite a bind too. I have to make an extra special effort not to be rude to old ladies who ring up for Billy Graham's autograph . . . Ring! ring! 'Hello. Billy

Graham? Not speaking personally, but will I do?' Hangs up
. . . I'm using a computer to write this letter. I had a course
on how to use it last week. It does all sorts of things . . .

One of the things it did was to leave that letter on record for
me to see. I had no alternative but to confront her with it. She
left the same day.

Another PA during this period was with me for only six weeks.
At that time, Marilyn was working with me in the office most
days. We usually got there about 7.15 a.m. and in order to save
myself a lot of time, she and I would go over the day's work
together. I would leave a number of instructions with her to be
given to my PA later in the morning when she arrived.

One morning this new PA came into my office and said: 'I do
not like taking instructions from your wife.' I said I was sorry to
hear that as I had already given Marilyn some instructions earlier
that morning. They were to be passed on to her. I said that if she
found that was a problem, we needed to think about the future.
She immediately gathered all her papers together and left the
office, never to return. She was the only assistant I had who had
difficulty with Marilyn's involvement.

Before any PA was appointed I gave them 'the Test'. This pro-
verbial trial was undertaken by everyone we employed. It origi-
nated in our American headquarters' office in Minneapolis
and was adapted from a staff selection programme devised
by the Psychological Corporation of America. It was in three
parts. Part 1 was a simple typing test to discover the speed,
accuracy and skill of the typist; Part 2 was a test of intelligence,
office procedures, mathematics, spelling, grammar and general
knowledge; and Part 3 was a test on decision-making. I used to
tell candidates that they did not pass or fail the test: they were
either employed or not suitable. They never knew their marks,
for there were none. The test simply analysed whether or not a
candidate could do the job. It assessed their speed of working,
their general capability and their leadership qualities. In my
experience the test never failed! Although my own assessment
was sometimes different and I would appoint someone the test
showed to be unsuitable, when I did so I was always wrong. I
lived to regret the day I appointed them. Conversely, if I felt
unsure about someone but the test was very positive, then I
never lived to regret employing them.

Part 3 of the test was especially interesting. It contained a hundred questions, becoming progressively more complex as you went along. The instructions were for the candidate to complete as many answers as possible in twelve and a half minutes. 'Do not delay on any question that you cannot answer: *above all*, do not get any question wrong. If you cannot answer a question, pass on to the next one.'

It would have been possible to gain top marks without answering a single question. This was because it was not a test of general knowledge: it was a test of decision-making. Therefore if you looked at the first question and decided – immediately – that you couldn't answer it and went on to reach the same conclusion with each of the other ninety-nine questions, you took the right decisions and you passed the test! But every wrong answer counted against you, because you took a bad decision. You had thought that you could answer a question which was too difficult for you. In all the years only one person came through all parts with a near-perfect result – my former colleague, Jean Wilson.

Eventually this sterile period came to an end with the arrival of Ruth King. Ruth had worked for several of the Billy Graham team in the USA and elsewhere. She was ideal for the job, and we were beginning to get our act together when she was taken ill and had to resign. None the less we have remained friends and stayed in close contact ever since. From time to time, she returns to help on special assignments.

Ruth was eventually succeeded by the legendary Liz Fane. Things were never to be the same again after the advent of Liz! She had come out of the Capernwray Hall/Hildenborough Hall stable and like all who have been through that training, she was exceptionally good (Rosemary Wheeler had also been trained at Capernwray Hall).

From the beginning Liz took command. She refused to let me do anything that she could do equally well. As I was already working under considerable pressure (mostly from 7 a.m. until 6.30 p.m. – and still taking work home to do), it was a wonderful relief to have someone as good as Liz at my elbow. She was backed up by an excellent young secretary (whom we both used), Elisabeth Jefferies. The daughter of a member of the UK Board of the BGEA, Elisabeth was a most delightful acquisition in the office, and another highly efficient youngster. Years later she told me that the most important thing she had learned in my office was to keep notes on five-by-three-inch cards.

Every morning I played cards on arrival! The rules of the game were very simple:

i.   Every note should be on a separate five-by-three-inch card.
ii. Never more than one note on a card.
iii. Never write on the back of a card (unless it is the continuation of a long note).
iv. Whenever possible, the card should be typed.
v.   Whenever possible include a telephone number for me to call back.

When I arrived at the office I immediately fanned through my stack of five-by-three-inch cards, pulling out those cards with jobs which must be done at once. The rest went into an elastic band for later attention. After action, the card was thrown away. Many of my secretaries adopted the scheme for their own programme in the days ahead. Elisabeth was one of them.

If Liz Fane was asked to name something special that she had learned from her work with me she would immediately say: 'the importance of *double-checking*'. On so many occasions I was to ask her if she had double-checked some event. The crunch came on the day of the presentation of the awards to the winners of the National Bible Quiz which had been sponsored by *Decision* magazine.

I had left Liz to make all the arrangements. (In fairness to her, I have to say that it was in her early days with me when the importance of double-checking had not yet been established.) The awards were to be given at a special luncheon, and Dr Walter Smyth (passing through London on his way elsewhere) was to be the honoured guest and he would make the presentations. Liz booked a room at the Post House Hotel in Hampstead. I asked her, on several occasions, if all was in order and she assured me that all the plans were well in hand.

The day came, and I drove up the hill from Camden. On arrival at the hotel I asked where our special room was. There was a deathly hush. 'There is no special room,' the manager said. 'We've put you in the public dining room.' At that moment, I think Liz wished the ground would open and swallow her up. It must be the only Post House Hotel where members of the public, eating their lunch in the restaurant, formed part of the audience to a presentation, and to the several speeches which were made. In years to come, I only had to refer to the occasion to send Liz rushing off to do her double-checking!

Liz and I had some five years of association together, terminated only by the closing of the London office on September 30th, 1987, the date on which all of the international offices of the BGEA were closed down.

But I couldn't lose Liz as easily as that! She has remained my personal assistant emeritus! Her immediate positive response to a special need is one of the great blessings that the Lord has given to me in my past associates. Marilyn and I have remained as friends to most of them, and whenever we meet it is rather like a family reunion.

Liz responded to an urgent appeal to help me through Mission '89. Together we ran the team office – and when Billy Graham came to Scotland for a mission in 1991, once more Liz responded to the call. The team were always delighted when I was able to tell them that Liz Fane had agreed to help me again. She is a wonderful team member and adds a lot to the atmosphere of any event in which she and I are involved. I am grateful that the Lord led her across my path.

Our first major involvement together was through the twelve-week period of Mission England in 1984. For this we had to set up an office in seven different locations – Bristol, Sunderland, Norwich, Birmingham, Liverpool and Ipswich – followed by Sheffield a year later. We were given the responsibility of looking after television, radio and the press, not something for which I was ideally suited. But tall Larry Ross, from the Walter Bennett agency in America, had come over to learn the ropes in Britain. We had first met him when Billy Graham came to Sandringham. On that occasion this seven-foot-tall young man was in his team. *Why* he was there, at first we could never understand. But he had a wonderful spirit, and commended himself to us. We learned later that he was to be the new public relations man for Billy Graham.

During Mission England we leaned heavily on his expertise.

There could not have been a better or more understanding colleague and we learned a lot from him. Liz entered into the spirit of the whole event like an old pro. She was an enormous strength both to me and to all of the team and together we kept the media involvement humming with innumerable interviews for the press, magazines, television and radio. Through this we met lots of interesting people, correspondents who had merely been names to us before, such as John Mortimer, Jean Rook, George Gale and Malcolm Muggeridge.

One of the most memorable activities we shared during those days is described by Derek Williams in his book about Mission England. It referred to the occasion when the one millionth person was due to attend one of the mission meetings at Ipswich. As the moment approached, I took Liz with me to one of the gates. Derek Williams takes over the story:

It was Friday, July 27th at Portman Road football ground, Ipswich. The fact that the millionth person was about to arrive was probably irrelevant so far as God's economy goes, but to human beings ... it was a little milestone they did not want to ignore.

The stadium staff kept a tally of the people entering Portman Road; when the figure was within a hundred of the number required to produce the one million, Maurice Rowlandson (with Liz Fane) went into action. Standing at the main entrance, he turned his back on the streaming crowd so that he would not be influenced by a face, and began the countdown as people passed him. Nervous team members prayed that the person upon whose shoulder Maurice Rowlandson's hand fell would be young and male. (Young and female on a newspaper front page might look embarrassingly similar to sales hype which spreads girls across car bonnets: old and either sex would be untypical of the high percentage of young people who came to hear Billy Graham.) The press men didn't care who it was so long as he or she was local.

At 7.20 p.m. Maurice Rowlandson sprang, and some prayers were answered. Alan Paget, looking a little older than his fifteen years, was escorted on to the turf to meet Billy Graham. He was presented with a bible and a

Mission England sweatshirt and the electronic scoreboard announced the magic number to the crowd.

What the team did not know was the near-disaster that accompanied my selection of the one hundredth person. The ninety-ninth person was a young black lad who had, in fact, come with Alan Paget. As I accosted Alan Paget, his friend turned to me and said: 'You're Maurice Rowlandson. I've been to lunch at your house. I'm a friend of your son Gary.' Had I selected one person sooner, I might have been laid open to the charge of favouritism to a friend – although I had to confess that, although I remembered the occasion of his visit, I did not remember him.

Mission England was a traumatic period, and needed some light relief! We moved the office seven times, which meant packing everything up; loading the car; driving to the next location (sometimes more than 250 miles); unloading on arrival and setting up ready for work the next day. Our living quarters were also moved at the same time. Thankfully, we were always accommodated in the same hotel as that in which the office was established – and we got to know the different styles and quality of our accommodation *very* quickly.

Liz and I had an easy way to establish the quality of the new hotel, at least as far as the food was concerned. The meetings usually finished around 9.30 p.m. and by the time we got back to the hotel and could get something to eat, it was often around 10.15 p.m. By that hour, much of the menu would be 'off', but the important factor was the chocolate cake – was it any good, and was there any left? If not, then that hotel went down in our estimation. We were unanimous in our agreement that the chocolate cake (and its availability) was best at the Hotel George Washington in Sunderland.

Throughout Mission England (including the extra week in Sheffield) we had had the help of a team of hunky policemen from the Christian Police Association. They were all volunteers who had given of their time to help in innumerable ways. One of them was Kelvin Ashley who was assigned to be the driver for Mr Graham. Kelvin had a great sense of fun, and was always playing tricks on the girls in the office.

One morning, I came into the team office around 7 a.m. and the phone immediately started to ring. I went to answer it, but found that it had been securely strapped down by parcel tape, and it was impossible to shift it. The phone stopped ringing, and a few seconds later a second phone in the office started to ring. I dashed across to it, only to find that that phone was also immobilised. Eventually a telephone in the room next door (used for relaxation) started to ring. I ran into the next room and, happily, discovered that the phone had not been tampered with. It was T. W. Wilson. 'Maureece,' he said, 'I've been trying to get one of you on the office extension, but no one answers. What in the world is happening down there?' How do you answer a question like that to a senior team member?

Later in the day, I was sharing this experience with Liz Fane and the other team staff. They went into consultation, and unbeknown to me they went to see the hotel management. Kelvin had the day off and had gone out, so the girls arranged for the hotel staff to clear his room completely. Every stick of furniture was taken out, including all his clothes and belongings. Later that afternoon Kelvin returned, with only a few minutes for a quick change out of his jeans and sweat-shirt and into a suit before he had to drive Mr Graham to an important engagement. When he opened the door to his room, he couldn't believe his eyes.

He went to see the reception desk – but they knew nothing about it. Kelvin tried to get some information, but the best he could achieve was a suggestion from the duty manager that he should 'have a word with Liz Fane'.

By then, time was running away with him, and he had to report for duty to drive Mr Graham. From one of his colleagues, he borrowed a suit jacket to make himself halfway presentable – but the sleeves were too short and he looked a bit like a waif and stray! None the less, he had to complete the job and tried to hide from Mr Graham the somewhat unorthodox clothes he was wearing. Meanwhile, the girls arranged for everything to be put back in his room and when Kelvin returned, they tried to persuade him that he had had hallucinations! At any rate, they felt that they had got their own back.

The whole team loved Liz and respected her. This was apparent in November 1991 when she sustained an accident. She was knocked down in the street by a hit-and-run driver and was confined to hospital with a broken femur and other injuries. No sooner had the news been circulated on the team prayer sheet than the messages started to arrive. First was a fax from

Billy Graham: 'Was so sorry to hear about your accident and we are all praying for a speedy and complete recovery. We love you in the Lord and appreciate all that you mean to us and to the Kingdom of God.' From Mr Graham's secretary, Stephanie Wills, came a separate message:

> Just this week I read again that 'No matter what comes our way, God is involved. All that touches our lives is filtered through the Father's hands . . . He is in everything – even the difficult times. He is working everything in my life together for good. He didn't say I would like it – I do not like anything about this, but no circumstance is so big that He cannot control it.'
>
> If the entire Billy Graham Crusade and Mission World Team could be squeezed into this page, they'd all be right there. Seriously, I'm praying that as God touches your body, the healing process will take place. May you have peace in your heart.

It is this closeness between all the team, and their wider associates, which counts for so much.

After one of my secretaries had left to get married (mostly in the summer months) or, sometimes, through some other unexpected event, I would be left without a secretary at a crucial period. Over the years I was able to develop a team of helpers upon whom I could call.

In 1988, such a situation occurred but none of my regular helpers was free. Just about that time, Marilyn and I were involved in one of our regular Holy Land tours. I decided to announce to the fifty-five strong group my need for secretarial help at the Keswick Convention.

Among the party was a twenty-three-year-old who had come on the tour through the generosity of an elderly lady, no longer strong enough to stand the rigours of such a tour. She had said that she would pay for a young girl – preferably not a Christian – who would come in her place. Marilyn and I, between us, asked no fewer than twenty-eight eligible girls before we found one who was willing and able to accept. My PA in those days was Alexandra Bullock, a girl sent to me by the Lord at a time of real need. She had a friend who filled the specification, so an invitation was extended to Amanda Bragg.

Her knowledge of religion was very sketchy. But Amanda was a delightful person. We soon discovered that she had little or no understanding of what the Christian message was all about. Later, she was to ask my son in all seriousness, 'Gary, what do I have to do to qualify to go to church?'

Amanda fitted in well with the tour group and she came to all of our evening sessions. She listened to all of the comments at the various sites we visited. But the message did not seem to get through. When I asked for someone prepared to help me as a secretary at the Keswick Convention that year, she was the first – and only one – to respond. After talking about it, Marilyn and I decided that we would invite her to come.

She did, and she was marvellous. As far as we knew, she did not attend a single meeting (although she may have slipped in at the back on an occasion or two). She may also have heard some of the messages over the office loudspeaker. But there was still no visible sign of the message getting through.

A year later it so happened that I was again without a secretary at the time of the convention. Out of the blue I had a call from Amanda, asking if I needed secretarial help once more at Keswick. It seemed too good to be true, and we were able to have her with us once more for the period of the convention – with the same results.

In 1991, Billy Graham came to Scotland for the missions in Edinburgh, Aberdeen and Glasgow. I was invited by Blair Carlson of the Billy Graham team to organise and run the team office. Liz Fane was already involved with me but we needed some additional secretarial help.

For family reasons, my own secretary at the time was unable to come for so long a period. Marilyn suggested asking Amanda if she would be able to come: she was and she did, and once more she gave sacrificially in both time and effort, helping me throughout the three weeks.

Unlike Keswick, she came to many of the Scottish meetings and in a poignant comment on the last night she said: 'Maurice, I so nearly went forward tonight.' I was reminded of King Agrippa's comment to the Apostle Paul: 'Do you think that in such a short time you can persuade me to be a Christian?' Paul replied: 'Short time or long – I pray that . . . you . . . may become what I am' (Acts 26:28-9). It may have been almost for Amanda, but God has His own time and there is a right time for Him.

It was interesting to see the mission through the eyes of an un-converted colleague. This young woman was deeply impressed with all that she saw and heard, and she exclaimed: 'Bev Shea's singing sends cold shivers down my spine!'

Her attitude throughout the mission had been impeccable and she had given such dedicated service that she would have put many a committed Christian to shame. A week later I had a phone call from James Barrett, a businessman who had given exceptional support to Billy Graham and the missions. He asked for Amanda's telephone number because he wanted to offer her a job. He said: 'I particularly want a committed Christian like Amanda!' It was a case of having the attributes but – not yet – the commitment.

Another area in which a full-time Christian worker has a special need is in his back-up staff. He must have a faithful and dedicated staff and in this the Lord has been gracious. He has sent just the right people at the right time. Many juniors have started their working life with us. Those in more senior positions have always been so helpful. We thank the Lord for every one of them.

Finding the right staff was not always easy. We fell foul of regulations on some occasions. You could not, for instance, advertise for a Christian: that was discrimination! So in order to sort out the sheep from the goats, we would introduce a number of significant questions into the first interview. 'Are you able,' we would ask, 'to lead a person to faith in Christ?' That threw a lot of those who had applied for a job in reply to our advertisement. Counselling was part of the work in the office, and it was important to have those who could help in this.

We were also required to employ those of other races and those who were disabled. In both areas we never had any problem. Rodney, a multiple sclerosis sufferer, was our packer for a long time. He carried on as long as he was able under great difficulties. Anthea, a spastic, was our receptionist for many years. All of our disabled did a great job of work.

For a while I had a black secretary. Desiree came from the West Indies and was an excellent colleague. She had phoned from Harrods, where she was working, to ask if we needed an AES operator. This was just at the time when I needed someone, and she came to me for two years before her family emigrated to Canada and she went with them.

On one of our Israel tours, she was able to use one of the free places we had been given. In Jerusalem she badly wanted to buy a T-shirt that she had seen in one of the Arab stores. But she was nervous about bargaining, and she asked me if I would go with her to buy it. I told her that if she really wanted it, she would have to pay more; but if she was prepared to lose it, then we would get it for a good price.

The trader asked for ten dollars. I told Desiree to offer two. The trader said, 'No – six dollars.' I told Desiree to stick at two. The trader said: 'You will make my family hungry at that – four dollars.' I said to Desiree: 'Stick at two dollars, and walk out of the shop.' As she and I left, the trader grabbed her arm and said, 'Three dollars.' Desiree replied: 'No! My father says two dollars!' She got it for her two dollars and it seemed that I had gained a relative!

In a strange way, there has been an ongoing relationship with many of the secretarial team which has been most humbling. So many of them have told us how they have looked back on their time with us as a highlight of their working life. At the Keswick Convention in 1991, I was standing outside the secretary's office when a young lady named Jackie Saunders (née Leeds) stopped to talk to me. She looked at me and then said: 'You won't remember me.' She told me her name and it rang a bell. She said: 'I'll always remember my time in the Billy Graham office in London. You were all so wonderful to me, and those days meant a lot to me.' Every day after that, during the convention, she passed by my office with a cheery smile.

Also in 1991 I received a letter from Christina Willis (née Duthie) in Kenya:

I can't for a moment expect you to remember me ... approximately a hundred years ago I was a little clerk at the BGEA, first at Bush House and then Camden Town. You'd made BGEA quite a family affair and we enjoyed the atmosphere there and meeting all your family. I was a very skinny (still am) school leaver in too much make-up and short skirts who was enthusiastic for Jesus (still am). Unbeknown to me, my attire was a bit over-the-top but you, kindly, didn't say anything. I was from a working-class nominal Christian background.

Your son Gary became a sort of friend, but I was in awe of all of you I guess, because of your lovely home and nice accents, so I kept my distance. I loved your daughter, Cherylyn. She was beautiful and fun and I felt such grief when I heard that she had gone to her Heavenly Father seemingly early!

Now I'm a mother of three teenagers and wife of a Missionary Aviation pilot working in Kenya . . . I just want to say 'Thank you' for your leadership at that time in my life, whether you remember me or not.

At Christmas time in 1990, Jean Wilson and I decided that between us we would organise a Christmas party for both her staff and mine, and that we would also invite any of those who had worked with us at the Billy Graham offices between 1955 and 1987. We sent out nearly 200 invitations, and just over 150 accepted. It was humbling to both of us that so many of them should have wished to come to the reunion. Most of those whose stories I have told were present, many of them with their husbands and children. Dawn Hedges (née Chandler) flew all the way from Canada just to be with us.

The work of the staff was backed up by a wonderful UK board of directors. For many years the board was large and under the chairmanship of Bishop Goodwin Hudson. But after the cutback in 1977, the board was reduced to six active members under an elected chairman; the former board were elevated to a Council of Reference. The Hon. Crispin Joynson-Hicks (now Lord Brentford) was the first elected chairman and he was succeeded two years later by businessman David C. Rennie.

The UK board was directly responsible and subject to the board in the United States. Many of the board members from the USA often came to Britain to visit us, and they were always welcome.

Until 1977, the US board had agreed a regular monthly subsidy to help maintain the work of the UK office. But in 1977 Bishop Goodwin Hudson was called to the USA to meet some of the board members and Billy Graham. They told him that, by the end of 1978, the UK office should be entirely free of subsidy and self-supporting. They added that they hoped the UK might even be able to begin to contribute something towards Billy Graham's ministry in other parts of the world. In fact, halfway through

1978 we were able to tell the US board that the subsidy could cease, and by the end of the year (and in every subsequent year until the office was closed nine years later) we were able to send substantial amounts towards the ministry elsewhere.

Most of this support came in response to the prayer letters sent out to the UK supporters three times a year. Written by Billy Graham, the letters gave up-to-date news of his activities, together with requests for prayer. He always outlined especially the financial need to accomplish the heavy programme ahead.

After he had written his letter, Billy Graham would send the draft to me to put into English. It was not that what he wrote was incorrect: it was simply that we in England often expressed things in a different way. Also the letters often referred to US-orientated matters and were not suitable for circulation in the UK. Accordingly, I would check through the letters and remove, or change, those parts which were not applicable. Then, sometimes, I would suggest an additional paragraph referring especially to the situation in the United Kingdom.

When he quoted heavily from scripture, the response to the letters was always greater than when he talked only about the work. When I first received the letters for circulation I could often predict the sort of response we would get. Often he was able to offer a free book to those who responded; other times he offered a music tape. Strangely, the offer of a music tape produced almost one-third more response than the free book. When there was no offer, the response dropped significantly. I suppose we are all human!

Another big source of financial help was legacies. For many years we advertised the work of Billy Graham in the *Solicitor's Journal* and other legal publications. This was on the advice of one of our board members who pointed out that, when people were writing their wills, they often asked their lawyer for information about Christian work which needed money. Lawyers, in turn, would consult their professional publication for details of suitable projects for their clients to support. Over the years we had a great many legacies.

It was in 1990 that this policy really paid off. A casual supporter of the Billy Graham Evangelistic Association had died and had left the proceeds of his estate to four different Christian charities, of which the BGEA was one. When his estate was realised, it amounted to a figure in excess of four million pounds. Certain family bequests had to be taken out of this, but when all was determined, each of the four beneficiaries received a substantial six-figure sum. It came at exactly the right time for Mission Scotland and was a real provision from the Lord.

In 1978, when the work of the office was cut back, I found that I had some surplus time. In the autumn of 1978 I heard that the Keswick Convention was looking for a secretary. It seemed to me that I could do the work involved while still retaining the oversight of Billy Graham's work in the UK. I wrote to Billy Graham himself, to George Wilson and to Dr Walter Smyth. All three of them encouraged me to apply for this work and Mr Graham himself pledged his support and said that the work could be done from the Billy Graham offices.

In due time I was interviewed by the Keswick Council and later appointed to commence work on January 1st, 1979. The two ministries seemed so complementary to each other. In the Billy Graham Association there was evangelism – bringing people to Christ. In the Keswick Convention there was teaching (especially about practical scriptural holiness), and the ministry at Keswick would build up and instruct the new converts. I found no conflict arising from this joint involvement and I enjoyed the maximum support from all of my colleagues on the Billy Graham team.

It seemed to me almost incredible that what had begun at Keswick in 1946 should have gone the full circle, and now I found myself back in the driving seat of the convention. For me, God had called . . . led . . . and involved me in a remarkable way over the years. In all the years there had been the influence of Billy Graham in everything I had done.

One thing is clear. In all of the work emanating from the office, the home team were co-workers together in the Lord's work. Whether it was one of the many staff members, a secretary, a personal assistant, a board member or a team member – or even members of the family – it was that sense of pulling together that counted. In all that we did it gave us a sense of achievement. To succeed, enthusiasm was an indispensable attribute. A positive outlook and a determination to get things done and overcome a problem were great gifts. Most of those who worked with us had those gifts. They had learned to let everything 'be done decently and in order' and to do 'all things for the glory of Christ'.

Had the original call not come at Keswick, there is no knowing how the story might have worked out. As it is, the response to that call, and a sensitivity to God's leading in the intervening years, brought me to an enviable position. I am able to tell this remarkable story of God's leadership and provision through many incredible sequences of events. None of them would have been so effective and so well done without that exceptional home team of co-workers. Thank God for every one of them!

8

The Away Team and Team Meetings

'If any of you lacks wisdom, he should ask God who gives generously' (James 1:5). If there is any area where God has given generously to Billy Graham, it is in the gift of wisdom in the selection of his colleagues.

There can be very few organisations which can show the same loyalty and longevity of their staff and colleagues as is displayed by many of the Billy Graham team members. There are those in the team today who were first associated with Mr Graham before the crusades even began. There are others who have come in over the years, and have remained with the team ever since.

The Wilson brothers, T.W. and Grady, were known to Billy Graham from the early days. Until his death a few years ago, Grady was a close associate and friend of Billy's, always at his side in every important ministry. T.W. still has an important function, often acting as Billy Graham's aide during times of high pressure, and on his visits abroad. He has fulfilled this responsibility ever since 1962 when, during the crusade in Chicago, Billy Graham was inspired to invite him to fulfil this important task.

George Wilson (no relation) was also involved from the time before the crusades started and remained as head of the Minneapolis office (the administrative headquarters of the team) until his retirement in 1988.

Cliff Barrows, song leader, choir director and so much more, is a henchman magnifique! Bev Shea, the soloist, is still singing strongly in spite of being over eighty years of age. Tedd Smith has a sensitivity on the piano which has commended itself to all who listen; Charlie Riggs (who first became known in Britain during the Harringay crusade of 1954) is still involved with the counselling. All of these, along with Mr Graham himself, have formed the platform team since the very first crusade.

Many have retired while still in the team ministry. Sherwood Eliot Wirt was editor of *Decision* magazine from its founding until his retirement. The retirement of Walter Smyth was announced in 1987 but he, like so many other members of the team in a similar position, has been recalled again and again to assist Mr Graham in special projects, especially in Eastern Europe and the Soviet Union.

When I was in charge of the London office, I often used to get letters from young men who declared that they had been called to work with Mr Graham. I would spend some time talking with them and ask them if they met the prime qualification to join the Billy Graham team. I said that almost everyone on the team had been known *personally* to Billy Graham for at least ten years before they were invited to help. It was certainly like that in my case. This factor usually thinned out the applicants!

There are several areas of responsibility in the team. There is the platform team who take a leading part in all the crusade meetings. There is the administrative team, responsible for all the work of the Minneapolis office. There is the associate evangelists' team; the *Decision* magazine team; the World Wide Pictures team; the crusade set-up team; the counselling and follow-up team; the overseas team; the telephone ministry (normally used during television specials); the team office team and several others. Each group has a specific responsibility for its own part of the overall work.

Altogether the number of those involved, including the day-to-day staff in the offices, must number between 400 and 500 members. Yet there is a family atmosphere between them all, even across the world. This is fostered by several means.

Years ago, there was a monthly publication called *Our Decision*. This news-sheet was circulated to everyone connected with the association throughout the world. It gave news of Mr Graham's programme; reports of crusades; vignettes of various members of the team; news of forthcoming programmes and events and many other items. Later, the cost of continuing this news-sheet became prohibitive, but its function was taken over by a monthly information sheet called 'Notes and Quotes', a publication which has been going since 1977.

In addition there is a gigantic prayer chain across the world. Almost weekly comes a blue sheet prepared and circulated from the Minneapolis office. It gives details of the team's prayer needs. Sometimes it is praise for answered prayer; sometimes it is a special need for one of the team family. Whatever it may be, the entire team is alerted and gets down to prayer for a loved and trusted colleague, or a member of that colleague's family.

So it was for us, when Jacky had her accident in 1982. Through this blue prayer information sheet, the news was sent throughout the world, and our colleagues everywhere were praying for us. It was the knowledge of that which gave us such strength at the time.

The prayer information sheet also generates correspondence. If some tragedy is experienced, or someone faces the trauma of unexpected serious illness, they can be sure of encouragement from their colleagues. It is an incredible feeling to be aware of the fact that these people care!

Not least among the carers is Billy Graham himself. He knows the names – and often the family history – of all those who have been associated with him for many years. Some of the newer faces take a little longer to recall, but he is always personally concerned for each one he meets. He gives the feeling, when you are with him, that you are the only one who matters to him. He tells you that the work you are doing is appreciated. He enquires about situations which have developed previously and asks about their progress. His memory and knowledge are prodigious.

Marilyn and I had a brief insight into the way in which this is achieved: there is perfect team-work between Ruth Graham and Billy. It happened for us at a time when their youngest son, Ned, came to school in Britain. We had strongly advised that he should go to Monkton Combe School in Bath, but Felsted School was chosen instead. A friend of the Grahams in the United Kingdom had told them that Monkton Combe was riddled with drugs and had recommended Felsted instead. Actually, very few public schools were entirely free of the problem in those days and Felsted was little different. Monkton Combe had certainly expelled a boy for using drugs, but that was the extent of the problem. Monkton Combe remained a Christian school with a tremendous influence.

Another factor which prompted our advice was that our younger son, Julian, was at Monkton Combe at the time. We felt that he could be a factor to assist Ned. But Felsted was chosen and we were asked to act as Ned's guardians while he was there. We were able to have him home at half-term holidays, and to visit him occasionally at school.

Whenever Ruth came to London, we would collect her from the airport and take her to Felsted for a visit to Ned. Then came the day when Billy and Ruth Graham came to London together and were able to visit him. Most of the drive from London was spent by Ruth briefing Billy, about the names of the people he would meet and their significance to Ned. So, by the time we arrived, he knew the headmaster's name; the name of Ned's housemaster; his teachers; his close friends and a wealth of other information which was helpful to him. Thus, when we arrived at Felsted, Mr Graham was able to make an intelligent and understanding contribution to the conversations, and could greet people by name. It was an impressive result of the care that Ruth had taken to prepare him. We enjoyed our meetings with Ned and were sorry when the time came for him to return to America.

Some years later when I was chairman of the British council of Trans World Radio, we were visiting their studios in Monte Carlo. One afternoon, Marilyn and I were walking along the promenade, quietly chatting, when a great giant of a man suddenly ran across and gave Marilyn an enormous bear-hug! I couldn't at first think what was going on – but then I saw that it was Ned. He told us that he and his mother were having a few days' rest in the nearby hotel. He took us back to the hotel to have coffee with his mother. It was a lovely experience.

In 1972, shortly after our daughter Cherylyn had died, I wrote to Capernwray Hall in Carnforth to ask if there were any American students at the Bible College who might like to spend Christmas in the home of a British family. We had, from time to time, had students from Capernwray over Christmas and it was always a rich experience. This time was to be richer than ever. How good the Lord is: He knows our need from the beginning and He provides in surprising and unexpected ways!

The answer came back from Capernwray that there were two or three students who would like to come – and one of these was Betty Ruth Barrows, the daughter of Cliff and Billie Barrows. You can imagine our delight when we learned that we were to have this fellowship with one of the Barrows family.

Betty Ruth's coming was like balm to our souls. It was our first Christmas without Cherry, and we were not looking forward to it. The love and warmth Betty Ruth shared with us helped to fill the vacant spot and made it so much more bearable. In fact she left a legacy of her visit which still reminds us of her today. She had missed the Christmas music which pervades American life as the festive season approaches. You hear it on the radio and television; you pass it in the streets, the stores and shopping malls. Christmas is still a magic season in America, and Betty Ruth was missing the magic. So she asked her mother to send over some tapes of Christmas music, and about four or five arrived at our home. They were nostalgic for Marilyn and beautiful for all of us to listen to. Our great joy was that, when the time came for Betty Ruth to return to Bible School, she left the tapes with us and told us to enjoy them in future years. We still do!

The other major contribution to the unity and fellowship of the team is the series of regular team meetings (later called Team and Staff Conference or TASC). Reference has already been made to them and especially to the very first one I attended, at Airlie House in West Virginia. A year later an invitation came to me (in my own right) to attend the team meeting in Miami Beach, Florida. This time, the invitation was extended to Marilyn also. The team meeting was held at the Miami Beach Hotel, a hotel owned and managed by Christian people, whose chaplain turned out to be Lex Smith – the young man who had first gone to America with me in 1948. He was one of the eight (of ten originals who had attended Northwestern from the UK) who had remained in America after the period of schooling concluded. Strangely, I was not to see Lex again until the Keswick Convention in 1991 – twenty-nine years later, and forty-two years since he had been best man at our wedding. I was standing at the doorway of my office in the Keswick Convention Centre when a man stopped in front of me and said: 'Do you know who I am?' I confessed that the face was familiar, but I couldn't put a name to it. I was incredulous when he told me who he was. It was thrilling to see him once again.

The following year it was decided to restrict the team meeting to just the team men only. It was held at the Hilton Airport Hotel in Atlanta, Georgia. So I went to America alone for this visit. There was such a strong reaction from the team members that wives had not been invited, that a promise was given that it would not happen again.

Many times, the team was able to go to unexpected locations for the team meeting. In theory they would sound far too expensive but often the management of the hotel was glad to have the team staying there as it was good publicity for them. In some places they provided the accommodation without charge; in others they would reduce the tariff to a level which made it impossible to refuse. So we enjoyed some team meetings in exceptional locations. One of these was the exclusive Greenbrier resort at White Sulphur Springs in Virginia. Situated at the foot of the Appalachian mountains, this magnificent centre was of five-star quality. The team was able to return there on a number of occasions in future years.

It was at a team meeting at Greenbrier, in November 1971, that Bishop Goodwin Hudson was asked to bring a greeting. At the time there had been the severe world-wide petrol crisis. For him, bringing a greeting meant a word of fun as well as a word of spiritual encouragement. On this occasion, he came to the microphone, and in his droll way described the situation – with a solution!

We've had a petrol crisis due to the Arabs deciding that they wanted to 'up' the prices. Since we last met as a team the price of petrol has gone through the roof. In Britain, we're frantically looking for oil in the North Sea to offset our dependence upon overseas suppliers. And I have been pondering the problem. I have been reading about the advantages of the camel [laughter] – just wait for it if you don't mind! – and I've been reading about its remarkable endurance. Apparently you only have to fill it up with water and it'll keep going for three weeks. So I thought this sounded like a solution to our problem: 'Buy a camel,' I said – until I realised that the Arab sheiks not only control the world's oil, but they also control the world's camels!

On another occasion, standing at the automatic podium always

used by Billy Graham he commented: 'This adjustable pulpit of
Billy's terrifies me, and makes me feel like the deep sea diver
who received a message: "Come up at once, the boat is sinking." '
Such was his mastery of the language that he was immediately
able to follow that story with a serious comment without it seem-
ing in the least bit incongruous: 'During these days together I
would have been very surprised if some emphasis of expectation
of our blessed Lord's return hadn't occurred. I would have been
very surprised. We often talk about it at home and my heart has
been warmed as I've found almost everybody – most of you –
have been aware that Christ is coming back again.'

The stories by and about Huddy are legion – but there is one
more which should be recounted. It occurred during an address
he gave to an earlier team meeting at Greenbrier in 1967,
shortly after his return from Australia:

> I want to share with you some of the problems of Australia.
> The continent has a population of 14 million people,
> 140 million sheep, 750 million rabbits and 750,000 civil
> servants. The 140 million sheep, with the help of 100,000
> people, produce wool worth 300-400 million pounds. It
> has been noted that the 750 million rabbits cost the
> country half as much as the wool clip. However, seven
> rabbits eat as much as one sheep. The 750,000 civil
> servants cost the country nearly as much as the 750
> million rabbits.
>
> Mercifully a virus has been found which helps to keep
> the rabbit population in check – furthermore, a civil serv-
> ant sometimes eats a rabbit (but a rabbit never eats a civil
> servant!). No way has yet been found to keep the civil
> servants in check!

The programme of a team meeting rarely changed. Each morning there would be a bible exposition. A renowned bible teacher
would come and open up the Word to us and they were precious
times. Then would follow the report sessions. The afternoons
were largely devoted to outdoor activities (whenever the weather
permitted) and in the evening we usually heard from Mr
Graham himself. Sometimes after the evening session, we would
have a fun time together. Grady Wilson was always ready to tell
a story, as were other team members. One of the favourite

stories was told about Mr Graham himself. In fact, it made the newspapers where it was told like this:

Billy Graham was on his way home from Honolulu to his home in Montreat. On Wednesday afternoon, he couldn't get out of Atlanta by air because of adverse weather conditions. So T. W. Wilson rented a car and set out to drive home.

Mr Graham, at the time, was recovering from a lung and bronchial infection, so he got a pillow and blanket and curled up in the back seat and went to sleep. T.W. drove to a small Georgia town called Jefferson where he stopped at a drive-in hamburger restaurant and went inside to ask directions to the new highway. Unwilling to disturb Billy in the back seat, he left the motor running. It was still pouring with rain.

In those few moments Graham awoke and needed the rest room [WC]. When he came out, there were the car's tail-lights disappearing to the north. Graham, who had little money, no raincoat or hat, and was running a fever, sat there and waited and waited for T.W. to return. Nobody recognised him.

Finally Graham asked the waitress if there was a taxi service. Well, there was a fellow a few miles up the road who drove people around. He came. He didn't believe Billy Graham was Billy Graham, but for twenty dollars he'd take him the eighty miles to Greenville, South Carolina in a 1950 Plymouth with a cracked windscreen.

Wilson, meanwhile, unknowing that his passenger was no longer asleep on the back seat, kept going.

At Greenville, the Holiday Inn where the evangelist hoped to stop was full; no rooms. There were no cars to rent except at Greenville Airport, so there Graham went and rented a car.

Still feverish, he drove slowly up the fog-shrouded mountain to Montreat. Mrs Graham, their children and Wilson were in the front yard when he arrived at about 1 a.m.

Wilson hadn't discovered he was minus his famous passenger until he'd had to stop in North Carolina for gas. They'd alerted the Highway Patrol, the Georgia police and heaven only knows how many other people. Billy

Graham said: 'T.W. thought I was in the back of the car asleep all the time!'

Whenever possible, the team meetings were held in the south – especially in Florida. The weather there was so good from November to February, the period during which the team meetings were generally held. Marco Island, on the gulf coast of Florida, was one such location. Many members of the team enjoyed a game of golf, and there were good golfing facilities at that hotel.

One feature of a team meeting was our name labels. Billy Graham always asked for our names to be in good one-inch to one-and-a-half-inch lettering, so they could easily be read at a distance and without glasses. Also, it was our custom to wear them on the right-hand side of our coat, rather than the usual left-hand side. The reason for this, as Billy Graham once explained to me, was because when you shake hands with someone, you naturally look to their right. If the badge is worn on their left, you get a crick in your neck, looking at the badge. After a while, it becomes natural to pin the badge on the right-hand side and I still do, whatever conference or convention I may attend.

We returned to Florida again in 1973, shortly after Spre-e '73 had been held in Britain. At the time, John Dillon had remained in London to help in the release of our latest film. John, with his wife Louise, had commended himself to the British through his contribution to the success of Spre-e '73. Mr Graham had asked him to stay on and supervise the future film releases throughout the country.

The meeting that year was held at Porte St Lucie and we were all enjoying the experience. Then one day, during a plenary session, some announcements were made that took us all by surprise. We were first told of a number of new appointments. Dr Walter Smyth was to be in charge of overseas offices in place of George Wilson. There was some sense in this because Walter was constantly travelling through many of the places where there were offices, whereas for George it was always a special trip.

Then we were told of new responsibilities – in America – for John Dillon. This put all the plans in Scotland and England into the melting pot, and we had to rethink our whole programme for the film releases. John Dillon told me afterwards that when

Mr Graham had asked him to accept these new responsibilities, it had been an agonising decision for him.

In 1976 the team meeting was in Orlando, Florida. I had an embarrassing experience upon arrival. I had just checked in at the reception desk and they had asked for an imprint of my American Express credit card. Marilyn and I then went to our room. We were busy unpacking when there was a knock at the door. It was Dr Walter Smyth, and in his hand he had my American Express card. I had left it on the desk at reception. To return it personally to me (without making any comment) was adequate rebuke for my carelessness, and I made doubly sure that such a thing did not happen again.

We arrived a few days early, to find that John and Louise Dillon had also arrived early. They kindly put themselves at our disposal and took us to Cape Canaveral one day, and to the Cypress Gardens another. We had a time of renewed good fellowship together. As Orlando was also the home of Disneyworld, there was an opportunity during the team meeting itself, on one of the free days, to pay our first visit to the famous theme park.

Two years later, we paid our first visit to Jamaica when in 1978 the team meeting was held at Montego Bay. At first we thought that we wouldn't make it. The pilot of our plane came in to land, decided that he wasn't in the correct position, and gave the engine full throttle. We went round a second time . . . and a third, and we began to wonder if we'd ever get down. But on the fourth attempt he landed safely.

Our accommodation there was in the Hilton Hotel. During our stay the hotel started to fall to bits! On our first night we were woken by a crash to find that the curtained wardrobe had fallen off the wall, totally covering all our clothes which had been inside. Then we discovered that nothing in our bathroom worked. We told the management about it, but it did not get repaired and we simply had to get by. Another day, when there was a heavy downpour of rain, the ceiling in the dining room came down, exposing a roof mostly devoid of tiles. Rainwater poured into the dining room, and some of the team had to move their tables to avoid it. Finally, we were all warned about the possibility of thieving from our rooms and advised to take extra precautions to secure our belongings. It was a little unsettling.

From Montego Bay Marilyn went to Phoenix to spend some time with her parents, who had moved there from Minneapolis. Meanwhile, I went on to Washington to attend the National Religious Broadcasters' Convention. My flight was to Miami and thence by another airline to Washington. On that second leg I found myself sitting next to an American Jewish dentist. We chatted the whole way there, and I discovered that he was a fan of Billy Graham's – though he had never heard him in person and certainly had never met him. So I invited him to come as my guest to the NRB Banquet on the last night at which Billy Graham would be speaking. I promised also to introduce him to Mr Graham.

He was very moved by Mr Graham's address, and delighted to meet him in person. The next morning I had a telephone call from him: 'How are you going back to England?' he asked. I told him that I had a return ticket on TWA from Washington. He said: 'You're an Englishman: you can't go TWA. You should be on the Concorde!' I told him that I would like to be, but I couldn't possibly afford it. He replied: 'You can't – but I can. I'd like you to take your ticket to the airline, and get them to upgrade it to a Concorde flight with my compliments.' He had already been on the telephone by the time I got to the airline offices and everything was ready for me. It was the first of several occasions when he made it possible for us to travel on Concorde.

That first flight was a wonderful experience. I'll never forget the one-up-manship of the Concorde pilot as we came in to land. Over the intercom he announced: 'Ladies and Gentlemen, we have just landed at Heathrow Airport in London. The Boeing 747 which left Washington half an hour ahead of us is just halfway across the Atlantic!'

Callaway Gardens near Atlanta, Georgia was the venue in 1979. It was there that I had one of the most embarrassing experiences that I had ever had with the team. I often got into trouble with inadvertent spoonerisms which crept in from time to time, like saying 'par cark' for 'car park' or 'you have just hissed the mistory lesson.' But this was worse. (Readers who are easily offended should skip the next paragraph.)

The hotel at Callaway Gardens was beside an old gravel pit, and the coffee shop (with tables inside and outside) was named 'The Pits'. One afternoon, I approached one of my team colleagues with whom I had not had an opportunity to 'fellowship', as the Americans call chatting together. As I saw he apparently had nothing to do, I went up to him, put my arm around his shoulder and said: 'Why don't you and I go and have *tea in the Pits*?' Only it didn't come out like that . . .

In 1984 the team meeting was held at a new hotel in Phoenix, Arizona. That was a real Wild West fiesta! We had a marvellous time in the bible reading sessions, and in the many report sessions. When they were all over, we relaxed together and had an outing to real cowboy country, culminating in a proper Western barbecue in the evening. It is at times like that the team really gets to know each other.

The most recent team meeting at the time of writing (1991) was at another magnificent location in West Virginia, known as The Homestead. The buildings were almost a quarter of a mile in length and had every facility one could wish for, including a swimming pool, bowling lanes and exercise rooms.

Three of the team members came to The Homestead with new wives. Bev Shea had married Carlene, a former member of the staff at the Montreat office. Montreat is the mountain resort where Billy Graham lives and a small office is maintained there for his secretary, Stephanie Wills, and for T. W. Wilson's staff. Bev's wife Irma had died some years previously, and Bev delighted us all with the news of his marriage to Carlene.

The second of the trio was Dr Sherwood Eliot Wirt. Winola, his remarkable wife of many years' standing, had died two years earlier, and Woody had met and courted Ruth Love, one of the secretaries of the association who had helped to set up many a crusade.

The third was our good friend John Dillon. Louise had finally succumbed to the cancer which had dogged her for many years. In the past year, John had met Betty, who had worked with him at the Amsterdam Congress the previous year, and now he brought her as his wife to the team meeting. We all rejoiced with the three of them who were themselves rejoicing.

It was there that another traumatic announcement was made. It was to change the lives of many team members including ourselves. Bob Williams had been setting up an office in Harrow, England, from which the new ministry of Mission World was to be organised. He had laid intensive plans for this event, and it was envisaged that it would be some three or four years before they could be realised.

At The Homestead, we were told that the whole of the Mission World organisation was to move to Minneapolis, and Bob Williams and his staff would transfer there from London as soon as possible. This was disturbing news for me because the remnants of the Billy Graham London office, together with my Keswick office, were located in the Mission World building. If that building was to close, then I too would have to move. (On my return I set about finding suitable offices and, with some help from Mr Graham, I found ideal premises just across the road and round the corner from Mission World).

The other announcement made at The Homestead was that the Burbank Studios of World Wide Pictures in Hollywood were to be closed down. There would be a reorganisation of personnel, and Bill Brown (then vice president of World Wide Pictures) would be invited to take early retirement. But like so many others who have retired, Mr Graham has called him back since to assist in many ways. Bill has graciously and humbly accepted whatever work has come from the association, and he has been an invaluable help to Mr Graham.

There is no doubt that the loving and friendly atmosphere which pervades every team meeting has contributed in a large measure to the family feeling that exists within the organisation. The first day or two, one is so busy greeting old and trusted friends that the sessions almost come as an intrusion! The sessions, none the less, are the kernel of the whole exercise. The expository bible reading each day is a great blessing to us. The rest of the day is taken up with reports from all the various sections of the work. I would report from the London office; similarly my colleagues in Australia, South America, France, Germany and all the other overseas offices would present their reports. There were reports from *Decision* magazine; the two radio stations owned and operated by the BGEA; from World Wide Pictures and from cities where the next crusades were being planned. There was also an opportunity to see the newest film which had been released by World Wide Pictures.

There was rejoicing over triumphs; a sharing of understanding with defeats. There was encouragement for those who were depressed, and it was uplifting to hear from each of the team members about their part in the overall ministry.

Among the guests at the team meeting would be the members of the American board and, sometimes, some of the British (and other) board members. Mr Graham would also invite some friends of the team such as Corrie Ten Boom (whose story was told in the film *The Hiding Place*) and Joni Eareckson, the quadriplegic girl who starred in the film *Joni*. Often several members of Mr Graham's own family would be present and it was a great delight to meet them.

At one of the team meetings (at the Miami Beach Hotel), George Wilson's long-time secretary, Esther Hawley, was married by Mr Graham to Harold LaDow, and all of us were invited to the wedding.

After the team meeting in 1971, Marilyn and I went on to visit her brother in Los Angeles. Paul Sandberg at the time was singing with the Haven of Rest Quartet, making regular broadcasts on many Christian radio stations in the USA. When we got to Los Angeles, we discovered that a day or two later there was to be the Rose Bowl Parade in Pasadena. The Grand Marshal of the Parade was to be Billy Graham. We simply had to go! Paul managed to secure some tickets for us in an excellent stand about halfway along the route.

We sat in Section 9, Row J, seats 7 and 8, which turned out to be a fairly exposed position in the block. In due course the parade started and eventually along came the car in which Mr and Mrs Graham were seated (it was an open car, and they were sitting on the back seat). Billy was waving indiscriminately. Suddenly, to our utter astonishment, he looked around in our direction and caught sight of us, way up in the stand. He stood up and shouted: 'Hello, Maurice!' and gave us a hearty wave as the procession moved on.

Russ Busby, the team's official photographer, has been a stabilising influence upon the team in many ways and for many years. There's no side to him, and he quickly demolishes any pomposity in others. It is impossible to be pompous when Russ is around and he always has a cheerful comment to make, whatever the situation.

At the Atlanta team meeting he planned to take portraits of all the team members. One by one we presented ourselves; we were duly made up and took our seat in front of Russ's camera. 'Which is your best side?' he would ask. 'Turn your head that way . . . now this way. You know, you haven't got a best side!' He managed to get pictures in all sorts of places, and accompanied Mr Graham to most of his engagements. His photographic record of the ministry is outstanding. Most of the photographs in this book – including the cover picture – are his.

The strange customs of England have sometimes caused problems to Russ. In the early days of his involvement in Britain, he was attending a VIP dinner in London. He had flown in only the night before and was tired and hungry, so he decided to have a good meal, and not to worry too much about pictures. Suddenly the chairman stood up and proposed the toast: 'Ladies and Gentlemen, the Queen.' Russ Busby ran madly to collect his camera, wondering how he could have been so foolish as to miss this picture of Her Majesty. No one had informed him that the Queen was expected. He was terribly disappointed when he found out that it had simply been the correct British way to drink a toast to Her Majesty!

In 1965 I had cardiac ischaemia: heart trouble. At the time it was quite serious. It demonstrated its presence to me by a constant severe pain in the region of the heart – so constant that I could not even cross the road without an attack. It slowed me down and I thought I had come to the end of my useful life.

The problem was diagnosed by my osteopath, Mr A. Rutland Webster, to whom I had been recommended several years before when I had slipped a disc. From time to time I went to Mr Rutland Webster for treatment to my back. On one visit I was describing these severe symptoms to him and he urged me to visit a Dr T. R. Williams in Harley Street – 'A sound man,' said Mr Rutland Webster, who obviously had great confidence in him. He made an appointment for me to see Dr Williams the same day.

That visit to the doctor resulted in a walk up Harley Street to a heart specialist where I was immediately given an ECG. Dr Williams came with me, and he discussed my case with the heart specialist. The specialist agreed with the proposed treatment which Dr Williams wanted to give me. He described it as a radical treatment which, he told me, was not recognised by the Heart Clinic, but which he had found abundantly successful over the years. He prescribed one vitamin E gel of 400 units (made by Bioglan) and a glass of wine a day. He told me that if I maintained this therapy for the rest of my life – and kept my weight down – I would be on course for a long life!

The treatment worked marvels: I am still on it more than twenty-six years later and my programme is, if anything, heavier than when I was a younger man. I have much to be grateful for, in the diagnosis and treatment by Dr Williams.

Russ Busby came to London shortly after my first consultation with Dr Williams and I shared this prescription with him. Johnny Lenning, producer of the radio programme *Hour of Decision*, was somewhere nearby and he overheard. Russ said he was going to follow the same therapy if a long life was assured.

A year later he returned to London. He told me: 'Maurice! That prescription you gave me is terrific! I've never felt better. I'm well on the way to a long life ... by the way, what did you say was the name of the pills I was supposed to take?' That was in 1966, but still in the early 1990s Russ keeps asking: 'How about those pills?' Johnny Lenning got the name some years ago and now asks: 'Still taking your vitamin E?' At any rate, I can testify that it is a treatment that really works. I thought I was finished in 1965; today I have more energy than I can use. Long live vitamin E!

On January 21st, 1984, when Billy Graham was in London for a number of pre-mission engagements, he was invited to a breakfast television interview on TV-AM with David Frost. Russ Busby and I, together with T. W. Wilson, took Mr Graham to the early morning appointment.

He was not first in the programme: just before him David Frost had interviewed a young London 'stripper'. As she came off the set, very scantily clad, T. W. Wilson remarked: 'Just look at that! Isn't it awful?' Russ Busby said to T.W.: 'T., remember, it's not the first look that is sinful, but the second look constitutes the sin.' T.W. replied: 'Man, I haven't finished my first look yet!'

✳   ✳   ✳

Sherwood Wirt, founder editor of *Decision*, wrote to me on one occasion when he was about to visit London. He wanted to know if Bishop Goodwin Hudson would like to invite him to preach at his church – but he didn't want to ask him directly. So he wrote to me:

Tell the Rt Rev., His Excellency, Your Grace, Blessed by Nothink A. W. Goodwin Hudson MA FRGS (A), whom I love in the truth with every cell of this tired body, that I shall be descending from the blue heavens above upon fair Blighty somewhere around October 1 or 2. That I might be induced, howbeit by pressure, connivance etc., to remain over until the Sabbath if there is any chance I might preach the Word, let's say on October 3.

He got his preaching engagement!

In the summer of 1986, crusade co-ordinator Sterling Huston and his wife were to spend a few days in London. We were glad to lend them our flat in Wembley because we planned to be at our home in Frinton during that period. However, on July 28th we had to return to London unexpectedly for an engagement and therefore went to stay at the Post House Hotel in Hampstead. We told our son where we were, in case anyone needed us.

We went to bed at our usual time (around 10.30 p.m.) and at 1 a.m. the telephone rang. At the other end of the line was the voice of a terrified American girl. She asked for help and protection. It turned out that, with a girl-friend, she had been touring Europe intending to visit the boy-friend of one of them. Unknown to him, the work to which he was assigned in Europe was for the CIA. When he found out what was involved, he opted out. Unfortunately that was after they had already shared some compromising confidential information with him. So the CIA agents were keeping track of him while he was still in Europe.

The two girls, of course, knew nothing about this, but when the CIA found out that the fellow and the girls had met, they thought that this confidential information might have been passed on to them. As a result, like the fellow, they too were followed everywhere they went and on one occasion the room where they were staying had been broken into and searched.

When they telephoned me, they were at a hostel near Euston Road where there was no room for them to stay. But they were too frightened to go outside because there were strange men hanging around and they were afraid they might be kidnapped. They had telephoned their parents in the USA and they, in turn, had requested help and advice from a friend of theirs, Dave Barr. He was the international representative for World Wide Pictures and had given them my number. The family had passed it on to the two girls. Our answerphone in turn had directed them to our son, who gave them the number of the Post House Hotel. I had to turn out in the middle of the night and go to the hostel to collect them. I was told to bring some positive identification, so that they would know I was the right person! When I arrived at the hostel, one of the girls telephoned her parents in the States and asked me to talk to them. I had to convince her mother that I was indeed Maurice Rowlandson. She asked a number of questions that obviously Barr had suggested she should ask, and in the end she released her daughter and friend into my custody. We obtained a room for them at the Post House Hotel, and the next morning I took them to the airport for them to join a flight home.

A day or two later their parents telephoned to express their thanks. Her mother told me: 'I guess we'll never know all that happened and we will have to leave it at that. We realised that you were able to help them at a time that was quite inconvenient to you!' Later still, Dave Barr wrote to say: 'Your experience with Donna and her girl-friend sounds like something out of a TV special on cops and robbers! We are grateful that you were able to help the girls, and I know that their parents are especially grateful.'

❊   ❊   ❊

The very first person I met who was to become a member of the Billy Graham team was George Wilson. When I met him first, he was the business manager of Northwestern Bible School and College of Liberal Arts. He was the person in charge of my affairs while I was there, and I have already told some of the stories associated with him.

It was an unbelievable invitation which he gave me at lunch that day in 1961. I still wonder at my brashness in asking that he confirm the invitation to join the Billy Graham Evangelistic Association in writing! It is a wonder to me that he ever followed through at all on that. He asked me what I wanted him to confirm; I mentioned things like salary, holidays, sick leave and pensions. I ended by saying: 'Oh yes, and I shall need a car.' All I needed was a small car – an Austin Mini would be adequate, I said. In the event, the letter of confirmation came but not one of the points I had asked for had been covered. But he did confirm the matter of the car – except that he wrote: 'You are authorised to purchase an Austin *Healey*!' At the time, such a car was about the top of the range, and very expensive. I hope he appreciated that I did not take him at his word, and chose only a Mini. Come to think of it, the Austin Healey is still due to me!

Over the years, George Wilson has been a loyal and true friend. Whenever he came to see us in the London office, it was rather like a royal visit. Everything was spruced up, even if it was already in fairly good condition. But we wanted everything to be just right. Rarely when he arrived was it as he wished. We always found that he could give us helpful advice, which meant that everything was kept at a very high standard. He was always candid in his comments – but candour in order to cure is very different from candour in order to hurt. Putting someone right is quite a different thing from putting someone down! He inspired in us a great desire to please, and this was true for all of those who worked for him. He may have been on the other side of the Atlantic, but he was very much with us – in spirit – in the office in London and in everything that we did.

The stories about him are legion. He inspired either a deep dislike or a deep love and trust among those with whom he worked: there was no middle course. There were, I suppose, some who saw him as a threat to their work. But he was not like that. If you were prepared to trust his judgment, things generally went right for you. But there were those of similar strong opinion, who found him hard to accept. None the less, as has been indicated earlier, even those who found him hard to get on with, sank their differences when the team got together. There was friendly banter among the group and no conflict ever went so deep as to cause friction or hurt within the team.

Tall Larry – Larry Ross – was a member of the team I always enjoyed working with. Strictly speaking, he was not a team member; he worked with the Walter Bennett Agency which handled much of the public relations work for Mr Graham. But his involvement was so central to all we were doing that we always thought of him as one of us. In order to cope with his great height – he was well over seven foot tall – I used to carry around what I called my Larry Box: I would stand on this box when I talked to him and speak eye-to-eye. It saved him the crouch and it saved me neck ache. He was a great soul and an inspiration to all of us who worked with him.

As with so many members of the team, I enjoy the fellowship of Larry's friendship when I can. It is hard to maintain friendships with the Atlantic Ocean between you, but Larry is one of those people who, when you meet him, takes up the conversation from where you left it last time. Occasionally there is an exchange of correspondence between us, or maybe a transatlantic telephone call (mostly replaced, regrettably, by a fax these days). It was always good to hear his voice. Usually he would telephone when there was something special he wanted me to do.

In 1986, I celebrated my twenty-fifth year with the Billy Graham Association. They kindly presented me with a gold badge with a jewel embedded in it to mark the occasion. Mention was made of the event in the team information sheet, 'Notes and Quotes'. Larry Ross saw the news and wrote to me: 'Congratulations are in order to you as well, mate, for your twenty-five years with the association. After first seeing your milestone in "Notes and Quotes" I was present in Minneapolis last week when, in chapel, they announced congratulations to you before the whole staff there.' Larry is a good friend, and one we have come to love and appreciate over the years. He has also given us some good laughs.

There are many more stories about every member of the team. Some of these stories have already been told in other books. Suffice it to say that every one of the team has meant something special to Marilyn and me. We thank God for the remembrance of every one of them.

It is one of the enduring privileges of my life that for so many years I have been associated with the Billy Graham team in this way. As in my family there have been disagreements; there have even been sharp differences of opinion. There are one or two team members who do not find the relationship with another member of the team an easy experience. But that is true in a family too. It does not detract from the inherent love and trust that flows through all the family units. It is the same in the team. Where there may have been disagreements, they disappear in the many opportunities of ministry which come to each of us. Consequently there is rarely an occasion when an irreconcilable situation arises.

Sadly, the only real breach of relationship comes about through marital problems (or, rarely, moral difficulties) and when this occurs there is a mutual understanding that the time has come to sever the relationship with the team. Of course, it is hurtful to everyone concerned when this happens. But as far as lies within their power, the team leadership try to be gentle: firm, yes – but gentle with it. Over the years these instances have thankfully been very rare and the main body of the team has been protected from such problems.

By and large, my work with the team has been an inexpressibly satisfying experience. The support and understanding of the team – not least of Billy Graham himself – is something which can only be appreciated from personal experience. It may sound trite, or even insincere, but it is utterly true.

I thank God for His leading which brought me into the aegis of the team. In a way it seems that He must have had this plan in mind from the beginning. That 'thin gold line' of my experience has never wavered. God has been in it from the beginning and He is still in the continuing relationships. For someone who has never had the privilege I have had, the story seems unbelievable. But I speak from the base where I stand and can only tell things as I found them. God has been good in bringing to Billy Graham, those of His choosing to share the responsibilities of the ministry with him. That God is in the centre of it all is the secret. This is not man's doing: it is God's and it is marvellous in our eyes!

9

Mission England and a Coma

By 1975, it had been eight years since Billy Graham had come to Britain for a crusade. Spre-e '73 had been a rather different event, and a whole generation had grown up for whom the stories of Harringay and Earls Court were but history. Yet the needs of the capital city for the gospel were as great as ever.

Out of the blue I had a telephone call from Earls Court. They told me that they had gigantic rebuilding plans which might destroy – for all time – the arena facilities. They thought it might be impossible to run another crusade after 1977. They asked if we were interested in staging another event before then.

I had felt burdened with the need for Billy Graham to return to Britain, and I shared this burden with my UK board. I told them about the phone call from Earls Court, and asked them if the time had not come when we should take the initial steps to promote another crusade. They supported me in this proposal and suggested various ways in which this might be done. In particular, they mentioned the name of Lord Luke.

The avuncular Lord Luke had always been a warm supporter of Mr Graham. It seemed appropriate therefore to recruit his support for any plans that we might have. I made an appointment to see him on October 1st, 1975. My PA, Rosemary Wheeler, came with me to take notes of the meeting.

He welcomed us warmly and made the suggestion that we should call a meeting of Christian leaders as soon as possible. He said that he would be glad to take the chair. He asked that the Reverend David Bubbers should be invited to speak, along with Michael Alison MP and Dr Raymond Brown. We planned the meeting for November 6th, 1975 at Church House, Westminster.

Back at the office, we started to compile a list of names of leaders to invite and eventually came up with around a hundred. Then one day, shortly before the meeting, I had a telephone call from Gordon Landreth, who was the general secretary of the Evangelical Alliance. He expressed his concern that all of those who had been invited could be construed to be those who would give unqualified support to the proposal to invite Billy Graham back. He pointed out that all of them were known friends of the association and that not everybody felt like that.

I asked him what he would suggest, and he gave me a list of around fifteen names of those he knew who would question the wisdom of organising another crusade in London at this time. I agreed to send invitations to those fifteen. Thirteen of them were among the 109 who actually attended.

Lord Luke took the chair at the meeting, in his delightfully hesitant way, and invited the three speakers to put their case in support of a crusade. David Bubbers gave a powerful address, as did also his two supporting speakers. Lord Luke then opened the meeting for questions and comments from the floor.

Almost every one of the thirteen participants who had been nominated by Gordon Landreth spoke – and every one of them raised questions and doubts about the wisdom of such a proposal. No one spoke from the floor in support. In due course Lord Luke looked at the clock and expressed his view that the time had come to wind up the meeting. He said that, in his opinion, the main call from those present was for consultation and he proposed that a select committee should be set up to examine the whole proposal and to make recommendations. Names were agreed for that committee which would meet under the chairmanship of Chief Inspector Robin Oake (see Appendix C). They held their first meeting on December 3rd, 1975 at the offices of the Evangelical Alliance.

During the next few weeks they met several times. Eventually they invited the Church of England Evangelical Council, the Evangelical Alliance and the Billy Graham Evangelistic Association to put together lists of names to form a consultative council. These three bodies agreed to do so and selected February 12th, 1976 as the date when the consultation would be held. Some 200 representatives attended the meeting which was held at the Friends' Meeting House in Euston Road. The participants at that meeting proposed many helpful ideas. Already it has been mentioned that the experimental crusade in Blackpool, the university missions of Oxford and Cambridge, and the concept of a multi-centre crusade grew out of that consultation.

Nevertheless we were not to know that, from that original meeting on November 6th, 1975, through innumerable committees and consultations, it would be November 2nd, 1981 before the plans would finally come to fruition with the first meeting of the National Mission Committee.

In the meantime the consultative council was followed by a working group which conceived a programme entitled 'Let My People Grow'. The blueprint for that programme was virtually a blueprint for a crusade – but nothing ever came of it.

On October 20th, 1976 there came the first meeting of the Lambeth Group, with a proposal by the Archbishhop of Canterbury that he should issue a call to the nation. He sought an assurance from Mr Graham that he would not accept any crusade invitation until after those plans had been implemented. These were announced on April 25th, 1977 when he issued a press release about the 'Nationwide Initiative in Evangelism'.

Eventually, the working group decided that they had no mandate to proceed, and disbanded on March 14th, 1977. After that meeting, Tom Houston approached me and said: 'Maurice, you have fulfilled all that was required of you in respect of consultations. It would seem that the way is now open to you to proceed with the organisation of a crusade.'

Shortly afterwards, on April 19th, 1977, Mr Graham was in Copenhagen for a crusade in Denmark. He sent an urgent message to me to ask that I should invite a group of evangelical leaders to meet with him there. The group was to include two Anglicans (the Reverend Richard Bewes and the Reverend Michael Cole), two non-conformist ministers (the Reverend Gilbert Kirby and the Reverend David MacLagan) and five laymen (the Hon. Crispin Joynson-Hicks, Eric Delve, Hugh Prest, Gordon Landreth and Clarence Jefferies). Two members of the Billy Graham team were also included (Dr Walter Smyth and Dr Bob Evans). Mr Graham and myself completed the group. He shared with all of us his burden and concern for the United Kingdom and we returned to the UK with a commitment from Gordon Landreth that the Evangelical Alliance would call a special meeting – which they did on May 3rd, 1977. It was at this meeting that the recommendation of the former consultative council was picked up. They had suggested that Mr Graham should accept an invitation to conduct university missions at Oxford and Cambridge.

Also at that meeting they formed a co-ordinating committee (see Appendix C), which by the end of the year had laid plans for the Evangelical Alliance's 'Decade of Evangelism'. Much of the time was spent in discussing the relationship between the Decade and the Nationwide Initiative.

Eventually things were brought to a head by an article by Gavin Reid in the Church of England newspaper. After setting out all the arguments which had been put forward in the past two and a half years, and deploring the fact that the process of consultation had taken so long and had got us nowhere, Gavin Reid continued: 'We haven't got Billy, and those who originally felt strongly about inviting him . . . are becoming dismayed with three years of ecclesiastical chatter.' It took time for the impact of that article to filter through but on February 5th, 1979, in the *Guardian*, the Reverend Peter Mullens wrote an article headlined 'Stay away Billy Graham; For God's sake, stay away!' The following week, the Reverend Ian Barclay replied with a strong presentation of the case for Billy Graham to come. Inevitably this confrontation interested the BBC, who invited both Peter Mullens and Ian Barclay to debate the issue on their Sunday morning radio programme.

So emotive was the debate that, unexpectedly, at the end of the programme the producer said he had decided to run his own national poll. He asked listeners to send a postcard to him to say 'Billy Graham YES' or 'Billy Graham NO' according to their viewpoint. A week later he gave the result of the poll: 14,990 cards, of which 13,825 said YES and 1,165 said NO! There had never been a response like that to a single announcement on the radio.

Moved by this poll result, the Evangelical Alliance debated the whole issue at their meeting on March 15th, 1979 when, with one dissenting vote, they agreed a motion to invite Billy Graham, and Gordon Landreth sent a telegram the same day.

Meanwhile, a group of Christian leaders in Birmingham were getting impatient with their London counterparts. At the same time that the Evangelical Alliance had been debating the matter in London, a Birmingham headmaster, Kenneth Barnes, had initiated a group based in the Midlands. In his letter of invitation he said: 'We have lost patience with the consultation procedures currently in progress.' His invitation was extended to representatives from other areas of the United Kingdom.

However, when they met, they heard of the action now being taken by the Evangelical Alliance and of the telegram which had been sent to Mr Graham. The steam went out of the meeting in Birmingham and they agreed simply to write a letter to Mr Graham to co-ordinate their efforts with those of London. A working party to represent both areas was set up and on November 12th, 1979 Mr Graham himself attended a meeting at London's Cora Hotel.

Much of the discussion centred around the impending university missions at Oxford and Cambridge, and Mr Graham said he would reserve his judgment about any further invitations until after those missions.

As far as the Billy Graham team was concerned, their efforts in Britain were concentrated upon the plans for setting up the university missions. With Blair Carlson and Walter Smyth I drove to Oxford and then Cambridge. We had been warned in advance that we would find a very proper committee in Oxford, and a very radical committee in Cambridge. In the event, the Oxford committee met us in jeans and sweatshirts; the Cambridge committee were smartly dressed in suits, shirts and ties! I was reminded of the Joe's Café syndrome. And so it turned out. Oxford was good but somewhat disorganised and had a more charismatically styled approach. Cambridge was sharp, well organised and conventional.

On that initial planning visit to Cambridge, Walter Smyth was involved with one of the committees while the young Blair Carlson and I took a walk along the River Cam. It was to be an occasion I would often think back to in future years. He picked my brains. He wanted to know all about working with the Billy Graham team; the problems I had faced; the joys I had experienced; the things I had learned to avoid and the things I had found to be important.

We covered many topics. We talked about the methods I had used and the ministries of Billy Graham in which I had been involved. We talked about systems and computers; we inevitably talked about five-by-three-inch cards. We discussed filing, letter writing and administration generally. I realised later that he was preparing himself, by gathering as much information as he could, for a future significant ministry with the Billy Graham team. It was a privilege to have shared that time with him, and I believe he benefited and enjoyed it as much as I did.

When we went back to Oxford for the mission on January 29th, 1980, we were somewhat alarmed at the style of the meeting. It was different from anything Mr Graham had been involved in before. Dance and drama, testimonies and worship singing formed a big part of each programme. Canon Michael Green would spend some time in prayer with Billy Graham each day. He was identified with the more charismatic position, and this came out in the planning of the meetings.

In Oxford we were particularly aware of opposition to the meetings. One night, the TV cables were cut; the fire alarm was set off, and when I came to leave, I found the police around my car, checking it for a suspected bomb. It turned out to be a hoax – but it was a comfort to know that they were so watchful.

While he was at Cambridge, Mr Graham found that it was impossible to eat his meals in the hotel restaurant. To do so gave him no peace, for there were so many in the close confines of Cambridge who wanted to talk with him. Many of the students, upon discovering the hotel in which Billy Graham was staying, would take their meals there in the hope of meeting him. So he ate in his room, and mostly T. W. Wilson would keep him company.

One day, after lunch, I had occasion to explain the difference in meaning and idiom between Cambridge English and American English. As I came up from the restaurant, T. W. Wilson was coming out of Mr Graham's room. He looked a little crestfallen, and I asked him: 'T., what's the matter?' (we always called T. W. Wilson either 'T.' or 'T.W.').

'Maureece,' he said, 'I think I've upset the chambermaid.' I asked him: 'What happened?' He replied: 'Well, Maureece, I was having lunch with Billy when I upset the tomato soup all down the front of my pants [American for trousers], so I went along to the chambermaid's room and I said, "Ma'am, can you help me? I've soiled my pants!"' I explained the English meaning of what he had said and he was devastated!

After those university missions the Evangelical Alliance formed an invitational committee which met in the Waldegrave Hall at

All Souls Church, Langham Place (see Appendix C). Mr Graham joined the meeting following his luncheon at Buckingham Palace with Her Majesty the Queen. He listened to the speakers and heard of the level of support for a mission in England. After that meeting, Gordon Landreth announced that there would be some delay in Mr Graham's reply.

Among other things, Mr Graham wanted to assess the situation among the youth of Britain, and Dr Walter Smyth asked for a youth committee to be established with whom he might consult. Twenty-three youth leaders met with Walter Smyth on April 29th, 1980. Three main points emerged: first, that those who invited Mr Graham to Harringay in 1954 were about the same age as those represented at this meeting; secondly, that if young people were to represent some 60 to 80 per cent of those attending any crusade meetings, they should be represented on the central committee; and thirdly, that this group of twenty-three supported plans for a crusade.

The same day, Walter Smyth met with the Reverend David Bubbers, the Reverend Gilbert Kirby, Gordon Landreth, David Rennie and myself to explain in depth Mr Graham's feelings about an invitation. He asked that a steering committee should be formed to guide things towards a possible crusade (see Appendix C).

On October 12th, 1980, after numerous meetings of that committee, they received a letter from Billy Graham giving a qualified 'No' to the invitation. Yet, at the same time, he left the door open for further approaches. As the steering committee disbanded David Bubbers suggested that we should leave a caretaker committee in place to follow through on any possibilities which might arise.

On January 14th, 1981, Mr Graham was again in London and met the caretaker committee – expanded, on that occasion, by the inclusion of representatives from other areas of the United Kingdom. At the unanimous wish of those present at that meeting – and with the approval of Mr Graham – it was agreed to reconstitute the steering committee and to ask them to update their findings.

On March 4th, 1981 there followed one of the most important meetings of the whole of the consultation process. David Rennie was in the chair for a steering committee meeting in the board room of the Leprosy Mission. The meeting took place at the time of the first efforts by Terry Waite to free a group of hostages in Iran. Terry Waite had flown out in person to see the Ayatollah Khomeini. That first face-to-face contact had been rewarded by success.

At this meeting one of those present was the Reverend Gavin Reid. He referred to the success that Terry Waite had had and commented: 'Gentlemen! Maybe that is the way to get things done. Maybe a face-to-face confrontation with Billy Graham will produce results.' It was a God-given inspiration. The committee latched on to it, and sought to find a time when a selected group of members could fly to America and meet Mr Graham.

In the event, it was discovered that Mr Graham would be in Europe, and that it would be more convenient to see him in Nice. A group of us, convened and co-ordinated by David Rennie, arranged to fly to Nice to meet him there. In addition to David Rennie were Gavin Reid, Clive Calver, Eddie Gibbs and myself. For Gavin, this was to be his first visit to the South of France, and his first experience of the Mediterranean. He was looking forward to seeing it and to the opportunity to stand on its shore.

On July 6th, 1981 we were met at Nice airport by Blair Carlson. He drove us straight to Mr Graham's hotel, three minutes' drive from the airport, and escorted us to a room in the basement. There for the next three hours we sat in deep discussion with Mr Graham, Walter Smyth, Fred Dienert and Blair Carlson.

Gavin presented the concept of a six-city mission (not including London) which, greatly to our surprise, Mr Graham accepted in principle, hook, line and sinker. He gave us the authority to continue our consultations in the six selected regions and promised that, as soon as there was a clear mandate and invitation to him to come, he would be ready to accept.

The meeting wound up; Blair Carlson took us back to the airport just in time for our plane, and all that Gavin saw of the Mediterranean Sea was out of the airplane window!

There are many other stories which came out of that lengthy period of consultation. At the very first meeting on November 6th, 1975 there had been those who had come expecting to sign an invitation to Mr Graham. They were discouraged by the result which, to them, seemed so negative. Many of them said as they left: 'I didn't agree with one word of what was said.'

But none of them had attempted to speak from the floor. It may have been a case of the silent majority – or it may have been that Lord Luke had terminated the meeting too soon, before there had been time to call them. It was frustrating to know that all of those who had spoken were our critics. But there was nothing that could be done about it – except to pray. On November 2nd, 1981, six years later, those prayers were finally answered. The Lord often teaches us patience!

Another story of those days emerged from two letters which I received. When it appeared likely that the time was approaching for an invitation to be sent to Billy Graham, I had a letter from a Christian leader in which he concluded by saying that he hoped my efforts to bring Billy back would be successful. He added that this country needed Billy's ministry, and that he believed that I should be encouraged in all that I was doing.

On the same date he wrote a letter to another Christian leader which he ended: 'Like you, I believe it would be a disaster for Billy Graham to come back to this country. I hope that you can do whatever you can to discourage those who would like to invite him!' That second letter was forwarded to me by the recipient, presumably to do his bit in discouraging me! The writer could never have known that I would receive both letters on my desk. I felt that it was a case of trying to be all things to all men and letting those to whom he wrote feel that they had his support, whichever viewpoint they held. I somehow felt that God could not bless that type of double-faced approach. (The letter writer has since declared a more liberal position.)

After we had returned from Nice the heavy work started! Our first task was to sell the idea of the nationwide mission to the six regions. We had to persuade the clergy, ministers and laity in each region that they should get involved.

My immediate task was to identify the key leaders in each of the six areas, and to invite them to an exploratory meeting at which we would share the whole project with them. Between October 21st and 24th, 1981 we travelled from region to region to present the plans.

We carefully assembled a team which included John Mallison from Australia. He had been deeply involved in the planning of nurture groups during the time of Billy Graham's Australian visit two years earlier. Nurture groups were intended to train the local churches, so that they would be ready to receive the enquirers.

Others who travelled to the regions with us were Billy Graham team member Walter Smyth, David Rennie, Gavin Reid, Clive Calver, Brian Mills, Eddie Gibbs, my secretary, Karen Wade, and myself. At each centre we established a tightly knit and well-conceived programme which included a short film extract from Australian television. Part of it was the dramatic interview that Billy Graham had had with David Frost, in which David had invited Mr Graham both to close the interview on television with prayer, and also to give an address to which viewers could write if they wanted further spiritual help.

There was a time for questions, and we soon discovered a very positive and supportive response from each area. During the tour, a delegation came from Norwich with a strong recommendation to divide the East Anglian visit into two parts. They pointed out that there was no easy communication between north and south East Anglia, and they recommended a three-day (later extended to four-day) visit to Ipswich. This recommendation was accepted.

Mission England was later to be extended yet again when a persuasive delegation came to Billy Graham to ask him to include the city of Sheffield. We found that it was impossible to expand the 1984 visit to include Sheffield, but their insistence was so great that Billy Graham later agreed to return to Britain in 1985 for a week-long mission in the city.

It was on this tour to each of the regions that Brian Mills conceived and presented his Prayer Triplets plan. This remarkable programme encouraged everyone to become involved in the mission long before Billy Graham was to arrive. Each individual was encouraged to think of, and to pray for, three unconverted friends, and to join with two others in a triplet – each member of which had also identified three friends for whom they would pray. The names of those nine prayed for were written down by each member of the Prayer Triplet, and the three together would pray for the conversion of these nine friends.

Many, many Prayer Triplets were encouraged when their friends were converted before Billy Graham had even arrived! Thus the practical effect of Mission England was felt before the mission itself had started. This Prayer Triplet scheme was later adopted by the Billy Graham team and used in every subsequent crusade. It was a most effective form of pre-evangelism.

The travelling team first visited the city of Newcastle-upon-Tyne, where they were confronted by a protest group from Northern Ireland led by Pastor Jack Glass. This protest group was to follow the team to each of the centres. The protest was directed against the co-operation (as they saw it) between the mission and the Roman Catholic churches. In fact, the protest group added to rather than detracted from the plans of the tour, prompting a closing of the ranks in each locality with a greater determination to make the mission plans work.

We left each of the cities with a firm promise that they would try to initiate an invitation from that area. After each meeting, we packed up all the equipment, tidied up the room, and left as a team for the next location.

It was hard going: Newcastle in the morning, where David Holloway was in the chair, then on in the afternoon to Preston. BGEA board member Clarence Jefferies was in the chair there. Next day it was across the country to Coventry where a local businessman, Ian Frith, welcomed us. Then we drove on to Bristol for a meeting chaired by Tony Dann. Our final meeting the next morning was in Norwich where Dr Peter English was the chairman, and where representatives from Ipswich joined us.

It was a gruelling programme which left us all exhausted at the end. The trouble was that all the members of the travelling team had to be fresh for the next presentation. But the Lord gave us strength and grace and we saw it through. At the end, we had the satisfaction of knowing that every place was with us – although the final confirmation did not come until a week or ten days later when a formal invitation to hold a mission came from each of the six areas.

The steering committee formally disbanded itself; the former working party joined with them in offering their services to the new national mission committee, of which the Reverend Tom Houston was to be chairman. A core group was established, consisting of the envoys who went to Nice and this bridged the gap until the first meeting of the national mission committee. Then Mission England was under way! All that now remained was to prepare and send a formal invitation from the regions to Mr Graham.

On March 5th, 1982 Billy Graham stopped at Manchester on his way back from Blackpool. At the Excelsior hotel, he met representatives from each of the six locations which had been selected for missions (see Appendix C). (Crusades were now to become known as missions in the UK because of certain ethnic connotations to the word 'crusade'.) After a time of prayer and discussion there was a unanimous decision to extend an invitation to Mr Graham for a nationwide mission in 1984.

Two or three of the group went into a huddle to draft the formal invitation. A typewriter was hurriedly borrowed from the hotel and taken into the room next door where, with the draft in my hand, I typed the formal document. Although it was all done in a rush, the invitation was a work of inspiration. It expressed the need, outlined the concept and extended a warm invitation to Mr Graham to accept. He graciously received it from Gavin Reid, and indicated that he would let us have his response within a few days.

While I was typing the invitation, we broke for lunch. When I came back to join everybody, I overheard a delightful conversation between one of the delegates, an Anglican minister, and Billy Graham. Surprised and a little overwhelmed at finding himself sitting next to Mr Graham at the buffet lunch, he searched around for a conversational opening. 'Mr Graham,' he asked, 'which day do you take for your statutory day off?'

'I beg your pardon?' replied Billy Graham. 'I'm not quite sure I understand you.'

'Well, I mean what day do you take to "do your own thing"? I mean, I usually take Friday off, but some ministers take Monday.'

'Oh my!' exclaimed Mr Graham. 'I don't think I've had a day like that since 1949!'

Lunch over, we returned to the conference table where the completed invitation was passed around and signed by all those present. Spontaneously, Gavin Reid led everyone in singing 'Praise God from whom all blessings flow' and we had a time of open prayer and dedication of ourselves to the task ahead.

It was the end of a long line of meetings: from the select committee of 1975, through all the many consultations to the final executive committee to get things done. But, looking back, God was in it all. From what we now know, 1977 or

1978 could not have been more wrong in timing; conversely, 1984 could not have been more right! So, although the process was painful, often frustrating and continually abortive, the end product was in the plan of God.

Bob Williams was appointed from the Billy Graham team to co-ordinate the planning nationwide. He was assisted by Greg Strand (Bristol); Mike Southworth (Newcastle, which finally confirmed Sunderland as the location); Blair Carlson (Liverpool); Norman Sanders (Birmingham); Dan Southern (Norwich) and Steve Huggins (Ipswich).

David Rennie, chairman of the British board of the Billy Graham Evangelistic Association, had recently taken over new factory premises which were intended for future expansion of the business – but he did not need the space immediately. He generously offered this space to Mission England, and the central planning office was opened in the Microlease factory in Harrow Weald. The space available was converted for use as offices, and became the power-house for the mission. It was there that we held the multitudinous meetings of the co-ordinating committee and sub-committees.

The full story of the mission is told in Derek Williams's book *One in a Million* and it is not proposed to repeat it here.

It was as the planning for the mission started, that Marilyn and I faced the second most traumatic period in our lives – just as it had happened in September 1972 at the start of Spre-e '73 ten years before.

It was August, and we had just travelled to our home at Frinton for a planned three-week holiday after the heavy pressures of the past six months. I had my heart set on sailing my Jaguar sailing ship *Summer Wind*. Marilyn had invited the son of one of her close friends to come and crew for me, and Paul Barker and I had had an excellent first day's sailing on the Saturday. Our daughter Jacky and our daughter-in-law Diana (Gary's wife) together with our grandson, Timothy, had been with us for the weekend and we had had a happy time together. On Monday evening, Jacky left us to drive back to Northwick Park Hospital where she was in the final year of training for her SRN qualification. At 10.45 p.m. we went to bed. Fifteen minutes later our lives underwent a dramatic change. A telephone call came and a strange voice asked if it was Mr Rowlandson. Was I, she asked, a relative of Jacqueline Rowlandson? With a sinking feeling in my heart I said I was. 'I am sorry to tell you that your daughter has met with an accident and is in Bishops Stortford hospital.'

In a strangled voice I asked if Jacky was all right – but the only answer I received was: 'I think you had better come.'

As I swung my legs out of bed, I remember saying to Marilyn: 'I can't go through all this again.' She replied: 'You may have to – but you'll have to trust the Lord to see us through.' Memories flooded in of the similar phone call we had had in 1972 – but then it had, tragically, all been over. This time there was hope: she was at least alive!

Rapidly we dressed. Marilyn telephoned Julian and Fiona to tell them the news, while I drove across to the marina to tell Paul (who was sleeping on the ship). Diana's father and mother, Peter and Rosemary English, were also moored in the marina, on Peter's ship, so I was able to tell them why Diana and Timothy would be on their own at the house.

On the way over to the marina I realised that the car was almost out of petrol. The yellow warning light on the dashboard was on, and I needed to fill up without delay. But where, at midnight, would I find a petrol station open? I had no idea. But the Lord was with me! Parked at the side of the road on the way to the marina was a police car. I stopped and asked them if they knew the nearest all-night garage where I could fill up. They told me of one in Colchester on the road to London.

I drove back to the house, collected Marilyn and with a prayer on our lips for Jacky, we drove to Bishops Stortford. Like the widow's cruse of oil, the last drops of petrol in my tank lasted us to Colchester and we were able to fill up. We arrived at the hospital just as Julian and Fiona drove up in their car. Julian had his bible open, and shared some verses with Marilyn and me. It was a great comfort to have members of the family stand with us like this in moments of crisis.

They took us in to see our dear battered and bruised Jacky. She was unconscious and the Asian doctor who attended her was very solicitous. We talked to Jacky and we sought comfort from the doctor. He told us that the accident had occurred at Start Hill Garage. A lorry driver had tried to go into the garage, but found the canopy too low. He reversed into the main road right on to Jacky's car and crushed it.

Jacky, of course, knew nothing about this, and she did not respond to our conversation. We kept watching for hopeful signs that she was waking up. She twitched and moved and was very restless, so she was obviously alive – but that was about all.

That doctor was wonderful. He said: 'We have a very good hospital here, but not good enough for your daughter. With your permission, I would like to move her immediately to St Bartholomew's Hospital in London. I have an ambulance and police escort waiting.'

Of course, we immediately agreed. Marilyn went with Jacky in the ambulance, and I followed in the car. The police told me: 'Keep up with us: we'll go through red lights, but follow close behind.' I did!

Their organisation was impeccable. The Essex police car which escorted us from Bishops Stortford could only go as far as the Essex border. There, the Metropolitan Police were waiting for us. As the Essex car departed down the slip road, the Metropolitan car pulled away – still at a high speed and with scarcely a pause in the journey.

It was a terrifying experience to travel so fast, especially through the empty streets of East London. True to their word, they did not stop at a single light; they went straight through everything and I followed close on their tail.

The staff at Bart's were expecting us. Jacky was immediately put on to a trolley and wheeled to the electronic scan which allowed the doctors to determine the seriousness of the damage. They also gave her an ECG which showed that the responses of her heart were in good order. As soon as they could they moved her upstairs to the W. G. Grace Ward where she stayed overnight, clinging on to life. The hospital advised us to get some rest because they did not know what we might have to face the next day. Nearby was the Royal Scot Hotel, and at 2 a.m. they were able to give us a room. But sleep did not come easily. As soon as it was light we were back at the hospital and made our way to the W. G. Grace Ward.

Most of the morning the doctors examined her, and they were a long time in consultation. Eventually they came to tell us that they had put her on a ventilator, and that they would like our permission to undertake some small surgery to her head to permit a sensor to be inserted to monitor the pressure on her brain. They would then move her to the intensive care unit.

When eventually we were able to see her she seemed very restless and her body would jerk constantly. It seemed as though she was reacting to the terror of the accident.

At the time she was connected to no fewer than sixteen monitors: cathodes, electrodes, catheters, probes and an ECG machine. They checked her pulse, blood pressure, breathing and the pressure in her skull, as well as many other minor functions. They told us what all the instruments meant: but for us, it was enough to know she was alive and we watched each flashing light, each moving needle and each LED read-out with great attention. A nurse was assigned to her full-time and every fifteen minutes she drained Jacky's lungs and checked all those instruments. Every slight variation seemed to us like an emergency! But the wonderful team of nurses treated it all philosophically.

The doctors took us off into a side room for a consultation. They told us they could not offer any promises – simply an expectation that she would pull through. Dr Watson, whom we had told of our faith in the power of prayer, said: 'I don't really believe in that, but I can tell you that I do have good vibes about your daughter. I believe she'll make it.'

That first morning a cable came from Billy Graham, assuring us of his prayer support. George Wilson in Minneapolis sent a cable to say that the whole Billy Graham team had been alerted and would be praying for us. Marilyn's mother, who herself was fighting the final stages of cancer, told us on the telephone that she had alerted all the praying members of the family in the USA, and also had told many of our friends. From Australia came a message to say that friends there were praying. Doug and May Brown, friends from our church in Frinton, told us that everyone in the church had been alerted to pray. Marilyn's Community Bible Study class was also alerted – a powerful group because they already had a prayer chain set up.

During those dark days, the wealth of prayer support was unbelievable. We had between six and eight key people to telephone each night, and they in turn passed on the day's news and prayer requests to countless others. We rang Walter Smyth who was in London; we rang George Wilson in Minneapolis and Marilyn's mother in the same city. We rang Doug Brown at Frinton; the office; our own family and two or three other key contacts daily. They each alerted many many more to pray.

Each day we were able to tell of special needs of which the nurses and doctors had told us.

It is strange how, sometimes, a very small thing can be of comfort and encouragement. I had to ask the ward sister for a medical certificate to pass to the hospital where Jacky was training. As Sister made out the form she said: 'I'll make it out for three weeks: then you can ask for another one.' That simple little statement gave me more encouragement than any other comment could have done. If Sister was talking about another certificate in the future, there must be hope!

The monitors flickered on. Our hopes and prayers rose and fell with the needles and numbers we watched. We had been told that one needle, in particular, needed to remain steady: it was the pressure in the skull reading. We were alarmed beyond all measure when one morning this reading started to rise alarmingly. The nurse spotted it immediately, and called the doctor, who came without delay. After examination, he discovered that the monitor was at fault; the proper reading was still acceptable.

During the first few days, we stayed the night in a room at the hospital. Then we moved back to the hotel room nearby so we could remain constantly on call.

Day by day there was no change. Inexorably the days passed by and we clutched at every hopeful sign – only to have that hope dashed the next time we came in. The hospital allowed us to spend 90 per cent of our waking hours with Jacky and the staff were marvellous.

They showed us how to help her. They told us of the importance of always talking to her – talking ... but receiving no response or reply. It is an uncanny feeling and hard to get used to. One of Jacky's friends came in to visit her. We told him to talk to her, and in two minutes he ran out of things to say. The next time he came in, he brought with him a card on which he had written down all the subjects to talk about.

We got a pillow speaker which we plugged into a cassette tape recorder. Then she could listen to speech and music tapes all the time. We were later to learn the significance of that.

One morning a lady came up to take a blood sample from Jacky. One of the nurses said: 'I think she knows you.' It transpired that she was the mother of one of my former secretaries. It was a small world. We got on very well with her and found that she had previously had connections with Hildenborough Hall. She had known us from that time.

One morning, on my way to the hospital from the office, I passed a shopping centre. A poster in the window of a dry cleaners declared: 'It's time you woke up.' I couldn't resist the temptation to stop the car and to ask the shop if they had a spare copy of that poster. They didn't, but a day or two later one arrived in the mail from the head office. We fixed it to the wall above Jacky's bed.

We had a visitor in the early days at the hospital. Sarah Whitfield was on the hospital staff and was the originator of a new hospital technique for caring for the relatives and friends of seriously ill patients. Her quiet and supportive nature meant a lot to us during those early days. In her we had someone to talk to about the treatment Jacky was getting.

Through her we were able to penetrate the bureaucracy and mysteries of the hospital. She told us the meaning of each new treatment; if we had concerns or worries, we could share them with her and we quickly learned that she would come back with an answer. It made such a difference and she was God's gift to us at a time of special need. We soon discovered that she was a Christian too. Fiona, Julian's wife, had told the Nurses' Christian Fellowship (of which Jacky was a member) and the NCF had alerted Sarah Whitfield.

The days passed and there was still no sign of her coming out of the coma. Gradually her physical condition improved as the body healed itself and day by day one or other of the monitors would be removed. It was strange how attached we had become to the monitors! How could she live without them? How could we know she was still alive and improving if we could not see the evidence on the monitors? One almost felt like asking the doctor to put them back – not for her, but for us!

Now the doctors began to warn us about her condition when she would finally wake up. She would be incoherent, they said. She would make uncontrollable noises and would not recognise us. After so long in a coma (now twelve days) we could expect very little from her. We alerted the prayer chains to pray that her mind would be kept away from this problem, and that God would give her normality when the time came.

One day we came in and the nurse said: 'Your daughter has opened her eyes: she's not conscious, and she hasn't come out of the coma – but it's a good sign.' We went in to see her, and it seemed impossible that those open eyes were not seeing us or comprehending anything. As the days passed, she was able to follow movements in front of her eyes – but she remained in a coma.

One of her visitors in the early days in the ICU was our own minister, Don Bridge from Frinton. He asked if he might pray for her and lay hands upon her. He asked us to be there in quiet prayer with him. He himself allowed the Spirit of God to flow through him and in silence he prayed for her. There was nothing mechanical about his approach; it was very meaningful and real. After Don Bridge left, Jacky seemed to have a new peace and quietness which was quite unbelievable.

One Saturday one of the nurses, who was twenty-one that day, told the unconscious Jacky that she was having a party that night, and afterwards would take her guests to see the Royal Ballet. On Monday morning she brought in a tape recording of the music of the ballet, which she allowed us to play on Jacky's cassette tape recorder.

The ventilator tube was eventually replaced when they performed an operation for a tracheostomy – inserting a tube in her throat. Later there came a day when they could no longer get an adequate vein for a blood transfusion. Marilyn and I were downstairs that day in the hospital church for the Sunday morning service. Out of the corner of our eye we saw Jacky's doctor come in and look around, but it did not seem that he was looking for us. When we went back to the ward after the service, Jacky's bed was empty. We were terrified that, after all, the worst had happened and that was why the doctor had been looking for us. But the nurse quickly reassured us. She said that Jacky had been taken to the operating theatre for a special insertion to be made in her chest to allow the transfusion to take place. It was a bit scary at the time, but Jacky was soon back in bed and none the worse for the operation.

It was a happy day when she could be moved – still in a coma – from the intensive care unit to an ordinary ward. Here, by comparison, she seemed to get no attention from the nurses. It was a hard adjustment for us to make, but they explained to us that she was improving so much that the intensive degree of nursing was no longer necessary.

Around the fortieth day, still in a coma, Jacky seemed to be showing slight responses. We developed these by changing our conversation. We would ask questions needing a 'yes' or 'no' response. We told her that a thumb up meant 'yes' and a thumb down meant 'no'. To our delight and incredible surprise, it worked! She got every question right and, a day or two later, was able to cope with more complicated responses. She was also able to be fed on normal food. It was all a good sign.

On the forty-ninth evening, several of her friends from Northwick Park Hospital came in to see her. Before coming to the hospital they had visited a McDonald's, and they came loaded down with hamburgers, French fries and milk shakes. Still in a comatose state, Jacky ate her fair share!

On the fiftieth day of the coma, Marilyn and I had been into the office first thing in the morning. We usually went there before going to the hospital; I could collect some work to take in and do during those periods when we could not be with Jacky. One of the staff, Margaret Birch, said to Marilyn: 'Fifty days: isn't fifty the time of jubilee and celebration?' Marilyn replied that she did not feel there was much to celebrate yet. The staff said that they would pray that today there would be cause for celebration.

I had to sit as a magistrate at Harrow Court that morning after leaving the office. Marilyn went to the hospital. After court I got a bleep on my bleeper. I had two numbers on the bleeper and this one meant that I was to ring the hospital. Such a bleep always caused my heart to stop because it was only used in emergencies.

I called the ward and the nurse answered. 'I have someone to talk to you,' she said. And there was Jacky on the line, lucid and clear – if a little husky and deep-voiced. 'Hello, Dad! This is your daughter Jacky!' she said. It was indeed a day of jubilee and celebration. Jacky had woken up on the fiftieth day after the accident. But more than that! Our prayers had been answered. She was not incoherent, she was not making uncontrollable noises – and she had recognised us.

Later, Marilyn told me what had happened. Day by day she had gone with Jacky for her physiotherapy treatment. She never knew if she might have to continue that treatment for a lifetime of unconsciousness, and she wanted to learn all about it. On this special morning, she was helping to undress Jacky when she ran her finger down the sole of Jacky's foot. She knew how much Jacky hated that, so as she did it, she said: 'One of these days, Jacky, you'll say "stop it" when I do that.' And Jacky instantly responded with 'Stop it'! And the miracle had happened! They were the first words she had spoken for fifty long days.

As soon as I got the message, I drove straight to the hospital and shared in the rejoicing which was going on around Jacky's bed. The prayer team was told and they gave thanks for answered prayer.

Later we heard that, at the very hour Jacky had woken up, Marilyn's prayer group had been in session for us. One of the ladies had prayed: 'Lord, let Jacky wake up – and let it happen now!' It would appear that the Lord answered that prayer instantly, because that prayer was spoken at just about the same time as Jacky said 'Stop it' in the physiotherapy room.

One of the first things we wanted to do was to establish how much Jacky could remember of the past. She had had her twenty-first birthday party at Frinton in May, and we first tried to see if she could remember that. She did – and then went on with this most surprising information: 'I remember it clearly. I took all my friends to the Royal Ballet.'

We remonstrated with her that she had done nothing of the kind, but she insisted she had and continued: 'I know I did, Dad, because I can still remember the music.' Then we recalled the nurse who had celebrated her twenty-first by taking her friends to the Royal Ballet and her kindness in bringing in the tape recording of the music for the unconscious Jacky to listen to. So both the words and the music had penetrated! We learned the importance of those days of sitting by her bed, constantly talking to her without response. Perhaps all our efforts contributed to the answered prayer that she should be lucid and normal upon waking up.

Jacky's recovery thus far allowed me to return to my responsibilities in the preparation for Mission England. During the dark days of the coma, my colleagues had been very kind and understanding, and had not made demands upon my time. I had managed to stay abreast of the day-to-day activity, but creative work had been put on stand-by! Now I was able to give more constructive time and help in the early days of planning for the nationwide event.

We still spent a lot of time at the hospital. Jacky needed

encouragement on a daily basis and we tried to help her in every way we could. One day I was sitting by her bed when I started to sing quietly to her, a song which we often sang together in the car: 'Toodle, looma looma, toodle eye aye.' No sooner had I started, than she joined in – word and tune perfect to the end. It was a further indication that her mind was clear and her memory of the Umbrella Song was mostly intact.

When we were visiting Jacky, we noticed that the agency nurses were required to wear sticky labels bearing their name. This helped the doctors and nurses to identify them. But often the labels were lost when they were brushed off the uniform by their arm. This was because the labels curled up so badly. One day I took the doctor aside and explained to him the difference between taking the label off the backing, and taking the backing off the label. The former method involved lifting a corner of the label and peeling it off the backing. Always it came off with a curl. On the other hand, if you placed the label face down upon your hand and peeled off the backing, the label remained perfectly flat. Used like that, it was never lost because it was not brushed off by the arm. The doctor was so impressed that he wrote the details in the ward instructions for everybody to follow, and we felt we had made some small contribution to the efficiency of the ward.

But the days of anxiety were by no means over for us. As she walked from her bed to the bathroom one afternoon, I noticed that she was limping badly. I told the nurse who immediately called the doctor. Apparently, Jacky had noticed this previously when she was in the physiotherapy department, and they too had told the doctor. Jacky was diagnosed as having a deep vein thrombosis in the left leg. In minutes they had the foot of her bed lifted up and a drip connected with a solution to dissolve the blood clot. It was in a dangerous position in the groin. If it moved from there, it might go straight to the lung which could cause instant death. We had some anxious days while we watched her progress.

Then, to compound our anxieties, news reached us from the United States that Marilyn's mother was rapidly going downhill. On Sunday, October 31st, we had two important pieces of news – one sad, one glad. A phone call from Minneapolis said that Mrs Sandberg, Marilyn's mother, had died that morning.

It seemed as though she had held on to life as long as there was a need of prayer for Jacky. Once Jacky had woken up and all seemed to be going well, it was as though she had felt ready and able to enter heaven, and she relinquished life. A little later the same day came a second call, from our son Gary, to say that his wife Diana had given birth that morning to our second grandson, Andrew Mark. 'The Lord gave: the Lord taketh away. Blessed be the Name of the Lord!'

Because of Jacky's condition, Marilyn had not been able to fly to Minneapolis to be with her mother during her last days. Now she wanted to go for the funeral and we felt that it was right that she should. She told Jacky all about it. Jacky wasn't too happy, but brightened up when she heard that our good friend Rita Payne would come and sit with her the first day, and Auntie Joyce (my cousin Joyce Bell) would come on the second day. So she accepted the short separation and was content with the arrangements which had been made.

We were all glad to see Marilyn back – not least Jacky. A week later there was a most moving event. On November 14th it was Remembrance Sunday. Many of the patients had walked (or, like Jacky, had gone in their wheelchairs) to the hospital day room. There was a television set there, and the patients wanted to watch the ceremony at the Cenotaph.

There were about twenty-five patients in the room in various stages of recovery – none, it appeared, as bad as Jacky, who sat slumped in her wheelchair. She was finding it hard to gather the strength to hold up her head, but when she did, she looked almost normal. The service at the Cenotaph proceeded to the point where Her Majesty the Queen was to arrive. As the strains of the National Anthem started, Jacky made a superhuman effort and – for the first time since her accident – stood by herself without any helping hand. She remained standing while the National Anthem played, and then sat herself down again. She was the only one in the room standing: most of the others couldn't, and there was scarcely a dry eye to be seen.

From then on it was all downhill. It was a question of building up strength and stamina. We were impressed with the way in which the nurses at Bart's respected Jacky's training as a nurse. They never talked down to her. When the doctor came to give her a pain-killing drug, he told her what was on offer and left her to choose which she would prefer. From her knowledge, she chose the one with the least problems and he complimented her on her choice. When she had the thrombosis the nurses told her that she had a DVT; it was she who translated that for us. One of her nursing chums from Northwick Park Hospital came in to visit her and saw Jacky's bed propped up at the foot. 'Whatever's wrong with you?' she asked and Jacky replied, in her post-coma deep-throated voice, 'I've got a DVT in my left leg!'

Shortly before Christmas she was judged well enough to be moved to the Regional Neurological Rehabilitation Unit at Eastern Hospital in Hackney. There had been plans to send her several weeks earlier, but the DVT prevented that. At Eastern they put Jacky through a rigorous recovery training programme. Each day they pushed her a bit more and bit by bit she fully recovered her faculties.

A week before Christmas they told us that she could come home for the festive season, and we prepared for that event. That Christmas was one of the happiest we had ever spent.

On Christmas Day the telephone rang and I answered it. It was clearly a transatlantic call because of the echo on the line, and there was Billy Graham. Surprised that he should call us on Christmas Day, I hardly knew what to say to him – but I needn't have worried. 'I don't want to speak to you,' he said, 'I want to speak to your daughter!' For the next twenty minutes they had a conversation together while we, as a family, marvelled that this wonderful man should have taken time out to make that telephone call. It meant so much to all of us, especially Jacky.

After Christmas it was back to Eastern Hospital in Hackney. By that time, our hearts were so full of thankfulness to God that we wanted to do no more than to share that feeling with all our friends. So we planned a Thanksgiving Service at St Paul's Church, Robert Adam Street. On March 19th, 1983, almost 250 people – relations, friends, colleagues at work, colleagues from the Billy Graham team, nurses and doctors – came to join us for that service.

Among the doctors was Dr Watson the consultant from the hospital whom we had seen the very first night. It was he who had said to us that although he didn't believe in prayer and all that sort of thing, he had good vibes about Jacky. His words had been a great encouragement to us that first day. Yet we had not seen him again throughout the time that Jacky was in hospital. So it was a special thrill for us that he had taken the time to come to the thanksgiving service – and we told him so after it was over.

Left:
1984. Billy
Graham appearing
on the BBC News.

Above:
The Billy Graham Board of Directors, 1984.
From left to right: Alistair Rennie, Barbara Smith, Ruth Rennie,
*Mark Smith, *Clarence Jeffries, *David Rennie, *Maurice
Rowlandson, *Walter Smyth, Lady Brentford, *Lord Brentford,
Ruth Graham and Billy Graham. (*Director)

Left:
Mission England, 1989.
The 1,000,000th visitor:
Alan Paget speaks to
Billy Graham.

Below:
Billy Graham as millions
remember him.

Above:
Maurice and
Marilyn
Rowlandson.

Right:
Marilyn
Rowlandson talks
with Ruth Graham
during Mission
England.

Above:
The Venturers'
Cruise. Henry
Hole is third
from left in the
back row,
Maurice
Rowlandson
second from left
in the front.

Above:
The Rowlandson family reunion. *From
left to right in the back row*: Rachel, Jacky,
Jeff Davies; *seated*: Fiona, Maurice,
Marilyn, Diana, Gary; *front*: Julian,
Matthew, Timothy, Andrew.

A few days before the service I had been driving to Frinton. As usual, I was listening to tapes in the car and among them was a tape of David Kossoff's *You Have A Minute, Lord?*. On this tape he had his poem about his younger son's remarkable return from a near-to-death illness. As I listened, everything he said exactly applied to Jacky's recovery – and with little changes I felt it would be exactly right to read at the start of the service.

Marilyn agreed, but said that she thought I ought to check it with David Kossoff first. We had met him on a number of occasions as a result of his book of bible stories and Marilyn was anxious that we did not offend him by making these changes. So I wrote to him and told him of our intentions.

A day or two later he telephoned me. 'I would be delighted for you to adapt the piece,' he said, and added, 'and if you wish I'll come and read it.' It was a generous and wonderful gesture and we appreciated it. So the service started with David Kossoff:

How lovely you look, how elegant our Jacky
    in your outfit light and stylish
Bought by your mother while
    you lay flat on a tilted hospital bed.
To you, dear Jacky, just another outfit
For your mother and dad, and all your friends, so much more.
    A symbol of hope, a sign of new life.
Celebration clothes for a given-back daughter.

For given back, you were, dear Jacky.
    Fought for, by young doctors and tireless
    nurses with swift competent hands.
You nearly died, dear Jacky; virtually you were dead.
    We will call things by their right names.
    You were dead; and then alive again.
    Gone away . . . and then brought back.
    By doctors and nurses . . . and God.

Monitor screens and tubes and
    pipes and wires and drugs, and God.
Intensive care technique and
    ceaseless vigilance and skill and God.
A quick and lively smile you had for dad,
    with his talk of thanks to God.

But we will call things by their right names,
   and the giver of life is God.

So back with the living you were,
   Model patient, uncomplaining with
   natural good manners and humour.
A fighting constitution, from strong
   and determined forebears, gave you swift recovery,
And the colour came back, and the mind
   awoke, unimpaired, and the heart, so recently
   nearly stilled, so nearly silent,
   beat again strong and true.

By your bed we sat, dear Jacky, and
   looked at a recently re-born daughter
   our family miracle.
Soon well enough to celebrate your
   recovery, in your hospital room,
With loving friends
   who came in many guises!
Our miracle daughter, soon ready to go home
   – and to resume a life of service

Soon to re-enter your world
   and life style
Soon to nurse others
   as you yourself were nursed
   – with skilful loving hands
   and careful watching.
Knowing that all depends on your vigilance
and competence – and God.

There was a real spirit of thanksgiving in the service. Jacky acquitted herself well in an interview with Mike Hawken, the curate from her church. The message of thanksgiving was brought by the Reverend Don Bridge, whose visit to her in the hospital had meant so much. All of those who took part were deeply moved by the occasion. Billy Graham had asked our dear friend Blair Carlson to be present. He willingly came and read a message from Mr Graham as well as adding his own reflections. We appreciated all of those who came and especially those who took part. Among them were representatives of the prayer teams and they told of the blessing in their own lives as a result of this involvement.

Jacky's recovery was 90 per cent: she was left with double vision in the left eye and restricted width vision, a factor which made it impossible for her to continue her training as a nurse. For one year after her recovery, she attempted to achieve a satisfactory result and, indeed, passed her hospital finals. But they would not let her take her national finals: they knew she would pass, and they felt some responsibility towards the patients she would be treating. With the handicap of her sight, they felt it would be unwise to register her. So she went on to another career as a teacher, and gained a Bachelor of Education degree with Honours from St Paul and St Mary College in Cheltenham, in 1990. During her third year, she married a young man from Cambray Baptist Church (where they both attended). She and her husband, Jeff Davies, a Welshman from the Abercyon Valley, made their home in Cheltenham. Two years later she presented him and us with Rachel Anwen, our first grand-daughter.

Now that she was fully recovered, I was able to return full-time to the work of Mission England. The focus was on the month of May 1984 when it was due to start in Bristol. Earlier that year, in January, Billy Graham had come to Britain to fulfil a number of advance engagements. In many ways these were all in anticipation of the mission to be held five months later. Not least of these was his invitation to preach at the Royal Chapel in Sandringham.

During the same visit, he appeared on several television programmes. One of these was the *Russell Harty Show*. This chat show host liked his guests to be seen sipping a drink. A letter a week or two later in the *Christian Herald* severely reprimanded Mr Graham for drinking alcohol on the programme. A correspondent replied the following week: 'We are writing in defence of Billy Graham. We wonder if C. C. McFee was watching the *Russell Harty Show* on a black and white television set, and didn't realise that Dr Graham's drink was clearly a deep red tomato juice as against the wine in the other glasses.' It was always a happy event when others leapt to our defence. Actually, we never replied ourselves to inaccurate reports in the newspaper. We always felt that it was better to let others do it for us – and generally they did. It was Abraham Lincoln who said:

If I were to try to read, much less answer all the attacks made on me, this shop might as well be closed for any other business. I do the very best I know how, and mean to keep doing so until the end. If the end brings me out right, what is said against me won't amount to anything. If the end brings me out wrong, ten angels saying I was right would make no difference!

People are very quick to write in accusation, and very slow to acknowledge they were wrong! If a report appears in the press, however inaccurate it may be, it is believed in preference to the truth. I have a treasured press cutting. A single column about eight inches long, it reports an event in which I was involved. In that brief report, there are no fewer than twenty-eight factual errors.

On May 4th, 1984 Mr Graham arrived in London for numerous pre-mission engagements. When I met him at the airport he could scarcely talk; he had a bad case of laryngitis. We learned that, at the recent crusade in Alaska, his voice had been so bad that in the middle of his address one of his associate evangelists had had to take over from him. It was the first time that had ever happened.

The first thing he wanted to do was to visit Dr Williams in Harley Street. Dr Williams had treated him on a number of earlier occasions and Mr Graham had great faith in him. It took only minutes for the doctor to decide that a consultation with an ear, nose and throat specialist was required – but it was the bank holiday weekend. Which one of them would be available? Dr Williams tried thirty-seven consultants and in the end contacted the top man of them all, Mr Ian Fraser. He was in town and would be glad to see Mr Graham. We were given an immediate appointment and T. W. Wilson and I walked with Mr Graham up Harley Street to Mr Fraser's consulting rooms.

It was precisely at 12 noon on Friday of the bank holiday weekend when the blow fell! After seeing Mr Fraser, Billy Graham came downstairs and whispered: 'He wants to do an operation on me, and he wants to do it right away!' Visions of all Mr Graham's appointments during the next seven days floated before me and I thought of the re-arranging that would be necessary.

A few minutes later, Mr Fraser himself came down the stairs and told me: 'I will operate on him at 8 a.m. tomorrow morning at the Royal Masonic Hospital.'

'Not there!' I exclaimed. 'Isn't there another hospital we could go to?' But no: that was where Mr Fraser operated, and that was where it would have to be. I remember telling T. W. Wilson: 'That will be good for some three hundred letters!' In the event I was not far wrong! As soon as the news got out, through the newspapers, the letters started to arrive. 'Is Mr Graham a Freemason?' was the most usual question. Many others wanted to know why he had gone there rather than somewhere else. There were even those who said 'better no operation, than an operation there!' Every one of them had to be answered as graciously and informatively as possible.

Years afterwards the Royal Masonic Hospital was implementing a new constitution, the adoption of which prompted the resignation of two members of the royal family. In reporting this event on November 30th, 1991, the *Daily Telegraph* commented: 'One Masonic source, however, said it was the Royal Masonic Hospital which cured Billy Graham, the evangelist, of a sinus infection in 1984. "Perhaps he can help," he joked.' Even many years later the incident was still with us!*

Early the next morning, T. W. Wilson and I collected Mr Graham and took him to the hospital. He was in surgery until about 10 a.m. and when he came back to the ward he was still very groggy. Mr Fraser came with him, and I said (in passing), 'I'll have to make arrangements to cancel his preaching engagement at Westminster Chapel tomorrow evening.'

To my surprise, Mr Fraser told me not to bother. 'He'll preach,' he said. 'He'll have recovered enough to do that – and all his other engagements this week.'

Around 10.30 a.m. Mr Graham began to wake up from the anaesthetic, and turning to T. W. Wilson and me he said: 'Now there's some things I want you boys to do.' He went on to try to tell us about the cancellations. T. W. Wilson gently told him: 'Now don't you worry about that, Billy. You just lie there and get some rest, and we'll be back later to see you.' With that, he ushered me out of the room and we did not return until the afternoon.

Mr Fraser was true to his word. Around 4 p.m. on Sunday, I collected Mr Graham from the hospital and took him to Westminster Chapel for a crowded 6.30 p.m. service. As he

* Mr Ian Fraser has stated that he is not in any position to comment on the reasons why members of the royal family resigned over matters relating to the constitution of the Royal Masonic Hospital. This is something for others to do. He has no connection with the comments in the *Daily Telegraph*.

preached – with slightly less fervour than usual – the hospital band on his wrist was clearly visible. He gave an appeal at the end of the service and there was a significant response. Afterwards we took him back to hospital.

The next day he left hospital for a short while to do a television recording for the programme *Sixty Minutes*. On Tuesday we collected him from the hospital for the last time. He was to have lunch with Rupert Murdoch and fourteen editors of national daily newspapers at the offices of *The Times* in Grays Inn Road. He was warmly received by them all, and the luncheon was a noteworthy engagement prior to the mission.

When we came to leave, the commissionaire on the door could not remember where he had parked my car. Nor could he find the keys. I was comforted that even high-powered business houses could make mistakes like this. Eventually he solved both problems, but we were delayed a little in getting away. This created a slight difficulty, as Mr Graham had an engagement at BBC Television at Lime Grove with the Reverend Colin Morris. He was to record four television programmes based upon Mr Graham's recent book *The Four Horsemen of the Apocalypse*. For someone who had just left hospital it was a strenuous agenda. Not content with that, when we arrived at the studios, we were told that the ten-minute programme recorded on the Monday had not been satisfactory and would Mr Graham please redo it.

On Wednesday he travelled to Bristol in preparation for the heavy schedule of engagements there. First was the press conference followed by a reception for the local committee and the rehearsal and dedication meeting on Friday. Then there was the opening meeting of Mission England on the Saturday night.

The planning and preparation was of the same high standard that we had come to expect from the Billy Graham team. It was no surprise, therefore, at Bristol to find the crowds streaming in on the opening night. It may not have been a surprise . . . but it was a most moving experience. What had first been a burden in October 1975 now came to full fruition with the opening meeting at Bristol. In between there had been gigantic traumas, frustrations, consultations and innumerable committees. But God had brought it all to happen in His own perfect timing.

One event took place in Bristol which deserves a mention. It was the arrival of my Executel on May 25th, 1984! My friends and colleagues have always regarded me as a gadget person and

I suppose I was. All the gadgets I used had to make a positive contribution to handling the work better, quicker and more efficiently. If that was the criterion, then my Executel fulfilled it superbly.

It came about because of our need to send telexes from the press desk. To use the hotel facilities was both expensive and slow. Furthermore, such a route did not provide the confidentiality which we often demanded. So we examined various portable telex machines, all of which had some flaw in our specification. Then, out of the blue, someone showed me an advertisement for the STC Executel. Basically, it was a combined computer and telephone. Numbers were recorded and automatically dialled; there was an alarm facility which reminded you of uncompleted calls; there was a built-in calculator, sixty-year calendar, diary facility, rapid-dial system, and so much more. But especially useful to us, there was the means to send and receive a telex.

Later I was to discover that I could get airline schedules, bank exchange rates, railway timetables and loads of other useful information for which I was constantly being asked. It also had an electronic banking facility. Immediately after we had installed it, it began to earn its keep and has been a godsend to me ever since. I take it everywhere.

Mission England in 1984 was by no means devoid of stories. In Sunderland, the weather was atrocious. Not only did it rain, but it was bitterly cold. Mr Graham struggled against the biting wind and in the end took to preaching in a cloth cap. A day or so later it got even colder and he announced from the platform that he was preaching in two sets of thermal underwear. This news even made headlines on the front page of *The Times*. On the radio, a commentator remarked: 'Could this be the gospel according to longjohns?'

Two things happened in Liverpool. First there was an earthquake. It measured 5.6 on the Richter scale. At the time I was sitting at the press desk in the team office. Everything shook violently. Later, John Wesley White (one of the associate evangelists) reported that he was on the diving board in the swimming pool. He wondered why the board was vibrating so strongly when he hadn't moved! Later he told us that he thought of the Scripture: 'There shall be earthquakes in diverse places.'

Also in Liverpool we got some exciting news: Larry Ross was engaged! Cliff Barrows announced it from the platform that evening and told how Larry had rented a fifty-foot advertisement hoarding in Dallas and had had it painted: 'Autumn, will you marry me?' She had borrowed a ladder and in red paint had painted the word 'YES' all over it! Johnny Lenning, Bev Shea and John Wesley White broke the news of her acceptance to Larry at 6.30 a.m. the following day. They brought him three trays, one with a gigantic steak breakfast (Texas style), a second tray with his coffee, and the third with some toast. Each tray had a letter upon it, spelling out Y–E–S. That same day, the Holiday Inn in Liverpool where we were all staying put a notice on their big announcement board outside the hotel: 'Autumn tells Larry "yes" '!

At the end of the mission came one of the best tributes of all to the planning and ministry of Mission England '84. It was contained in a letter addressed to Gavin Reid, and came from the Archbishop of Canterbury, Dr Robert Runcie:

> I wanted to thank you for all you have achieved with this ambitious project. It has certainly been a massive undertaking, and I have heard many exciting reports about its success in all kinds of ways. I have heard much too about your own central part in it all. You have evidently worked with enormous dedication and industry, and I would like to express my own personal and sincere appreciation.
>
> Of course, it will take time for the full fruits of Mission England to ripen, but I am confident that we have in this country a rich harvest to look forward to.

And that about summed it up. It was a lovely tribute to receive to wrap up all the hard work and planning that had gone into this remarkable year.

As I stood in the centre of the pitch at the Ipswich football stadium and let the last meeting permeate my soul, I said to myself: 'Maurice, drink it in, and remember it. This may never happen again in your lifetime.' I wanted to remember an era which had meant so much in my life, and to record, in memory, this last mission meeting.

A year later Mr Graham unexpectedly responded to an invitation to conduct a mission in Sheffield. On the last day of those meetings I stood in the centre of the pitch at the Sheffield football stadium, and said to myself: 'Maurice, drink it in, and remember it . . . !' The folk in Sheffield had been disappointed not to be included in the 1984 plans, and they had presented such a good case to Mr Graham that he consented to return to Britain for that one special week in 1985. It became an out-of-season mission meeting! But it was again remarkable and singularly blessed by God.

During the latter part of that mission, the Reverend Richard Bewes, Vicar of All Souls Church, Langham Place in London, began to make noises about the major spiritual needs of the capital city. He gathered around him a group of Christian leaders and a united approach was made to Mr Graham to come once more to London. Once again, the case they presented was so good that Mr Graham could not refuse and in 1989 he came for a unique series, organised from the centre, but held in four locations: West Ham football stadium, Crystal Palace, Earls Court, and a final one-day meeting in Wembley Stadium. All the locations were a total success. Once more, the full story has been told elsewhere. The whole programme went like clockwork under the overall direction of Blair Carlson.

At Crystal Palace, on the opening night, there was a total transport strike in the London area. This did not prevent the gathering of the largest crowd ever to have attended an event at Crystal Palace, when more than 30,000 people packed in.

Earls Court was full night after night, with many leaders and people with wide influence attending. One night, in June 1989, among the VIP guests were the Bishop of London (the Right Reverend Graham Leonard) and Cardinal Hume. They came to a special reception first, to which all VIP guests were invited. Shortly before the meeting started, Mr Graham sent me round to the VIP room to bring them in to see him. That room was on the same level as Mr Graham's platform room, but around two sides of the building. As we walked together from the reception to Mr Graham's room there were innumerable doors to pass through. I apologised to my two guests, each of whom deferred to the other at each doorway. It became quite confusing. As we reached the last pair of doors, I told them we were almost there. Cardinal Hume turned to the Bishop of London and said: 'Your grace, is this doorway an Anglican one, or a Roman Catholic one?' as he stood back to let the Bishop of London go through first.

After Billy Graham had greeted the two men, I escorted them to a box at the side of the arena. I later learned that both men were deeply moved by the meeting – in Cardinal Hume's case, especially by Billy Graham's invitation to the audience to come forward and to make a commitment to Christ.

During Mission '89 someone drew a cartoon picture which they presented to us in the office. Whenever there is a mission, Mr Graham is accommodated in a different hotel from the rest of the team. That way he can rest between engagements without always feeling under pressure. To avoid the press locating him, we never give out the name of that hotel; it is always referred to as 'the other place'. One of our drivers would be assigned to take any items to 'the other place' and he alone knew where it was. This cartoon was of a tombstone, and on the stone was the name of Billy Graham, with the epitaph: 'He is not here, he's at the other place.'

If 1955 had been Wembley in the rain then 1989 was Wembley in the torrential rain! No sooner had the meeting started than the heavens opened and we saw rain like Noah must have seen in the flood. It came down so heavily that at times the platform, on the other side of the stadium, was almost obscured. Then, just as we reached the offering, the thunder and lightning came. Gavin Reid had come to the microphone and had just said: 'Now I want to talk to you about money . . . ' and as he reached the word 'money', a thunderbolt struck the microphone boom immediately in front of the platform. Like a bomb exploding the thunder roared with an instantaneous bolt of lightning. Gavin Reid could scarcely have sought a more dramatic introduction! But the rain did not deter the audience. When Mr Graham gave the invitation, they poured out across the turf from the stands, leaving the comfort of protection for the extremes of exposure to the weather. It was a moving and remarkable sight.

At Wembley, I stood in the middle of the famous turf, and I said to myself: 'Maurice, drink it in, and remember it . . . ' because this time, it really must be the last. Only two years later I was standing in Celtic Park, Glasgow, saying it all over again. It seems that God is keeping us on our toes.

At both Mission '89, and at the Billy Graham in Scotland Mission, I had the privilege of being invited to run the team office. In 1989, Liz Fane was my main sidekick; in Scotland she helped again for part of the time, until Sally Lambert and Amanda

Bragg took over. It is always a highlight experience for all of us when we are able to serve in the team office in this way.

There was an occasion during Mission '89 when, as part of the team office responsibilities, I had taken Jean Wilson's car to have it cleaned and polished ready for her to use with Ruth Graham. I collected the car in the afternoon and promised her that I would deliver it to a parking space near to her flat in the West End and put the keys through her letter box that evening.

I found a good parking place, but when I went to deliver the keys I couldn't remember the number of her flat. For a moment I was puzzled about what to do. Then I spotted a telephone box on the street corner – and I remembered her telephone number. So I dialled the number and then dashed into the block of flats to find in which one a telephone was ringing! Through remarkable resourcefulness (if I may say so) the keys were safely delivered.

For mere Sassenachs, the Scottish crusade was difficult. The culture is different and the approach needed to be changed. Yet the Scots welcomed us all very warmly, even if the weather in Aberdeen was as cold as any we had ever experienced.

The warmth of our fellowship in the team office made up for the cold weather. Not least was this due to our friend Pek Gunn. He was an eighty-eight-year-old American from Nashville, Tennessee. In earlier years he had organised train parties from Nashville to any city in America in which Billy Graham might be conducting a crusade. Every train party always invited local dignitaries and all the crusade committee members to a Tennessee Breakfast in one of the local hotels.

Pek brought a planeload (not a trainload) to the London crusade at Earls Court in 1966. As usual he laid on the Tennessee Breakfast, this time at the Hilton Hotel in Park Lane. Breakfast consisted of a thick gammon steak, egg and grits (a Tennessee speciality) and sorghum sauce over it all. All the ingredients, except the eggs, had been flown in with the party from Tennessee.

Unsure whether the chefs at the Hilton would know the right way to cook a Tennessee ham, and almost certain they would not know how to prepare grits, Pek Gunn went through to the kitchen and stood over them while the work was done. This unusual and tasty breakfast was served to some 800 guests.

Now, at the invitation of T. W. Wilson, Pek Gunn had come to Scotland. He was a dear old man whose eighty-eight years were belied by his energy and enthusiasm. There was something about him that drew out the motherly instinct in all the girls on the staff and team. They looked after him, even in some of the strange requests he made. One evening, at dinner in the hotel, he looked at the menu and turned to Liz Fane. 'I believe I'd just like a bowl of cereal,' he said. Off went Liz to talk to the waitresses and, of course, they were able to provide what he wanted.

He was a poet: he entertained many of us at the table with his delightful recitation of poetry which he himself had written. At the end of the mission he gave each of us a book of his poems. Some were humorous, like this one entitled 'Calisthenical Neglect':

> If I had worked to keep in trim
>   By going often to the gym
> To exercise and swim and bowl
>   I wouldn't have this bulging roll!

Others were philosophical. This one was called 'Integrity':

> You won't go very far
>   If the person you are,
>   Is not trusted
>   And true and tried;
> And I'll wager a guess
>   That the door to success
>   Will be closed,
>   And your entrance denied.
>
> You can go mighty far
>   If the person you are,
>   Is trusted
>   And tried and true
> And the door to success
>   Will be open, I guess,
>   And the keeper will
>   Pass you right through.

When we had finished in Edinburgh, we moved the team office up to Aberdeen. Liz Fane had arranged for all the cars and the minibus to be transferred, while the rest of us moved the equipment. As in Mission England, we packed up the office in one place overnight, and opened the next office in the new place by lunchtime.

Pek arrived in Aberdeen and immediately started talking about taking a plane to Wick. Apparently there was a Gunn family Museum in Wick, founded by an ancestor, and Pek simply had to see it. Someone had given him the name of a hotel in Wick and from the telephone on my desk he called the number. He was told that the hotel was completely full. 'Give me the name of another hotel,' he asked, and was told that as Wick was a very small place, there was no other hotel. Pek replied: 'Well I guess I'll just come on up anyway. If nothing else, the manager can always move out of his room!' There was a seat on the flight to Wick, and to the concern of each of us, off went Pek Gunn with his little bag and no one to look after him. Worse still, he had no assured accommodation.

Shortly after he left, we needed to use the minibus, but we could not find the keys anywhere. There were several boys helping us as drivers and I made each of them turn out their pockets. We emptied the wastepaper baskets to make sure they hadn't fallen in there, and we went through the desk drawers. The keys were nowhere to be found. Suddenly we remembered Liz Fane. After completing the transfer of the office, Liz had had to return to London. We decided she must have taken the keys with her. As soon as we judged that she would be home we telephoned her – but no, she didn't have (and couldn't remember handling) the keys. So there was nothing for it but to call the AA and ask them to break into the minibus. None of us stopped to think that, even if we got in, we would need a key for the ignition.

No sooner had the AA man succeeded (after a struggle) in gaining access to the minibus than the telephone rang. 'Is that Maureece?' – it was Pek. 'Say, Maureece, are you missing some keys?'

It transpired that, when he had sat at my desk making telephone calls, he had picked the keys up with his papers and put them into his pocket. We learned that they had found a room for him in the hotel in Wick – how could they have failed? And the keys? Pek handed me over to the manager of the hotel. 'So you've got Mr Gunn with you?' I asked. 'We have indeed,' he replied in a broad Scottish accent. We talked about how best to get the keys back to us. The manager said that there was a bus from Wick to Aberdeen the next morning, arriving at Aberdeen at 1.40 p.m. He asked that someone should be there to meet the bus. He would give the keys to the driver, he said. And there were the keys for us the next day – an example of Scottish efficiency in the simple things of life! Four days later Pek returned with a shining face and endless stories – and poems – about his trip.

A second story, also set in Aberdeen, is told about Pek Gunn. One morning, shortly before we were due to pack up the office and move to Glasgow, Pek came to me and said: 'Maureece, I'm an old train man. I believe I'd like to ride train from Aberdeen to Glasgow. Would that be OK?' I told him that it was a delightful idea, and that I was sure he would enjoy it. On the spur of the moment, he looked at Amanda Bragg, the twenty-six-year-old secretary who had been helping me, and said: 'Amanda, you'll come with me?'

'Of course, Pek,' she said, 'if you'd like that.' It could have been no other way. I think that, if Pek hadn't invited her, she would have invited herself, for they were all concerned about Uncle Pek going by himself on the train.

That night, in the VIP room at the mission, Pek came up to me and said: 'Maureece: you know that young Amanda says she'll ride train with me to Glasgow. Do you think that's all right?' I assured him it was perfectly in order, and that I was glad he'd have company. 'Well, that's all right then,' he said, and added, 'You see, I just didn't want folks talking!'

Marilyn was able to take a couple of days off from her study work for her leadership of the Community Bible Studies in London. She flew up to Glasgow to be with us. On the morning I went to the airport, Pek asked if he could ride along with me 'to meet your lady wife', he said. I told him I'd love to have him with us. When Marilyn arrived, he made her a bow and said: 'I'm going to make you a queen,' and he lifted her hand to his lips and gave her a kiss. Then all the way from the airport to the hotel, he recited appropriate poetry to her.

When it came time to say goodbye to Pek, he taught us the Pek Gunn farewell handshake. It consisted of six movements, and took quite a bit of learning:

First, you linked right hand little fingers in an S hook;

Second, while still linked you brought the ball of each
   thumb together;
Third, you released the little fingers and slid the hand
   into a conventional handshake;
Fourth, you slid this around to grasp each other's thumb;
Fifth, you let go and hooked all four fingers and gave a
   gentle pull and push;
Finally you let go once more, clenched your fist and gave
   a friendly punch to your opposite number, fist to fist.

Pek will live long in our memories!

Mission Scotland was a memorable mission. The message
had been preached, and the Scots had responded – despite
warnings to the contrary – by coming to the front in great
numbers. The enquirers were counselled; among them was a
senior police officer. It was all very thrilling and humbling to
have been involved in this way once again.

We left Scotland conscious of the fact that there were no more
outstanding invitations to Mr Graham to return to Britain. It is
hard to contemplate that it will never happen again, unless . . .

10

Occasions of Honour

Discretion has always been an essential part of Billy Graham's contact with international leaders. That has been equally true of those special occasions when he has been honoured with an invitation from our own royal family.

In all the occasions when I have had the privilege of driving him to and from such an appointment, I have never heard any comment on his conversations with them. He rigorously resists the temptation to tell it all: most of us would have a hard time not to share everything that happened!

His first contact came in 1954 after lengthy correspondence between Mr John Cordle (later a Member of Parliament for Bournemouth) and Mrs Olivia Mulholland, a lady-in-waiting to Queen Elizabeth the Queen Mother. Mrs Mulholland had been invited to a luncheon with Billy Graham. On April 7th she wrote to say that, having met Billy Graham, she would like to go to Harringay.

About a month later, Mr Cordle wrote to Mr John Colville and suggested a constitutional approach to Her Majesty the Queen to extend an invitation to Mr Graham to meet her. Mr Colville advised John Cordle that a far less formal approach would be appropriate and that the Queen might meet Billy Graham in Scotland while he was on a short holiday there.

A day or two later, John Cordle had an appointment with an old friend at Buckingham Palace to discuss the possibilities of a meeting, as a result of which Sir John Carew Pole (a close friend of royalty and a personal friend of Brigadier Sir Norman Gwatkin, Equerry to King George VI) intervened. His advice to

John Cordle was to wait until Mr Graham returned to Britain in 1955.

This advice was accepted and Mr Graham later received an invitation to visit Clarence House and to meet the Queen Mother. On May 17th, 1955 he accepted that invitation and met both the Queen Mother and Princess Margaret. A few days later a further invitation came for him to meet the (late) Duchess of Kent. She later attended one of the meetings at Wembley Stadium.

The *Daily Express* gave coverage to an invitation which followed the Duchess of Kent's visit to Wembley. They reported that Mr Graham had been invited to preach at the Royal Chapel in Windsor Great Park on May 23rd, 1955. Present at that service were Her Majesty the Queen, Prince Philip, the Queen Mother and Princess Margaret. Afterwards Mr Graham and his wife Ruth were invited to luncheon with the Queen and Prince Philip and members of the royal household at Windsor Castle.

Four years later he received a further invitation to visit Buckingham Palace where a newspaper recorded, 'he had a long private talk with the Queen'.

In June 1966 an invitation arrived for Billy and Ruth Graham to have lunch with the royal family at Buckingham Palace, one of several similar invitations to come in future years.

My own involvement in the connections of Billy Graham with royalty did not arise until October 1971 when he asked me to organise a special dinner party for him. During the 1966/67 meetings, Princess Alexandra had shown a great interest in the crusade and had invited the Grahams to dinner. In 1971, Mr Graham was invited to address the National Institute of Directors' annual meeting in the Royal Albert Hall. He decided to use that visit to London to reciprocate with an invitation to the Princess and her husband. He asked me to book a private room at the Dorchester Hotel and gave me his list of guests to be invited. These included the then Foreign Secretary, Sir Alec Douglas-Home; Mr John Watson, the American ambassador and Mrs Watson; Mr Michael Alison MP and Mrs Alison; and singer Cliff Richard. There were around twelve guests in all.

As the day approached, Billy Graham arrived at London Airport and I took him to the London Hilton. Because he had a special privileged card at the time, he was able to stay there without any charge other than meals. On October 31st,

the day on which the dinner was to be held, I spent some time
with him during the day and he bombarded me with questions
about the evening. How should he address the Princess? Where
should everybody sit? Should he speak first, or should it be
the Princess? What about Angus Ogilvy – where should he
sit? He was quite anxious about the whole affair, and hoped
it would work out smoothly. The main problem was that he
didn't have Ruth with him. She had been unable to come
to London, and he was unused to dealing with these special
affairs without her help. So it was left to T. W. Wilson and me
to advise him as best we could.

At the right time we collected him from his room at the Hilton
Hotel, and walked with him up to the Dorchester. He was like
a cat on hot bricks during that short walk but immediately we
walked into the private room at the Dorchester he relaxed. It
was a lovely, quiet room with wall panelling, and there was
something about it that breathed tranquillity.

As the first guests arrived, he turned to T. W. Wilson and me
and said: 'You can both go back and have your dinner with
your guests now. Thanks for coming over with me,' and we
were dismissed. T. W. Wilson turned to me saying, 'Maurice,
I didn't like that. I wanted to stop and meet the Princess.' He
then led the way to the front lobby of the hotel, and indicated
to me to stand back with him in the shadows. 'We'll wait here
and watch her come in,' he said.

In a few minutes, through the revolving door came the Princess . . . alone. The porters went over to her, but she waved them
away and stood near the door by herself. T. W. Wilson said to
me: 'Maurice, I think a rescue operation is appropriate; come
with me.' He led the way over to where the Princess stood and
then graciously offered his hand: 'Ma'am, I'm T. W. Wilson, Mr
Billy Graham's associate, and this is Maurice Rowlandson, our
associate from here in London.'

For the next ten minutes we had a stimulating conversation
with the Princess while she waited for her husband, who was
parking the car. Eventually, he came in through the revolving
door; we took our leave of the Princess, who first introduced
us to her husband, and then returned to meet our own guests
(David and Ruth Rennie, Bishop and Mrs Goodwin Hudson,
Billy Graham's secretary, Martha Warkentin, and my wife) for
dinner at the Hilton Hotel.

Some three hours later, T. W. Wilson and I walked back to the Dorchester to collect Mr Graham. When we arrived, only three guests were still there: the American Ambassador and his wife and Cliff Richard. Mr Graham was talking to the ambassador, so we went to Cliff and asked him if he had enjoyed the dinner. He obviously had! 'Imagine it!' he exclaimed. 'Me, sitting next to the Foreign Secretary and talking as though we were old chums.'

When Billy Graham had said goodbye to his guests he turned to T. W. Wilson and me and said, 'I meant for you fellows to get here earlier, so that you could meet the Princess.' T. W. Wilson replied: 'Don't worry, Billy. We took care of it in our own way!'

On December 9th, 1975 another invitation was extended for Billy Graham to have lunch with Her Majesty the Queen at Buckingham Palace. On this occasion he asked me to drive him there.

Remembering Major-General D. J. Wilson-Haffenden's advice to me that 'Time spent in reconnaissance is rarely wasted,' I spent the early morning on a dry run to and from the palace; I timed the journey and, on arrival there, stopped to speak to the policeman on the gate. I told him of my commitment later in the day and he checked his daily list. As soon as he had confirmed that I was expected at the lunch hour, he suggested to me that I should drive in the palace gates and around to where I would have to deliver Mr Graham. This was an unexpected bonus, which was exceedingly helpful.

It was a strangely reminiscent and a somewhat poignant experience to drive through the central archway into the courtyard behind. I had done this before – but I had not remembered it until then. Shortly before she died, our dear daughter Cherylyn had gained her Duke of Edinburgh's Gold Award and had been invited to attend Buckingham Palace to have it presented by the Duke himself. The instructions said that only one parent could accompany the recipient of the award and we agreed that Marilyn should go. But I was able to drive them there and to park in the courtyard until it was all over. This visit brought back all those memories.

On my way back to the office through Hyde Park, I ran into a police census point. 'Where have you come from?' was the first question. 'Buckingham Palace,' I replied. 'Come off it,' said the WPC, 'everyone says that.' I explained that, in my case, it happened to be true and she apologised.

Later that morning, I collected Ruth and Billy Graham from their hotel and, with a nicely cleaned and polished car, drove them to their engagement. On this occasion I was waved through the front gates without delay. My earlier visit had proved its value. I delivered the Grahams to the main entrance in the court-yard where two pages were waiting to greet them. I was shown where I could park during the lunch hour – a rather isolated and lonely feeling to be the only car in this vast courtyard.

Some two hours later there was activity around the doorway and a page stepped out on to the roadway. With a flick of the wrist he summoned up 'the chauffeur' with the car, only to realise when I got out that I was not the chauffeur but obviously an associate of Mr Graham. He apologised to me for any lack of courtesy – but how was he to know?

Five years later, on March 24th, 1980, there was another invitation in very similar circumstances. The chief difference was that, on this later occasion, Mr Graham was on his own, and the luncheon was held in the private apartments of the royal family. This time Prince Andrew joined his parents at luncheon.

Once more I ran over the ground earlier in the day and this time I was directed to the archway to the right of Buckingham Palace known as the Garden Entrance. This led through into some beautiful gardens.

Paul Whybrew was a young man from our church at Frinton-on-Sea. A few years earlier, when he was aged sixteen and still at school, he had decided to write to the palace. He says he did it for a laugh. A friend of his at school had seen a picture of the Queen in a magazine and, knowing that Paul was an ardent royalist, had jokingly suggested that he should drop the Queen a line to ask if someone like him could work at the palace. To his astonishment he had a reply asking him to complete an application form. Up until that point he had not told anyone of his enquiry. The first his parents knew was when a red-crested letter arrived for him before he left for school one morning. So he had to spill the beans to his parents and within a month he had started work at the palace.

He was tailor-made for the job of footman. Very tall, he was dark and handsome and had an air about him which was exactly right. This time when I took Mr Graham to luncheon at the palace, Paul was on duty at the door.

After I had delivered Mr Graham to the private entrance, Paul Whybrew indicated where I could park the car. He then invited me to come in for lunch in the staff room. It so happened that I had brought some sandwiches with me, and I was conscious of the fact that Mr Graham felt most comfortable when he was confident that his colleague was always ready in the car. For this reason I declined the invitation, and ate my sandwiches parked in those beautiful gardens and within sight of the door to the royal family's private quarters. While I was parked there, a plane must have flown overhead taking pictures. Some weeks later, in one of the glossy magazines, there was an aerial picture of Buckingham Palace, and there – parked in the gardens – was my car.

Paul Whybrew was to meet Billy Graham again on several occasions. In San Francisco, the Queen and Prince Philip were entertained at a State Banquet by President Reagan, and a day or two later returned the compliment by inviting the President aboard the royal yacht *Britannia*. Paul was with the royal family in California at that time and he had an opportunity to introduce himself to Mr and Mrs Graham. He told them that he knew me, and found a warm response. Ever since then, Mr Graham has often asked me: 'How is the young man from your church getting on?' Some years later, Paul achieved fame by apprehending the intruder who broke into Buckingham Palace and reached the Queen's bedroom.

In May 1982, just as we were beginning to set in motion the means to organise Mission England, there was a conference of the International Christian Leadership group at Cumberland Lodge in Windsor Great Park. Marilyn and I had invited Blair Carlson to join us for the weekend and we had some great fellowship with him.

It was an important occasion for him, because he made many useful contacts for the forthcoming mission. On the Saturday afternoon he and I went for a walk through Windsor Park and found ourselves approaching the polo ground, where it appeared as though a match was about to start. We found that the Prince of Wales was due to play with his team, so we obtained some tickets in the spectators' stand and stayed most of the day to watch this most intriguing game.

During the lunch interval, Blair went 'walkabout'. Dressed in his grey slacks, blazer, and collar and tie, he must have had a certain distinguished look about him for when he came back later to join me in the seats, his eyes were shining. 'I can't believe this, Maurice,' he said, 'but I've just been speaking to the Princess of Wales!' Apparently on his walkabout he had wandered into the private enclosure where the players' horses were being attended to. Remarkably, he was not challenged – he must have impressed those who watched him with his regal air. As he wandered around he found himself standing next to the Princess's car. If my memory serves me, she was having difficulty in starting it. Blair saw the opportunity of a lifetime and had a chat with the Princess. By the time he came back to me, he was over the moon. The next day his experiences were compounded by our visit to the Royal Chapel where the Queen and members of the royal family were worshipping. After the service, Blair had the opportunity to mingle with the guests of the Queen outside the chapel. Altogether it had been a very special weekend for him.

During the days of planning for Mission England in 1984, Billy Graham received an invitation from Her Majesty the Queen to preach in the Royal Chapel at Sandringham. In addition, he and Ruth Graham were invited to spend the weekend there with the royal family.

On January 13th, 1984 a party of us drove from London to Shipdham in Norfolk, to stay for the weekend at the Shipdham Manor Hotel. Mr and Mrs Graham were due at Sandringham in time for tea on the afternoon of Saturday 14th and we went up early to allow them time to rest. On the Saturday morning, T. W. Wilson and I, together with Larry Ross and Russ Busby (Billy Graham's photographic associate), drove to Sandringham to reconnoitre for the journey in the afternoon when I would be taking Mr and Mrs Graham. On the way I had a puncture and I hoped that such a problem would not recur later in the day! Mid-afternoon, T. W. Wilson and I left Shipdham with Mr and Mrs Graham for the drive to Sandringham. As always, they had been expecting us on the gate and we were able to drive straight to the front door. There we were met by one of the footmen, who explained about collecting Mr and Mrs Graham on the Monday. He suggested that we might like to come for a 'spot of breakfast in the footmens' room', but I declined the invitation and said we would arrive around 8.45 a.m. He replied, 'Well, come and have a cup of tea anyway.'

T. W. Wilson had arranged that Walter Smyth would drive to Sandringham with me on the Monday. When we got back to Shipdham Manor Hotel, he said to Walter: 'Walter, Maurice has just talked you out of breakfast at Sandringham House!' How can you expect to make and keep friends when your colleagues do that to you? Walter was not too pleased.

The next day news reached us that, on the Sunday afternoon, Mr and Mrs Graham would be brought from Sandringham House to have tea with the Reverend and Mrs Gerry Murphy. When Walter heard of that, he passed the word around our party that, as soon as we had finished lunch on Sunday, we would all excuse ourselves and return to Shipdham.

The service at Sandringham was packed out, and there was a large crowd outside. As we waited with them after the service had concluded, we were able to watch the Queen and the royal family as they mingled with their guests outside the church. Among them was the inevitable BBC interviewer with his microphone. Approaching one lady he asked: 'Did you enjoy the service?' 'Yes,' she replied. 'Why?' the reporter asked. 'I heard Billy Graham preach,' said the lady. 'What was so special about that?' persisted the reporter. She replied: 'He preached about the Lord.' 'What was so special about that?' came the final question. 'You must not know Him!' replied the lady.

With T. W. Wilson, Walter Smyth, Russ Busby, Larry Ross, Blair Carlson and myself, we were a fairly large party. There was not room for all of us in the church, so the service was relayed to one of the large rooms in the vicarage. We were joined by many of the Murphy family and friends, all of whom (about thirty-five people including us) were invited to lunch at the vicarage afterwards. Joy Murphy gave us a right royal reception. We had a delicious meal, at the end of which all of us – mindful of Walter Smyth's earlier instructions – began to excuse ourselves and to get ready to go.

Joy Murphy came to T. W. Wilson and me and said: 'I want you two to stay.' Both of us were long-standing friends of the Murphys but we did not feel it right, on this occasion, to trade upon that friendship. So T. W. Wilson replied: 'Thank you, ma'am, but I believe we should return to Shipdham with all the others. I think Walter Smyth would prefer that.'

We continued to put on our coats. Eventually, when we were sitting in the car with Walter Smyth and some of the others, Joy Murphy put her head in through the window and, addressing Walter directly, she said, 'Gerry and I want T. W. Wilson and Maurice Rowlandson to stay for tea.' Without hesitation, Walter Smyth said: 'Of course,' and then turned to T. W. Wilson and me and told us to get out of the car. 'What are you waiting for? Don't keep the lady standing in the cold.' So the two of us returned to the house.

That evening, when we got back to Shipdham, we expected some sort of uncomplimentary comment – and we were not disappointed. But it was all in good humour, and in a friendly spirit.

In any case, the next day I was able to redeem myself. When T. W. Wilson and I were at the tea party, Mr and Mrs Graham had been brought from Sandringham House by Lady Abel Smith (the Queen's lady-in-waiting) and Lieutenant Colonel Blair Stewart-Wilson who was an Equerry to Her Majesty the Queen and Deputy Master of the Queen's household. Joy Murphy was the perfect hostess and made sure that all of her guests met one another, so we were able to spend time in conversation with each of those who had come from Sandringham House.

They were deeply interested in Mr Graham and his ministry and asked many questions. Lieutenant Colonel Stewart-Wilson said how much he would have liked to have had a tape recording of the morning service. I was able to tell him that a recording had been made, and I promised to send him a copy. We had a pleasant time with the Murphys and were greatly honoured to have been allowed to join their guests.

On the Monday morning, Walter Smyth and I set out for Sandringham House. As arranged, we arrived at around 8.45 a.m., and the footman who met us escorted us into the footmen's room for the promised cup of tea. One of those on duty that morning was Paul Whybrew.

When the time came for us to return to the car, the footman who had met us was about to take us back through the outside door. Paul intervened, saying that he would take us through the inside corridors to meet Mr and Mrs Graham. He escorted us along interesting corridors to the drawing room which had a very warm and friendly feeling about it. On top of the grand piano was a partly completed jigsaw puzzle, and there was also a card table on which was left the remains of a board game. It had all the feel of a family room, and we had an opportunity to look around while we awaited the arrival of Mr and Mrs Graham.

The door opened and in they came escorted by Lady Abel Smith and Lieutenant Colonel Blair Stewart-Wilson. They immediately recognised me from the tea party the previous afternoon and warmly greeted me as they would an old friend. In turn, I was able to introduce them to Walter Smyth, and they spent some time in conversation with him. That experience was more than adequate compensation for missing the footmen's breakfast.

We left the house and returned to the car. As Mr and Mrs Graham were settled in, a footman came out with a cardboard box: 'A brace of pheasants from Her Majesty the Queen, for Mr and Mrs Graham,' he said. I put them in the back of the car and told Mr Graham what he had been given.

'What in the world am I going to do with those two pheasants?' he asked. The problem obviously disturbed him, because several times en route to London he raised it again. He was conscious of the fact that the pheasants were a gift from the Queen. In the end, I said that when we arrived at the hotel, T. W. Wilson should take them to the chef and ask him to pluck, prepare, stuff, roast and serve them to Ruth and Billy in their room. T. W. Wilson left the car with the cardboard box under his arm.

Fifteen minutes later he was back, the cardboard box in his hands. 'Maurice,' he said, 'Billy thinks these pheasants are historic. He thinks they should be stuffed and mounted.' And stuffed and mounted they were! I returned to the office in Camden Town and called in the indomitable Michael Sage. Mike had come to us some years previously as our packer/driver and general odd-job man. One thing had become clear: Michael was never beaten, he always knew someone who could do whatever we wanted. So it seemed to me that Michael was my best bet.

When I told him the story of the pheasants, as I expected, Michael said, 'I know someone who can do that,' and off he went with the box. Ten days later he returned with the most magnificent glass case in which the two pheasants had been stuffed and set in a cornfield. A beautiful blue sky background was complemented by the two birds pushing their way through the corn stalks. The whole effect was superb.

I asked Michael Sage: 'Where in the world did you get that done so well?' He replied: 'I couldn't think of anywhere better than the Natural History Museum – so I took them there!'

Down in the corner of the glass case was a small brass plate with the legend: 'Pheasants from the Sandringham Royal Estate, presented to Mr & Mrs Graham by Her Majesty the Queen: 16th January 1984'. Billy was delighted, but my problems were not yet over. The next day he decided that he would like them shipped to his home in America. When the box arrived at American Customs they telephoned me in London, wanting to know what type of pheasants they were, their common name as well as their scientific name, and their country of origin – had they, for instance, flown in from another country? Somehow or other we satisfied their questions and the box was allowed in.

A few months later, Bob Williams (who was directing Mission England) decided upon a staff retreat so that we could have a time of fellowship and prayer together in preparation for the major mission ahead. He asked me to make plans for it to be held at Cumberland Lodge, in Windsor Great Park. On April 6th, 1984 we assembled there and had an excellent weekend together. Among other things, I was able to introduce some of the team members to the delights of Christian Croquet which those who took part greatly enjoyed. On the Sunday we were invited to the Royal Chapel in Windsor Great Park. The chapel is in a security area, and we had to give our names for the appropriate passes to be prepared.

The chaplain was the preacher, and he referred in the service to our presence and used one or two of the well-known crusade hymns. The royal family sit behind a curtain and are not visible to the congregation. The preacher can clearly see both areas. As the service ended and we came out of the chapel, the Queen and other members of the royal family were mingling with the worshippers and spent some time talking to them. The Queen had one of her attendants bring Bob Williams over to her so that she could meet him. It was a tremendous encouragement to all of us – and to Bob especially – to think that there was this interest in the mission in high places.

Five years later, and prior to Mission '89, Billy Graham was invited to preach at the Royal Chapel in Windsor for the second time. He and Ruth were also invited to have lunch with the royal family at Windsor Castle after the service. Security-wise we would be allowed two carloads of passengers. Mr and Mrs Graham and T. W. Wilson would be with me. Another car would convey Mrs T. W. Wilson with Blair and Elizabeth Carlson and Mr Graham's secretary, Stephanie Wills. That left one spare place in that car, and after lengthy discussions, it was arranged that the place should be used by a member of the staff, representing all the staff. Ingrid Holdsworth, who was working with the counselling and follow-up team, was selected.

In April I had had a telephone call from Mr Graham in America. He had asked if I would hold myself ready to be his driver on that occasion, to take him both to the service and to Windsor Castle afterwards. When the time came, young Mark Jarvis (who had worked with us on a number of events) was given the task of planning the car arrangements for Mr Graham's engagements. Some four or five days before the event, Mark came to me and somewhat diffidently asked if I would be willing to drive Mr Graham to Windsor. I think he was not sure if it was right and proper for him to ask me as his senior! I had not said anything to him (or anybody else) about Mr Graham's phone call in April, as I preferred events to take their natural course rather than to count upon privilege. So I was thrilled to be asked by Mark and felt it to be a confirmation of Mr Graham's own wishes.

On Saturday, June 10th, 1989, there was to be a cricket match at Lords between Eton and Harrow schools. As a member of the MCC I was entitled to book a box for that match. I decided that it was about time my American colleagues had some culture and education! Accordingly I booked a box and invited any member of the team who would like to come, to join Marilyn and me for a picnic lunch at the match. In the event about twenty of them came and we had a delightful day of fellowship and fun. To help them to understand the match, I wrote 'A Beginners' Guide to Cricket', a two-page description of the important facets of the game. I sent it to Philip Hacking (chairman of the Keswick Convention and a great cricketing fan) asking him to look it over and correct any errors. He declared it a masterpiece and said I should publish it. So it appears as Appendix B to this book.

The match over, Larry Ross invited a number of us to tea at the Ritz Hotel. It was the first time I had ever been there and it rounded off the happy day together. As this was so close to the beginning of the mission, I felt I should go back to the office to make sure nothing had cropped up during the day. When I arrived, the telephone-answering machine indicated that a message awaited me. It was from Canon Treadgold, Chaplain at the Royal Chapel. Would I please ring him?

He told me that he had received an invitation from the Queen Mother at the Royal Lodge, asking if the members of our party coming to the service would accept an invitation to meet the royal family afterwards.

In the event, when we arrived at the Royal Chapel it was already full, but we were assigned seats on the far side. As always on these occasions, the Queen, Prince Philip and the Queen Mother mingled with their guests after the service.

Approximately sixteen to eighteen people were invited back to the Royal Lodge afterwards and we felt very privileged to be among them. After some forty wonderful minutes we excused ourselves and took leave of Her Majesty and made our way back to the cars. I learned that one of the Queen's cars would take Mr and Mrs Graham to Windsor Castle, but that I would be expected to collect them there at 2.15 p.m.

All of us involved had lunch together (with Larry Ross, Russ Busby and others) at the Bridge Inn in Eton. Promptly at 2 p.m. I excused myself and drove up to Windsor Castle. At the gate I was expected, and was directed to the inner precincts of the castle. As I approached the Augusta Tower and the gated roads, the gates swung open, and I was allowed in. I felt very honoured that I should have been asked to fulfil this task.

As I waited at the door for them to leave, there was in front of me a tall window which obviously fronted a stair-case. In due course I saw the party descending this stairway and the door opened. Prince Philip and Sir William Heseltine escorted Billy and Ruth to the car.

Over the years there have been other occasions when the Grahams have been honoured with invitations from royalty. There was an invitation to them in 1954 to attend the Royal Garden Party at Buckingham Palace when Mr Graham was presented (for the first time) to the Queen Mother. In 1984 Princess Alexandra paid a visit to one of the Mission England meetings and followed the example of the late Duchess of Kent who had attended one of the Wembley meetings in 1955. In

1989, she sent an invitation to Mr Graham to visit her at her home one morning. Mr (now Sir) Angus Ogilvy and the Princess were living in an apartment attached to St James's Palace at the time. A small duplicated map was sent to me from the Princess's office with a note that the bell for the flat was to be found on the left-hand side of an iron gate in the corner, marked with a red star on the map. I found it, and rang the bell for Mr Graham to be admitted. Then, as usual, I sat in the car to wait for him to reappear.

It was about an hour later when the door opened and the Princess and her husband came out with Mr Graham. They walked him to the car, and when Mr Ogilvy saw me sitting there, he exclaimed: 'You should have come up with Mr Graham. I didn't know you were sitting waiting for him down here.' I offered my sincere thanks, but explained that I was quite used to waiting for Mr Graham while he met various people. But I was touched that they should have thought of me.

Apart from our own royal family, there have been occasions when he has met royalty in, or from, other countries. There is only one such event in which I have been involved, and that came as rather a surprise.

On one of his visits to London, Mr Graham wanted a quiet lunch and took T. W. Wilson and me to the Connaught Hotel. As we entered the dining room, we were surprised to see Mr Graham make a beeline for a table near the window. A tall, attractive lady rose from her seat and warmly embraced Mr Graham. He called us across and introduced us to Princess Grace of Monaco. She was a charming person: so warm and friendly that we were deeply impressed with her.

A few years later, I had a short note from her secretary, requesting a copy of *The Pilgrim Times* – the special publication which we had prepared for the Pilgrim Fathers' Meeting in the Royal Albert Hall. Mention of the publication had been made in the *Daily Telegraph*; Princess Grace had apparently seen it there and completed the coupon in her own handwriting.

In spite of all these royal occasions I have been impressed with the way in which Mr Graham has remained humble and reticent. He never talks about them: he never shares confidences about them. For him, they are just another opportunity to share the gospel. He does so, I know, in a discreet yet effective way.

For me, to have been associated with him on these occasions

has always been an honour and a privilege. I count them among
the very special events in which I have been involved. As I
have watched Billy Graham, it has been a lesson to me. I have
learned a lot from his humility, his discretion and above all
his desire to bring glory to the Name of his Master. In the
goodness of God he has been allowed to mingle with and
meet those in high places and he has neither traded on, nor
abused, those special occasions.

11

Overseas Ministry

It seemed inevitable that whenever an event took place in Europe, I would, in some way or another, become involved. The proximity of the London office to Europe meant that we often became the base for team members passing through London on their way to the Continent.

The first major event in which I was involved was in 1966. It followed a direct invitation from Mr Graham himself. He telephoned me one day and asked if I was planning to go to Berlin to share in the crusade and to attend the World Congress on Evangelism which was to follow. When I replied that I had no plans to do so, he gave me an invitation and encouraged me to accept it. Actually, I did not need much encouragement! The whole programme sounded incredible, and I made my plans to go.

In the event, I arrived in time for the last two days of the crusade meetings. They were *very* German, with brass bands and a formal concept which was quite different from any other crusade I had attended. It was Mr Graham's third crusade in Berlin and, of course, he spoke through an interpreter. That, for me, was a new experience. I had expected a somewhat jerky message, but in the event you quickly forgot about the foreign language and concentrated on the language you understood. His interpreter was Peter Schneider. In his younger days he had been an active member of Hitler Youth, but he had had a dramatic conversion and Christ had become real to him. In later years he became an associate of the team. Like all Mr Graham's interpreters, he seemed to be imbued with the uncanny knack of giving emphasis where Billy gave emphasis, and even made the same gestures (without looking to see what Mr Graham had done). Years later in Stockholm where Elon Svanell was to be Mr Graham's interpreter, the newspaper headline the next morning declared: 'Where would Billy Graham be without Elon Svanell?' It was remarkable how well the translation came across.

The World Congress in Berlin was sponsored by the magazine *Christianity Today* to mark their tenth anniversary. But the Billy Graham Evangelistic Association was deeply involved. Two of their number – Victor Nelson and Stan Mooneyham – were loaned to the magazine to co-ordinate and plan the event. That planning took three years. Some 1,200 delegates came from all over the world.

The congress was held in the new Kongresshalle (nicknamed 'the pregnant oyster'). Dominating the entrance hallway was the great Population Clock which, as the seconds ticked by, also displayed the net increase in the world's population. It amounted to a considerable number by the end of the congress.

The event attracted great interest in unexpected places. Among those who attended was Emperor Haile Selassie from Ethiopia, whose visit was arranged by Stan Mooneyham. It formed part of a semi-official visit to Berlin that coincided with the congress. In his address to the delegates the Emperor said that a person without Christ would drift and be wrecked like a ship without a rudder, and concluded: 'Therefore, O Christians, let us arise and with spiritual zeal and earnestness which characterised the Apostles ... let us labour to lead our brothers and sisters to our Saviour Jesus Christ who only can give life in its fullest sense.'

Especial interest focused upon two Auca Indians (Kimo and Komi) who arrived barefoot from Ecuador. They were the now reformed and converted Aucas who, a few years previously, had massacred Nat Saint and Jim Elliott, and other American missionaries to the Auca Indians. It was a moving experience to meet them.

Every big event must have its times for relaxation. That is one way to refurbish the body, and to revitalise the mind. In a free period when I had no other responsibilities, I took a walk up the main shopping centre and there, in a showcase at the side of the pavement, was an advertisement which described a studio where a souvenir facial mask could be made. It sounded intriguing, so I booked an appointment for my next free day.

At the appointed hour, I presented myself at the studio where I was made to lie on a couch: a straw was placed up each nostril to enable me to breathe, and a cardboard disc was placed around my face. The lady who made these masks covered my face with a plaster of Paris mix. Then she told me that I would find it would become rather warm inside. In fact, it became very hot: just at the moment I thought I could stand it no longer, with a deft move she lifted the cast from my face. A week later I went back and collected the finished mask. Today it hangs on the wall of our home – a somewhat macabre reminder of Berlin!

Years later it was to be complemented with a far nicer curio. In New York, on a similar occasion, I passed a shop where they advertised Solid Photography. Again it sounded intriguing and I went inside. You were made to sit on a chair surrounded by surrealistic cameras and instruments under a very bright light. The cameras clicked, and shortly from the machinery alongside emerged a delightful bust in black wax: I am told it is a perfect likeness of me! The family regard these items with generous forbearance, and understand the idiosyncracies of the man.

The plans in Berlin included a March of Witness through the city. This was held on Reformation Sunday. The East Berlin officials had refused permission for the congress to make a pilgrimage to Luther's Wittenberg, so the celebrations were confined to West Berlin.

During the ten days of the congress, Billy Graham chaired the sessions each evening and he gave the final address as the congress came to an end. He concluded: 'I'm going to ask that you kneel with me. There's room at your seat. I want you to make things right in your life, and make it a moment of rededication.'

There is no doubt that the Berlin congress paved the way for similar events – some of a regional nature, and some drawing delegates from every continent. Ultimately these congresses were to lead to the great Lausanne Congress on World Evangelisation in 1974.

In 1970 I received an invitation from Dr Ben Armstrong, then secretary of the National Religious Broadcasters of America. He asked that I should travel to Washington DC to give an address at the 1970 NRB Convention on the topic of 'Religious Broadcasting in the United Kingdom'. The convention was held at the Hilton Hotel in Washington, and I was invited because of my connections with the European and British broadcasts of *The Hour of Decision*.

I was asked to submit my paper in advance, which I did, and in due course the travel tickets arrived. Much to my surprise they were first class. Naturally I appreciated this gesture and the extra comfort that it afforded. With them were my full instructions to join in the convention. I flew over by TWA via Chicago and Minneapolis, in order to spend two days with Marilyn's parents before I flew to Washington.

On the plane over, I had been served lobster. When I arrived at Chicago, and while I was waiting for my onward plane, I was suddenly attacked by a dreadful bout of giddiness. It passed and I went on to Minneapolis. There, in the middle of the night, I was most dreadfully ill. In fact I did not properly recover for the rest of my time in the USA. A doctor in Washington declared that I had a serious case of food poisoning, undoubtedly the result of eating that lobster!

I returned from Minneapolis to Washington and struggled to get to the convention. It was a dreadful experience. On arrival at the Hilton, I collected all my registration papers and the programme for the convention. I examined the timetable carefully, but could not see any mention of the session in which I was to give my address. I sought out Ben Armstrong and asked for clarification because by then I was certain that I would only be able to manage that engagement: the rest of my time in Washington I would spend in bed.

Ben Armstrong went pale. It was clear that he had entirely forgotten to include my contribution, but said it would be added to the programme for one of the seminar sessions. He was full of apologies. So at the appointed hour, I went back to the Hilton ready to give my address. But, in the event, I was never called! I had suffered the food poisoning in vain – indeed, my whole journey was in vain. But the greatest surprise was yet to come. In the monthly *Journal of NRB* (Religious Broadcasting) the next month, there was my address published 'As given at the Convention last February'!

As a postscript to that story, upon returning to England I complained to TWA that I had suffered severe food poisoning as a result of the lobster I had eaten on the way over. I pointed out to them that my visit to America had been largely abortive because I was incapacitated. It transpired that other passengers had had the same problem, and to avoid any danger of lawsuits, TWA readily refunded the price of my ticket – which I was able to return to NRB.

In later years, Marilyn and I attended the National Religious Broadcasters' Convention regularly and we always had a good time. But I never forgot that first experience! In 1990 they were good enough to give me the International Award for Religious Broadcasting, so I could never feel any malice towards them.

One of the first European events to follow Berlin was the conference held in the Rai Centre, Amsterdam from August 28th to September 4th, 1971. There were 1,064 delegates from thirty-seven countries. On this occasion I was given two assignments, so there was no question as to whether or not I should go. First I was to be director of information, running the information desk. I was also given the responsibility of organising the stewarding.

Almost all of those who came were from the various countries of Europe and the congress made a great impact on them. It enabled the Europeans to sort out their affairs after the earlier congress in Berlin. They really needed an opportunity to get together to share experiences, and this European congress provided the ideal medium. It was sponsored by the Billy Graham Evangelistic Association.

For me it had a twofold impact. Dr Victor Nelson had been appointed as director of the congress, but his wife was taken ill and he had to return to Minneapolis. Harvey Thomas was appointed to take over his work, and he desperately needed secretarial help. I asked Dawn Chandler, my secretary, if she would be prepared to be seconded to Amsterdam for this period, and to work for Harvey. She agreed, not knowing that for her it would be a feat of endurance! At one point, her step-father; Dudley Brient, button-holed me at Frinton and said: 'Maurice, can't you get Dawn out of that dreadful situation in Amsterdam?' While I knew what he meant, I felt that Dawn was quite capable of handling the responsibilities – and, in any case, the event was almost upon us. While Dawn worked in Amsterdam, I used other members of the staff to help me with my secretarial work.

Harvey Thomas had worked with the Billy Graham team since the crusade in Manchester in 1961. After that he became another of those young men whom I had encouraged to study at Northwestern College in Minneapolis. While he was there, he also worked in the Billy Graham office and later was appointed to the team radio station on the island of Hawaii.

It was from there that he came to join me on the administrative team of the Greater London crusade in 1963. Later he went on to similar responsibilities in Australia and Dortmund. He found himself in the driving seat at Amsterdam, and was given the task of bringing together this vast enterprise.

He remained with the team until Eurofest '75, after which he left to fulfil a programme of freelance work which ultimately led him to the peak of his achievement as a consultant to Mrs Margaret Thatcher during her years as Prime Minister. He received the honour of a CBE upon her retirement.

The second factor for me was that the event occurred just at the time when Marilyn's father and mother would be visiting us in London from Minneapolis. I had a bright idea! I invited her father, Arvid Sandberg, to come with me to Amsterdam and to help me on the information desk. He accepted the invitation and we had a great time together.

Just one night throughout the whole event, the two of us took an evening off and had dinner (with another friend) in a downtown restaurant in Amsterdam. The next day we were glad we had. Some sort of virulent food poisoning had hit the congress following the dinner the previous night. Almost every delegate had the runs! Most of those attending the congress were men, so it was announced that all the toilets – men and women – would be available to the men. Dawn never heard that announcement. Later in the morning, she went into the ladies' toilet and found it full of men. Confused, and thinking she had gone in the wrong door, she dashed out and in the next door, only to find the men's toilet also full of men! She turned up at the information desk with a very red face, and asked me what was going on.

The congress meant a great deal to every participant. At the end of the day, the Reverend Gilbert Kirby (who edited the post-congress report) said:

> This unity of spirit and purpose was evident in the warm relationship which was enjoyed from the very outset . . . Dr Graham was invited to give the opening keynote address. Who has shown a more passionate concern for evangelism

in this present age, and who has done more for evangelism in Europe than Dr Graham? He was reluctant, as an
American, to speak but it was a unanimous invitation from
the committee that persuaded him.

Mr Kirby concluded (in his foreword to the congress report):
'Our on-going task remains unaltered – we are to be witnesses
to Him.'

The next major event to which we were all looking forward,
and which occupied our time and attention for the next two
years, was the Lausanne Congress on World Evangelization in
1974. The planning for this event had gone on for some twelve
to eighteen months before it took place. Dr Donald Hoke
from America had been appointed by the team to handle all
the administrative work. He visited London on a number of
occasions, and we had sessions together to discuss the things
which needed to be done.

Poor Don was handicapped by some degree of deafness. He
did not always hear what you said to him – and sometimes
misheard, with the result that things got done differently from
what you intended. But from the beginning of 1974 I scarcely
saw him. By then he was deeply involved in Lausanne.

George Wilson, in Minneapolis, who at the time was responsible for the London office, had told me to hold myself ready
to go to Lausanne. 'There will be work for you to do,' he said.
But as the time got closer and closer, there was still no news
of my involvement. In the end I checked with George Wilson
and he said I should go anyway.

I booked my ticket to travel across the Channel on July 12th,
1974; the Lausanne congress was due to start on July 16th. On
the afternoon of July 11th I had a telephone call from the London
Bible College: did I know of anyone travelling to Lausanne by car
during the next two or three days? I told them that I was going,
and would be leaving the next morning. They said that there was
a student who needed a lift, and they would appreciate it if I
would oblige. I asked that they should tell the student involved to
telephone me to make the arrangements. Half an hour later there
was a lady on the telephone: 'I am Wendy Leith, and I gather you
have offered to take me to Lausanne.'

For some reason I had never imagined that the student would
be female! This was not quite so easy and I explained that I would

be travelling alone, breaking my journey in Paris overnight and possibly somewhere else if I got tired driving. I said that I could not confirm the offer until I had spoken to my wife.

I telephoned Marilyn and told her all about it. She encouraged me to be the good Samaritan and to fulfil the offer I had made. So I telephoned Wendy and told her that I would take her. We arranged to meet near Waterloo Station.

On the morning of July 12th I set out for the Continent and duly met Wendy Leith as arranged. I discovered that she was from South Africa, and that she had spent a year at the London Bible College. As soon as I knew that she would be with me, I had reserved an additional room at the Novotel in Paris, where we were to stop overnight. Once we had arrived in Paris, she went her way and I went mine until we met up again the next morning, ready to continue the journey.

As we drove south, it got warmer and warmer, and around 4 p.m. I began to find driving tiring. We were just about to reach Dijon, and it seemed best to try to find accommodation there for the night. Looking around I found a suitable pension and I left Wendy in the car while I went in to book the rooms. Madame spoke no English, so I had to try my best French: 'Avez-vous deux chambres pour moi et la fille?' The trouble is that, when you try to use imperfect French, the other party tends to pour out voluble French of which you understand only every third or fourth word.

At any rate, I got the drift of what Madame was saying: 'Deux chambres, monsieur? Une chambre pour vous et mademoiselle.' I remonstrated as well as I could. I definitely wanted two rooms! It might be France but I had a reputation to protect, and whatever Madame said, it had to be two. In the end she gave up and handed me the keys to two rooms – but when I went to examine them, one was a communicating room off the other. So back I went, and tried to explain that I wanted two rooms, but on different floors. Poor Madame! She really couldn't understand the strange ways of an Englishman. Shaking her head in disbelief, she eventually gave me two rooms – one up and one down.

The next morning I came down to breakfast to find Wendy talking to Madame in fluent French, and having a long conversation with her! She hadn't told me that she spoke eight languages fluently. Conversing with Madame was no problem whatsoever. If only I'd known! Apparently Madame had been telling Wendy about the strange ways of Englishmen who booked two rooms when one would have done. Wendy explained to her that this Englishman worked for the evangelist Billy Graham, and told her what that meant. Madame embraced me and exclaimed that *now* she understood! It was all very confusing. We drove on to Lausanne where we arrived about 11 a.m.

On that journey we had shared experiences of our work for Christ. Wendy told me, eventually, that she was returning to South Africa to meet again a young man who had been courting her. She said that she was disturbed because he wasn't a Christian. She asked me what I thought.

I told her that the Scripture was quite clear: 'Be not unequally yoked together with unbelievers.' I pointed out to her that there were rocks ahead on which the relationship could be wrecked. I gave her three reasons which I felt were paramount in considering any involvement – as a Christian – with a non-Christian partner.

The marriage relationship always needs to be worked at, I told her, and there are always times when there are disagreements – even battles. They are hard enough for Christian partners to resolve. There is the added hazard where one is a Christian and the other not. If something really comes between you, the non-Christian partner might say: 'And I thought you were a Christian.' In a way, he uses that commitment against you, and it provides an intolerable pressure which ought not to be there.

Furthermore, I said, a marriage should be a sharing experience between the partners. How could it be, I asked, when one was deeply involved in Christian things, and the other not? There would always be an area where the relationship would be strained because of a Christian commitment.

Finally there was always the hope and expectation that the non-Christian partner could be led to Christ. In experience, however, this rarely happens. Tragically the reverse is often true: the influence and ministry of the Christian partner dissipates, and becomes less effective.

Wendy received this advice with some reticence. It was clear that she loved the boy in South Africa. When she returned she wrote to say: 'I do so much want the Lord's will to be done, in every respect. I'm doing a good bit of dating, and I have very much in mind our talk together in the car. I am finding it hard because I love him so much. But I am sure you are right and that I must not allow the relationship to develop while he is unconverted.'

Some years later Marilyn and I had a telephone call. It was from a John Millin, who was visiting England from South Africa and he asked if he could take us to dinner. He told us that he was Wendy's husband and wanted to thank us, in person, for all the counsel we had given. He was not the original boyfriend but he was a wonderful Christian man and Wendy had given him strict instructions to see us. She wanted him to tell us that the Lord's provision of a partner was far superior!

When we arrived at Lausanne, Don Hoke was standing on the steps of the Palais de Beaulieu. When he saw who it was he exclaimed: 'Maurice! I've been waiting for you. I knew you were to arrive some time today. You're to be in charge of security, stewarding and the catering arrangements.' With that he disappeared before I had time to reply!

There was no time to unpack the car, or to check in at the accommodation I had reserved. As soon as I entered the doors of the Palais, a number of people expected instant answers. The trouble was that most of them spoke no English – and I spoke *only* English. Suddenly the answer flashed to my mind – Wendy! She had vanished by that time to try to find her own accommodation. I spent the next two hours looking for her. Eventually we met up, and I asked if she would like to act as my ad hoc personal assistant for the congress. She was thrilled to have a job, and from then on we operated as a team.

With her knowledge of languages, there were very few people with whom we could not communicate. Wendy would speak to them in their own language and would instantly translate for me. Then she would translate my reply back to them. It worked like a dream, and once more the Lord had foreseen what would be needed and had supplied. 'Before they call I will answer!'

With only two days left to go before the delegates arrived, our work was cut out to get all the organisation in place. Nothing – bar nothing – had been done in any one of the three areas for which I was to be responsible. Everything had to be planned from scratch. Security was the most important aspect, and we first laid down the principles by which we would work. In fact, throughout the congress those principles worked well, and we had only minor breaches of security.

Feeding arrangements were the next in priority. Catering was already laid on, but we needed to plan the most speedy means of shifting several thousand people through the lines. Between us we devised a plan which almost worked from the beginning, and once it had been updated and honed up, it worked well.

Stewarding (or ushering, as my American colleagues call it) was old hat. I had done this since the Harringay days, and we simply put into practice the old, tried and proved routines. But because we were dealing with so many nationalities, I could not have done it so efficiently without Wendy's language expertise. She was a godsend.

Before I had left England, there had been a meeting at the Evangelical Alliance offices. To it were invited as many as possible of the British delegates to the congress. I found it to be a most depressing meeting. It was negative from start to finish. 'Why is the congress being held at all?' they asked. 'What possible good can come of it?' 'Think of all the money it will cost!' No one could think of anything good to say about it and all that was prophesied was doom and disaster.

Of course, as so often happens in these things, precisely the opposite occurred. The Reverend A. Morgan Derham, after the event, said: 'Beforehand there was all that controversy in England about Lausanne, and there were people opposed to it. They were tending to say "What has Lausanne got for us?" but I wonder whether we should not have been asking "What have we got that we can share with the world?" – in a thing like Lausanne. The congress presented a bridging operation between different worlds: between extremes of evangelicalism – and the British had a major contribution with several of the keynote speakers.'

The British group, of course, lost out by being insufficiently prepared. Because they had expected failure and a disaster, they had put little time into preparation. Consequently there were many positions of leadership resulting from the congress, which went to other nations. Had the British group gone to Lausanne with a more positive approach, their input could have been even more effective. The greatest British contribution came from Dr John R. W. Stott, who spent long hours drafting the Lausanne Covenant, a document which has become enormously significant since the congress. He was assisted in the editing by the Scotsman Dr Jim Douglas and others.

Simultaneous translation was installed at the congress. But in the smaller groups, that had proved too expensive. So they relied upon live interpreters who would be able to assist the speakers. In one such seminar with French and English present, the lecturer was Bishop A. W. Goodwin Hudson. He put up with the translation for the first ten minutes of his talk, then he paused and said: 'Can everyone here speak English? If so, we don't need the interpreter. Raise your hand if you don't understand English.' Without giving the interpreter time to translate that instruction to the assembled audience the bishop looked around and saw no raised hands. So he thanked the interpreter and dismissed him! Probably many of the French delegates were thoroughly mystified about what had happened, as they simply had not understood Huddy.

Billy Graham gave the opening and closing addresses, and was present at most of the sessions. His input was invaluable, not least in providing much of the financial needs of the congress. He said: 'I cannot prophesy what is going to come out of this conference. I can only hope.'

There were great challenges from Christian leaders from around the world. One of these was given by the Reverend (later Canon) Michael Green from Oxford. In his address he said: 'You must remember that it is Christ and not Lausanne that holds the key of David. It is He alone who shuts, and no man opens, and opens and no man shuts. And we must not organise Him out of the picture.'

Looking back nearly twenty years later, it is clear that Lausanne became a watershed for evangelicals. Once it had happened, there was no going back. The growth of the influence of the evangelical wing can be largely traced back to that congress.

The occasion was also used for team consultations in many spheres and it was in Lausanne, with Dr Walter Smyth, that I drew up the initial plans to close the London office. We recognised that there could be no continuing ministry for the association in London, once Mr Graham had gone to glory. So it seemed right to plan what should be done in that event. Ultimately these plans were put into effect in 1987, while Mr Graham was still very much alive. All the overseas offices were closed at that time. Our closure was directly based upon the guidelines that we drew up at Lausanne.

Halfway through the congress, Marilyn arrived with our daughter, Jacky. They spent the remainder of the congress with me, and it was a strength to me to have them around. Jacky went on to stay with friends in Switzerland, while Marilyn and I returned to England. We left the afternoon that the congress finished. We drove, that first afternoon, as far as Dijon. Searching out the same pension I had used on the way out, I confronted Madame. 'Avez-vous une chambre pour une nuit?' I asked. 'Monsieur,' she remonstrated, 'une chambre?' with an emphasis on the 'une'. 'Oui,' I replied, 'c'est ma femme.' 'Oh monsieur!' she exclaimed and welcomed us very warmly.

The great Spre-e and Eurofest events in Europe dominated our programme for the next few years and these have already been described in an earlier chapter. Their effect upon young people was unquestionable. There are innumerable stories and testimonies from those events. Many are covered in the pictorial booklet prepared afterwards by Dave Foster. In it, the Reverend Richard Bewes says:

> I am constantly meeting Eurofest participants and reading some of their letters as well. What amazed me at the time was the warmth of appreciation and the earnestness of intention . . . it was obvious that we had more than a great time. There was a marked preference for Bible expositions and . . . the participants would cheerfully stay sitting on the floor (no chairs were provided!) with their Bibles and notebooks open for lengthy expositions. The Word of God had a central place in the planning and, as the Scripture says: 'My Word shall not return to me void.'

I was involved overseas sometimes in events not organised by the BGEA, but at which I was asked to represent the association. One of these was the International Christian Communications Conference, again held at the Rai Centre in Amsterdam. Marilyn and I went to this event with some trepidation because we were not as deeply involved in Christian Communication as some of our peers. Yet it was important for a report to be given to Billy Graham on what was happening.

In the event, the communications conference distinguished itself by a lack of communication! For example, at the opening banquet there were two main speakers. One was Dr Everett Koop (introduced as Dr Dr Dr – the Dutch are very particular about those things, and he had three doctorates). He was a medical expert from America and later in charge of the American national health service. The other speaker was Dr Francis Schaeffer from L'Abri. In true Dutch fashion, the programme was interspersed between the courses of the meal. So we started with a solo and immediately afterwards, Dr Koop gave us a stirring address on the importance of life right from the womb, with special reference to the Christian attitude to abortion. He overran his time a little, and the first course followed.

Next came Dr Francis Schaeffer. He seriously overran his time (having started late anyway), but no one had communicated this fact to the kitchen. Thus, precisely at the appointed hour the row of kitchen doors opened, and out came an army of waitresses with armfuls of hot dinner plates. Noisily they moved among the tables, putting a hot plate in front of each participant. Meanwhile, Dr Schaeffer was still in full flow. There was an immense scrambling at the top table, as an attempt was made to restrain the waitresses from causing further interruption. But by then their job was almost complete. Dr Schaeffer continued for another fifteen minutes to conclude his address on Truth in Communication. Back came the waitresses to serve the meal on the now-cold plates.

The next evening there was to be a special concert to honour the members of the conference. It was to take place in a concert hall in the centre of Amsterdam. The programme included the first performance of a new work especially commissioned for this conference and it had been heralded as a major musical event. Because of the importance of the concert, it was to be recorded both for the production of a record and for a later broadcast on Dutch radio.

As the evening approached it was clear that we were once more running behind schedule. The session after dinner again overran its allotted time and there was a great scurry to get to the coaches as soon as it was over.

We arrived at the concert hall where the performance had already started. They wouldn't let us in – although we were the group that the concert was supposed to honour – until the first break in the music. It transpired that the concert director had seen a group of people come in, and had assumed it to be us. No one had told him that we were delayed! There were other similar examples of a lack of communication throughout the conference. I could not help remembering an old adage which was constantly repeated during my days in the Royal Naval Reserve: 'ninety-five per cent of the world's problems arise through a lack of proper communication!'

From 1973 onwards, we organised and led tours to Israel. The tours were planned as part of the ministry of *Decision* magazine and followed the general pattern of a similar series of Israel tours led from America by Dr Roy Gustafson, an associate evangelist of Billy Graham's. He was an inspiration to us and the tours that we organised were always very popular. John Corts (a team member who has since succeeded George Wilson as the administrative head of the BGEA) took time off from his duties in preparation of Eurofest '75, and came to give the bible readings on our second tour. Other years we invited various bible teachers to come with us and lead the spiritual side of the ministry.

Through the tours we made a lot of good friends for the association. Each time, the return rate was high as numbers of those who had been before came back to join us again – often with their friends. The tours gave an opportunity to share, in depth, the ministry of the Billy Graham Association and there were many whose interest was maintained for many years as a result.

We also organised tour groups to European cities where Billy Graham was conducting crusades. These gave an opportunity for people from Britain to share in the ministry in a positive way. Over the years we took groups to New York, Dortmund, Copenhagen, Gothenburg, Stockholm and Paris. The team always gave us a warm welcome to the crusade. It was good to see them again on these visits. Very often Billy Graham would be happy to meet the party. It was always a highlight when I was able to announce that he would either come and meet our group or we would be able to go to his room before or after the meeting.

Quite the biggest, and the two most effective events took place in the mid-1980s. They were the two International Congresses for Itinerant Evangelists. 'Evangelists', note, not 'Evangelism' – which had been the keynote of the Lausanne Congress and other similar events. These two ICIE congresses in 1983 and 1986 were the brainchild of Mr Graham. He was anxious to bring together those from around the world who had a ministry similar to his own.

In the first instance, only 1983 was planned: but so many applied to come, that there was no way they could all be accommodated. Many were disappointed when their applications were turned down that year. In 1984 Mr Graham took the decision to repeat the event in 1986 for those who had been unable to come in 1983.

In their essential organisation, the events were similar. The 1986 meeting was considerably bigger than 1983 as we were able to use the largest halls in the Rai Centre in Amsterdam. Both events had plenary sessions, seminars, discussion groups, demonstrations of methods, and plenty of time for fellowship. In addition a clothing exchange was organised, where delegates from poorer countries could help themselves to any clothing they needed. Many, many books and study aids were given to the delegates from Third World countries. For some there was a free distribution of equipment, including overhead projectors, film projectors, tape recorders and bicycles. The delegates came empty-handed, but went away laden down! Great care had been given to the type of equipment supplied: for example, recognising that in many isolated areas there would be neither electricity nor the ready supply of batteries, a cassette recorder was supplied which generated its own electricity simply by the turn of a handle. The delegates were delighted with the provisions that had been made for them. It was not an unusual sight to see delegates making their way back to their hotels or lodgings in sophisticated Amsterdam with their gifts stacked high on top of their heads in their normal native fashion!

Dr E. V. Hill had the delegates on their feet after an address when he called upon the evangelists to 'preach Jesus'. With a voice full of emotion, and rising to a high crescendo he said: 'How do we reach the masses? For an answer, Jesus gives the key: He said: "I, if I be lifted up from the earth, will draw all men unto me."[John 12:32] Lift Him up! Lift Him up! By living as a Christian should. Let the world in you the Saviour see. Then men will gladly follow Him who once taught "I'll draw all men unto me." Pray, my brothers: much prayer . . . much power. No prayer, no power. But when you get through praying – preach! Fast, my brother, but preach! Meditate, my brother, but preach! Preach, and preach Jesus; preach Jesus; preach Jesus!'

It was this International Conference of Itinerant Evangelists which presented me with the first serious conflict I was to

face, between my work for the BGEA and my work for the
Keswick Convention. A similar conflict was to follow a year
later when Mission England overlapped with the convention.
But my commitment was first and foremost to the ministry of
Billy Graham. So how could I handle this problem? I told the
Keswick Convention council of my dilemma and recommended
that they should allow my elder son, Gary, to step into my shoes
for these two years. They agreed.

In July 1982, Gary came to Keswick, and worked alongside
me throughout the convention. He made copious notes of all
that happened, and I introduced him to the local people who
would be so helpful to him. By the end of the convention we
had compiled procedure sheets running to many pages. I felt
that if Gary could follow through with those, the convention
would run smoothly. And it happened like that: both years
he contributed an enormous amount to the success of the
convention, and commended himself to speakers, trustees and
council alike. He did a good job!

The overlap in 1983 was just a few days. The conference in
Amsterdam was for ten days from July 12th to 21st: Keswick
released me on the 15th. On arrival in Amsterdam at 7.30 a.m.
on the 16th, I made my way to the Novotel where I was to stay.
No sooner had I parked my car outside and walked in, than
I ran into Blair Carlson. He looked at me and said: 'Maurice
– you're just the person I need. Can you help me with the
organisation of the Hungarian choir who are having breakfast
here, and a press conference afterwards?' So I was immediately
put to work. I don't think Blair realised I had only just arrived
in Amsterdam! But it was a good feeling.

After the Hungarian choir had departed, Blair greeted me
properly. He said that he had some good news and some bad
news for me – which did I want first? I said it was best to get
the bad news out of the way. He told me that my PA (who had
come over in advance of me, to get all the information I would
need when I arrived) had not worked out. In fact, she did not
seem to capture the spirit of such a congress. During a heavy
schedule of that nature the hours you worked were countless.
For her, however, there seemed to be a time when she switched
off. Blair was not too impressed.

'However, the good news,' he said, 'is that Mark Jarvis is
magnificent.' He told me that young Mark had done a splendid

job: he was reliable, hard-working and enthusiastic. Blair really appreciated him.

I came out of the hotel to drive to the Rai Centre, and found that my car had been broken into and the cassette radio had been ripped out. Not a good start!

When I went to the Rai Centre to report in, it took me a long time to find my PA. When I did, I found that everything Blair had said was true. She had collected none of the material I needed, nor was she able to give me any sort of briefing. It was a disaster. Much of it may have been my fault. I may not have given her adequate training for such a vital job. But I had imagined that it would come naturally to her (as later it did to Liz Fane, and others who worked with me). So it took a little longer to get into the event than it would otherwise have taken.

Because I had arrived late, I had no specific job at the congress. I spent most of my time helping out wherever an extra pair of hands was needed. Different team members soon discovered that I was available, and within two days I found it hard to fit everything in. Sometimes I was helping Jean Wilson on the bookstall; other times I was taking a duty on the exhibition stall for the BGEA. There were conferences with team members – especially Walter Smyth – and some opportunities to attend the sessions. But mostly it was hard work.

During the congress the Billy Graham Evangelistic Association had undertaken to subsidise those delegates who needed financial help. This was chiefly to make it possible for Third World delegates to attend. It was generally assumed that they could not afford to travel to Amsterdam, let alone pay for their accommodation and food.

One day, four totally subsidised participants arrived in Amsterdam and checked in at the accommodation they had been given. This was in the vast Jaarbeurs Exhibition Hall, some thirty miles away from Amsterdam. (Jaarbeurs was a remarkable place. Some 3,000 to 5,000 delegates were accommodated there under the watchful eye of Mark Jarvis, who had organised the whole operation.)

These four congress participants came back into Amsterdam where they rented a self-drive car and then drove to Paris for the weekend. On their return they were startled to find Bob Williams, the congress director, waiting for them at Jaarbeurs. He told them that he wanted five hundred pounds from each of them towards the cost of their accommodation and travel. He said: 'If you can afford to rent a car and drive to Paris, you do not need to be totally subsidised!' They all paid up.

About two and a half years earlier, on January 15th, 1981, I had faced the biggest conflict of all between my joint involvement with the Keswick Convention and my commitment to the Billy Graham Evangelistic Association. It was the only time it was irreconcilable. Walter Smyth had asked me to join him for breakfast at his hotel in London. He invited me to become the organiser of the 1983 International Conference for Itinerant Evangelists to be held in Amsterdam. It was a heart-wrenching decision that I had to make. I so much wanted to accept that invitation, yet at the same time I had an unquestioned responsibility to Keswick. My commitment was first to the Billy Graham Evangelistic Association: but in this instance it would mean *totally* deserting Keswick. Commitment and responsibility were in conflict. I realised that this was an invitation and not an assignment from Walter Smyth. In other words, he was asking me if I would be prepared to accept it, rather than drafting me to do the work. I saw that as an escape clause. I told Walter how deeply I appreciated the invitation – and shared with him the enormous conflict that was going on in my mind. I asked him for time to pray about it, and as I did it became abundantly clear where my duty lay. I was conscious (as I had so often been before) of 'the voice behind' saying: 'This is the way, walk in it.' In the end, I had to say 'no', for the good of the Keswick Convention. I got the impression that Walter Smyth was very disappointed in me with this reply.

The team then invited a German team associate, Dr Werner Burklin, to do the work. Actually, as things turned out, he was probably the Lord's man for this task. To organise a congress on the mainland of Europe really required more than just the English language. With only a smattering of French, I would have found it very hard to get by. As Werner was a German national, he spoke one European language already; he also spoke some French and was fluent in English. All that language capability was a great asset to him. After the congress was over, he returned to other ministries in Europe.

Three years later came the second congress which, this time, was organised by Bob Williams of the Billy Graham team. The dates were mostly before the Keswick Convention, so I went to

Amsterdam first and then on to Keswick where I arrived at the end of the first week. Once more, Gary had held the fort in my absence.

His willing spirit and readiness to step into the breach were deeply appreciated – not only by me, but by others also. The Reverend John Caiger, a trustee of the convention, wrote: 'Gary did a splendid job in running the Convention and looking after the office. He was helped in so many ways by Marilyn and Jacky – and then I found Julian appointed as my helper in communion service – so I was surrounded by helpful members of your family!' I was proud of all of them.

I arrived in Amsterdam several days before the congress started. I had been assigned to three big jobs: first, I was to be chief steward; secondly, I was to be a 'walking information desk'; and finally, I was given the task of organising the communion service on the last day. There was much planning to be done before the congress started.

On the day when the first delegates arrived, the team and staff watched them come through the door of the vast administration hall, and they all stood to applaud them. It was the culmination of months of hard work and planning. Most of those in that first batch were from Central Africa, and the emotion among the staff was such that there was scarcely a dry eye.

The numbers attending were greater than in 1983 and the logistics for accommodating and feeding that vast crowd were horrendous. But Bob Williams had it all in hand and did a magnificent job. Everything went like clockwork. He had the knack of getting the best out of unlikely people. Such was his leadership that he inspired those who worked for him with the desire to do a good job. He knew what he wanted to achieve and he knew the right way to get there. I had first met Bob Williams at the Lausanne Congress in 1974. It was there we spent some time together in discussion about the administrative details of the congress's organisation. He was another of those younger men who wanted to glean all the information he could from his elders. Such was his humility and his desire to serve well, that I found it an enjoyable task to share experiences and expertise with him.

Many years after Lausanne, he had been given the job of organising Mission England in 1984. Now he brought the experience he had gained over the years to this new task at the

ICIE. In the future he was to be appointed as the director of Mission World – a huge programme designed to cover the whole world with evangelism, by video, satellite and film.

The opening exercises at the Rai Centre in Amsterdam were dramatic. They included flaming torches carried in from each corner of the hall. They met at a central pedestal and there, together, they kindled the symbolic flame which was to burn throughout the congress. On the last day, when the dismantling and clearing up were going on, I was on my way to the car park when I passed a rubbish skip. There, lying on top, for destruction, were three of these torches. It seemed such a tragedy that they should be lost in that way, so I clambered into the skip and rescued one of them. It now hangs on the wall of my office and is above me as I write these words. It is a wonderful reminder of such a strategic conference.

Billy Graham was the keynote speaker at the opening meeting, and he spoke again at the end of the congress. During the ten days we were there, he often appeared on and spoke from the platform. He said that there was one word which was the same in every language: 'Hallelujah'. He would have the entire audience at the plenary sessions rise to its feet and he would say 'Hallelujah' and 5,000 delegates replied 'Hallelujah'. Immediately he repeated this twice more, and it became a hallmark of the congress.

It took a little time for the speakers to get used to an unusual phenomenon which occurred. Billy Graham, or one of the other speakers, would often make a joke during an address. There was an immediate low-key response of laughter, followed seconds later by a major burst of laughter, just as he was moving on to his next point. It took time to realise that, with every speech being translated into a myriad of languages, it was a few seconds after the comment had been made before it was heard and understood by everyone. When they heard it, they laughed.

The day the congress started it was a delight to welcome Julian and Fiona, my son and daughter-in-law, who came as guests for the first three days. It was always a joy to have the family involved in any event for which we carried responsibilities. They were always ready to help wherever needed and it was wonderful to have two extra pairs of hands available.

One plan did not work at all well on the opening night. Headphones had been provided for every delegate, to enable them to hear the addresses translated into their own languages. This meant the distribution of thousands of headsets – all of which had to be collected back immediately after the service. In 1983, delegates had been allowed to retain the headsets throughout the congress, but when the congress ended many of the delegates thought they could take them home with them. We were charged for the missing headsets and the resultant expense was horrific, so it was determined that, in 1986, the headsets would be issued and handed back on a daily basis.

That first day we established some four or five points where the headsets would be distributed, but these were far too few. The resulting congestion became frustrating, and it took the delegates a very long time to get into the hall and find their seats. At the end when the headsets were collected back they were literally thrown on to tables and it took six of my stewards until about 3 a.m. to sort them out ready for the next morning.

Observing this difficulty, I appointed a team of four stewards to work out a better and more effective plan with me. I put them in total charge of the headset issue and collection. We organised a system of channels through which the delegates would pass on their way into the meetings. As they went in, a steward would hand each of them a headset; it was a much quicker system than allowing everyone to help themselves. At the end of the meeting, we simply reversed the procedure, rapidly collecting the headsets as they left. There were no more tangles after that.

In the middle of the congress there was a free day. David Rennie had invited a group of us to spend the day on his ship, *Forbes*. David had come to Amsterdam in his ship, and it was moored in Amsterdam harbour close to the railway station. Along with myself, there was Liz Fane (my PA), Elisabeth Jefferies (my secretary), Walter Smyth and some of his family, and team member Bill Fasig. The day was glorious: David treated us right royally and we had a magnificent lunch while cruising from Amsterdam up to the Zuider Zee (now known as the Ijsselmeer). It is on occasions like this that true fellowship leads to a deeper friendship, and you get to know your colleagues and understand them. In the middle of so intensive a period of hard work, David Rennie's ship was an oasis to all of us.

My final responsibility at the congress was to organise the communion service. Logistically alone, this was a major event. We needed 5,000 individual cups of wine, and bread for everyone.

It was the feeding of the 5,000 all over again and there were basketfuls left over. Our main task was to serve communion without fuss, and with the least interruption to the atmosphere.

A team of my stewards spent all day preparing the bread, counting the cups of wine into baskets, laying out the bread and wine in the appropriate places, and holding briefing sessions for everyone involved. It was a somewhat complicated plan which needed direction throughout. So I stationed myself in the balcony above the platform, where all my stewards could see me. By predetermined signals they knew exactly when to start, where to help out in an area of difficulty, and how to request more bread or wine. They were a grand team. Every one of them kept their eye upon me, and the predetermined signals worked well and were easily and quickly understood. The whole service went like clockwork. The participation of the stewards in this way contributed to the atmosphere of worship.

To have a team of workers like this is a special bonus to a chief steward. Every one of them was sharp, smart and alert. They had a 'team consciousness' which made my job very easy. There is something special about a group of workers who keep their eye on their leader and who know instantly how to respond to a signal. I found it a great blessing to work with these dedicated folk.

Following the event, I received two letters: one was from my colleague Daniel Southern, who had been in charge of the arrangements at the Rai Centre. The other was from Bob Williams himself. Daniel said:

I just want to thank you for making the ushering at Amsterdam '86 such a smashing success. More than anything I appreciated your humility and willingness to flow with the situation which – at times – was very *dynamic*! I know the Lord is going to continue to use you in the days ahead even though there are immense changes in the works for the London Billy Graham office. May God continue to bless you and work through you as He has done in the past.

Bob Williams expressed very similar thoughts in his letter:

Thank you, dear Maurice, for your tremendous commitment to the details and specifics required with the Ushers (or Stewards as you would call them in England!) necessary to service the people in the Europahal. Many a time I passed by your work area in the 'Executive Tower' and felt a sense of gratitude because I knew that the Ushers were well taken care of in your hands. Truly God has been glorified in Amsterdam '86 and it is exciting to think how the Conference will aid in spreading His Message. May the Lord bless you for the part you've shared in this ministry.

Both of these tributes were wonderful to receive. Often, in the event, you feel that you are out on a limb: that no one knows the amount and intensity of the work that you are doing. You rest in the assurance that the Lord knows that everything is done for His glory. But it is only human to enjoy appreciation received in this way. This recognition has always been a hall-mark of involvement with the team. They never fail to express appreciation after an event is all over.

One feature of any event organised by the BGEA is their careful planning – not only for the event itself, but also for the breaking down and clearing up afterwards. So often we put all our energies into the success of the event itself, then we forget that everything needs to be cleared up afterwards. How often, for example, after an event in church, are the minister and the church secretary left to clear up and put the chairs and tables away? With the Billy Graham team, as much careful thought and planning goes into the post-event activity as into everything else. A team of helpers is recruited to plan the breaking down, with as much importance attached to it as the building up in the first place. It is a lesson we could all afford to learn.

I left Amsterdam early on the morning it all ended. I drove to Rotterdam and boarded the Norland Ferry (which had recently returned from service in the Falklands Islands war) to Hull where I arrived the next morning. From there I drove straight to Keswick where I arrived on the Tuesday morning of the second week. That evening Philip Hacking, the chairman, asked me to tell the convention all about Amsterdam. I was able, especially, to introduce them to the three-fold 'Hallelujah' that Billy Graham had used. I had the whole Keswick congregation on their feet to share in fellowship with Amsterdam in this way.

While overseas events like these were taking place, the London office was in the capable hands of either Jean Wilson or my current PA. Jean was often involved in running the bookstall at an overseas event, so the day-to-day office responsibilities frequently had to be left to our wonderful and competent team of staff members. Each day they would open the mail and then send it on to us wherever we were. By this means we were able to keep more or less up to date with the office work. It also kept us in touch with what was going on at home. Because of our confidence in those we had left behind, we were certain that everything was being done decently and in order during our absence. We were never let down.

12

The Work of an Evangelist

I sat in the bows of the Sail Training Ship, the STS *Sir Winston Churchill.* It was dark, but above us there was a myriad of stars. They seemed to shine much more brightly out here at sea. There were no other distracting lights except for the red and green of the port and starboard navigation lights, and a slight reflection from the mast-head white light.

'There must be someone out there who made all this,' said a voice in the darkness. It was a marvellous opening to talk about God: His love for the world, and the reason that He sent His Son, the Lord Jesus Christ, to earth. Questions are easy in the darkness. Because they were asked intelligently, the answers were pondered and considered. We had a long talk – one of many with a variety of young men who sailed as volunteer crew aboard the ships.

It was the ninth voyage I had made, sailing either on the *Sir Winston* or her sister ship, the STS *Malcolm Miller.* The initial introduction came through my service with the Royal Naval Reserve and I fulfilled my exercise commitment by serving aboard as purser. In that capacity you got to know all the boys very well, unlike the watch officers who mainly knew the boys in their own watches.

Eight months later, at the Central London reunion, he was waiting near the doorway, hoping I was going to attend – the voice in the darkness. His face lit up as I came through the door. 'Purser,' he said, 'I hoped you'd be here. You see I became a Christian three months ago – and all because you started me thinking in those talks that we had on the ship.'

As the scripture says: 'Cast your bread upon the waters and it will return to you after many days.' The excitement of an odd word dropped here and there, which later bears fruition, is only known by those who have experienced it. We are called to be faithful, to sow the seed – in whatever situation God may put us in – and He will give the increase.

Although my whole life has been centred on evangelism, Tom Rees gave good advice when he told me many years ago to concentrate upon those areas where God had given me special gifts. It was right to develop the talents for administration and to leave the ministry to those to whom God has given the preaching gift. But that does not exempt anyone from using an opportunity that God lays before us. I have never found it easy to talk freely about my faith. When questioned, I can respond; but aggressive evangelism has never been my style. So I am always glad when I am handed a situation on a plate like that which occurred on the ship.

Over the years, directly – but more often indirectly – God has used me to bring a number of friends to Christ. Sometimes they are able to tell me that it was something I said; sometimes it is something I did. Mostly I was given the privilege of starting the ball rolling, and someone else was used by God to enable them to make a decision for Christ. I thank God for those opportunities He has given to me.

I have often said that, as someone who was brought up in a Christian home and who made a decision for Christ at a very early age, I really have no idea what it means to someone who has never had that advantage to become a Christian. I will never know what it means to walk from darkness into light. I can only share that experience second-hand from hearsay evidence. The excitement of suddenly finding out all about what Christ has to offer, to someone who has been searching in a vacuum for some form of truth, is an experience for ever denied me. Gordon Glegg, son of evangelist A. Lindsay Glegg, used to say: 'A man without Christ is like a blind man, in a dark room, looking for a black cat that isn't there!' That incredible groping for truth is very real to a person who has experienced it: it is absent from the person who has been a Christian from very early days.

The decision I made at seven years old was very real to me. I cultivated a thinking that was Christ-centred, even though I was very young. At school I lived in a world of my own, because I was shunned by most of the other boys. I was the holy Joe around the school playground, but in an odd way it was clear that they also respected me for it.

But as I grew older and entered my teens, I could easily have been in rebellion against my faith had it not been for the ministry of Dr S. Maurice Watts, minister at the time of Union Church, Mill Hill – a church affiliated to the Congregational Union. Maurice Watts assumed his ministry during the 1939–45 war, and we grew up within the fellowship of that church during those difficult days. He concentrated upon a ministry to young people and started a weekly minister's class. It was held each Sunday afternoon at 5 p.m. and none of the young people at the church would have missed it. Dr Watts took us through all the teachings of the bible, through doctrine and theology and he related it all to practical Christian living each day. It was he who taught us that the whole of life should be a prayer: 'When I breathe I pray,' said the hymn-writer – and he taught us that hymns were not just words to sing. Every word, every line had something to say – either to us, for us, about us or was something to be said by us. Every hymn should be sung with meaning: 'Jesus my Saviour, Guardian, Friend, my Prophet, Priest and King' became 'Jesus my Saviour (pause), Guardian (pause), Friend (pause), my Prophet (pause), Priest (pause) and King.' You were made to think about the words, and the hymns we sang became meaningful.

He endeared himself to all of us as he taught us the importance of Christian living. He wore a Geneva gown with his academic hood, and the rustle of the silk as he moved to the pulpit is a memory that lives with me today. It was he who tamed the rebellious spirit and directed it into right channels and I shall always be grateful to his memory for what he meant in my life.

In many ways he prepared me for that first visit to Keswick. I was ready for the call when it came, and I knew how to respond. Strangely enough, he was not a full-blooded evangelical: he always described himself as a liberal evangelical, by which he meant that he believed in the gospel, he preached for commitment to Christ, but he did not hold the view of the inerrancy of scripture. He tried to teach us tolerance, but I fear I was not a good pupil. I had a different and more fundamental view of scripture and in some areas I was not receptive to his teaching.

In chapter 1, reference is made to the five young people from our church (of whom I was one) who went on their first visit to Hildenborough Hall. Shortly after we returned, we were at church one Sunday evening and Dr Watts preached on the topic 'Don't be afraid of being in the minority.' We looked at each other and felt that this was a message for us. We asked to see him after the service and explained that we were in the minority he had been talking about – so without fear we told him where we disagreed with him. He was very gracious and said he understood our concern, but he was too old to change his views now! We promised him we would pray for him!

Like my father, Maurice Watts tried to encourage me to attend a theological college. It was here, probably, that my rebellious nature showed itself most vividly. But I had a good reason for refusing. I had seen some of my friends whose entire ministry had been stereotyped or made impotent by a college training.

At the time a real star in my firmament was the Reverend J. Sidlow Baxter. My father had brought him to London from Edinburgh (where he was the minister of Charlotte Chapel) to conduct a series of meetings. I had never heard a speaker like him. He was a bible expositor of the highest order; he captured my teenage attention and gave me a love for the bible and a confidence in its truth which I have never lost.

Later we went on a visit to Edinburgh and spent some time with him in his home. He was a magnificent pianist and one day, in his house at 14 Ravelstone Dykes, he and his wife were entertaining us to tea. While we were waiting for the kettle to boil, Sidlow was telling me a story, using the piano as his illustrations. The story was of a burglar entering a house and every criminal action was faithfully reproduced by a piano interpretation which he extemporised. I was fascinated. My mother said: 'Don't, Sidlow! It's awful. It sounds so realistic.' Just then, the telephone rang: it was a message from London to say that we had just had burglars in our house! My mother held Sidlow responsible. At the time we had a lovely African grey parrot which talked its head off. When the police arrived at the house, the parrot was already saying, in a hushed sort of voice: ' 'urry up, mate! 'urry up!' It would have been a perfect story if we could have said that the police identified the burglars from the voice! It was not long afterwards that my mother died, and the parrot died a week later. The vet told us it was from a broken heart.

Sidlow Baxter was one of those who had become a great preacher without theological or academic training. He once said: 'The church has demanded men with degrees ... and by degrees they have emptied the churches.' Lively, virile and effective young men I knew had had the spark extinguished in college or university. Their ministry was changed; their enthusiasm and drive were dissipated and they had little effect.

On the other hand, I had watched men such as Stephen Olford, Tom Rees, Alan Redpath, even Gypsy Smith, whose ministry I admired. None of them had had academic theological training. I always wanted someone to do a thesis for their doctorate or masters degree on 'The impact and influence of the non-academic upon the evangelical world'. It would have been a startling treatise! Years later I was to have my view confirmed by seeing how two men I knew had so differed in their ministry after one of them had received academic training. Billy Graham and Chuck Templeton had both spoken at the meeting in Westminster Chapel on March 31st, 1948. Both were leaders in the Youth for Christ movement. Both had a powerful delivery. Later that year, Chuck Templeton had succeeded in gaining a place at Princeton University – and he tried to persuade Billy Graham to go with him. He felt that both of them needed disciplined study, but Billy Graham had many commitments. In any case he was already the President (principal) of a big bible college. How could he go back to university? So Chuck Templeton went alone and the historical and literary criticism of the bible changed his whole ministry.

For Billy Graham the Word of God was totally dependable. If it were not, then he had no message. His conviction stood the test of his own experience, and of the experience of many others. Only as faith was exercised did it become strong, and for him if any one part of scripture was suspect, then it was all suspect. For him there was no doubt: it was the Word of God, unquestionably right, totally inspired and inerrant. 'Holy men spake as inspired by God.' His duty was to proclaim the truth of that Word and rest upon his constant declaration: 'The bible says ... '

We can praise God that Billy Graham never yielded to the pressure of his friend, for to have done so would undoubtedly have changed him. Many believe that any further academic studies would have ruined him – and certainly the course of international evangelism would have been irrevocably changed. Billy's reliance upon the guidance of God prevented what could have been a disaster.

I have already explained how central was the concept of God's guidance in my life. Often I have not been able to see clearly the will of God but in later years, looking back, I can see that He did indeed guide me in oblique ways of which I was not always aware at the time. A reliance on 'the voice behind' was very real. Sometimes that guidance came through events which shaped the future. Sometimes it was through the intervention of a friend or colleague. Occasionally it was intuition or a 'gut feeling' of the right direction to follow. Sometimes it was through scripture which I read regularly. But in this I had a hang-up.

Throughout my boyhood, family prayers had been an unchangeable institution which took place wherever we were, and whatever else we may have been doing. They were paramount to the morning's planning. We had breakfast and then adjourned to the lounge for this daily ritual. This was in the days of family retainers. My family had a housekeeper, housemaid and a chauffeur/gardener. They all lived in and they were expected to join us for this daily event. The bell was rung to summon them from the kitchen, and they all appeared, glorious in their uniforms! Each of them was a committed Christian, so they were glad to come in.

We started each day with a scripture reading, followed by a comment. This was usually taken from the Scripture Union notes for the day. Then we all knelt while my father led us in a round-the-world prayer. He went through everything every day, and covered all the needs of the world: the King and all the royal family, our leaders in government, missionaries overseas, and the work of the church at home. He finished with a commendation of the family and the staff to the goodness of the Lord for that day. On Sundays, additionally, we sang a hymn. My father was a good extempore pianist and we sang all the old-fashioned church hymns with great gusto. Moody and Sankey, Mrs C. F. Alexander, the songs of Gypsy Smith (who, along with other visitors to our home, would sometimes take our morning prayer-time for us). Once, when Gypsy Smith was staying, I taught him a chorus. We were on our way to church and I, aged five, was sitting on his knee.

He told the story of that event in his book *The Beauty of Jesus*:

> Children are always delightful. When I was campaigning in London a tiny chap (Maurice Rowlandson) used to accompany his father when the latter brought his car to take me to a meeting. He wasn't shy to be riding in a car with a gipsy, for we had only just started when he began to teach me a chorus which he liked, and soon four people in that car were singing something like this:
>
> > The birds up in the tree-tops sing their song
> > The angels sound His praises all day long,
> > The flowers in the garden lend their hue
> > > So why shouldn't I
> > > Why shouldn't I
> > > Praise Him too?

As a day boy at boarding school I was encouraged to bring boarder friends home for the weekend. But I rarely did so, because of that morning prayer-time. I had a hard time living it down the next week at school: 'Do you know what old Rowly's parents do each morning? They *pray*!' And although I was glad in my heart that the day started with the Lord, I crawled inside when I had to face the ridicule of my peers. At that age it was a hard burden to bear. But there was a saving grace.

Because of his deep puritanical convictions, my father was against all the usual no-no's of the evangelical world of those days. No smoking, drinking, dancing, cards, billiards, make-up, theatre and a host of other prohibitions. He was also very reserved. He never spoke of sex. In many ways, for him, I suppose it didn't exist. When I was about to leave England to go to America to get married, he gave me the only sex instruction I ever had. As I said goodbye to him at the airport, he slipped a small brown paper package into my hand and said, sotto voce: 'You may need that when you get to the hotel.' Later on the plane, I opened the package to find inside a small tin of Vaseline.

Among his prohibitions, of course, was the cinema. In this he was rather more wise. He offered me the option of either attending film shows or being given an electric model railway. He pointed out the transient nature of a cinema visit as compared

with the permanency of the railway layout. I chose the railway!
And my friends from school were always happy to share it with
me. It was installed on a vast table-top around three sides of the
wall in our upstairs room. It was a magnificent layout for those
days, and I was able to have five trains (six at a pinch) running
at the same time. That was a real delight, for which my friends
would put up with morning prayers.

I suppose that much of my father's reticence was due to the
loss of my mother when I was ten. I was not allowed to go to
her funeral, but my father had a magnificently bound book
prepared for me, entitled *Radiant*. It contained the text of the
funeral service, together with many of the letters of condolence
he had received. It is clear from reading these that my mother
must have been a remarkable woman. I wish I had known her
in more mature years. Two years after her death, my father
married her sister who had lived with us (as a kind of nanny to
me) ever since I could remember. So it was not too different in
the household. Years later, in the late 1960s, when she died, he
offered to marry the only remaining spinster sister, who lived
in North Wales: she declined. If my mother was a remarkable
woman, my father was also a remarkable man!

But that concept of morning prayers left me with a hang-up
that through all my life I have never been able to dismiss. My
father would have been devastated.

Because of my hang-up about those morning family prayers,
I never felt that I could continue the same institution in my
own family. It would bring back too many unhappy memories of something that was intended to be the main source
of strength for the day. From time to time, with our growing
family, we tried to implement a similar programme, but one
factor or another seemed to get in the way. None the less,
we never failed to train each of our youngsters to have a
private devotional programme. I confess that my prayer-time
was mostly in the car on my way to work. Taking a leaf out of
Jean Rees's book, I remembered that it was perfectly possible
to pray while driving a car and I tried to redeem the time.

The scripture readings were mostly in the form of tape-
recorded talks. In this connection, one of the best things that
ever happened to us as a family was a visit to Calvary Chapel in
Costa Mesa, California. It was the church of which Chuck Smith
was the pastor. There we learned that Chuck was accustomed

to preach through the bible and that all his messages were on tape. I watched my son Gary's eyes light up when he heard this. The long and short of it was that we returned to the UK from California with some 196 cassette tapes in our baggage – the whole bible à la Chuck Smith. We were horribly overweight as a result, and Gary prayed that we would get a sympathetic clerk on the TWA check-in desk. His prayers were surprisingly answered when, without being asked, the clerk lifted our baggage right over the scales, and put them straight on to the conveyor belt – so that the weight of the cases was never a problem.

Those tapes provided our bible lessons for many years to come. Chuck's simple exposition of scripture brought it to life, and all our family's lives were strengthened as a result of listening to them. That was many years ago, but we still continue to listen to those and many other bible teaching tapes. They provide my daily diet of biblical teaching.

It has always been a miracle to Marilyn and me that in spite of us, all our children have responded to the teaching to find Christ as their own personal Saviour. That, in itself, has been an answer to our continued prayers, and we have never ceased to thank the Lord for answering so abundantly. In many ways we did everything that was wrong: we did nothing that was 'in the book' and by all normal standards, we should have raised a bunch of tearaways. But God had other plans and He circumvented our weaknesses to show us His power in the lives of our children.

So what has been the source of strength to me? Apart from the human angle – the support of family and friends, to which I have already referred – my strength has been in the knowledge of God's constant presence with me, in the person of the Holy Spirit. 'Practising the presence of Christ,' said Thomas à Kempis. That is one of the secrets.

I learned this from my friend Tom Rees. To him, life was always lived in the consciousness that 'it is not I who lives, but Christ who lives in me'. He had learned, in whatever situation he faced, to recognise that he never faced it alone. There was always that unseen Presence with him. That was where his strength lay. It is in a day-to-day realisation that alongside us in every experience is the reality of Christ. He is interested in all that we do. He shares our joys and He shares our sorrows. He was with us each one, as a family, when we lost our dear Cherylyn. He was with us in the days of anxiety over Jacky. He is with us today in the expected and in the unexpected. Therein lies our strength: in the consciousness of His presence.

In day-to-day life you meet someone you like, someone you respect and whose company you enjoy. Then you realise that they are without Christ. Suddenly any relationship takes on a new dimension as you seek to share with them the greatest of all discoveries that you have made. It seems frustrating when they do not seem to understand the central motivating force in your own life. To have Christ is the most important thing in life – and when you have something good, you want to share it. It always seems a puzzle that they don't understand – until you remember that the scripture says: 'The god of this age has blinded the minds of unbelievers.'(2 Cor 4:4) Our task is to intercede with the Holy Spirit that their eyes may be opened. That is what evangelism is all about.

It was in this context that the thin gold line which has continued through all my life has been important to me. I can never thank God enough for allowing me to have crossed paths with such a man as Billy Graham.

When my full-time association came to an end in 1987, it was as though a major part of my life had been cut out. I did not know then, of course, that you never give up work for the association. Since 1987 there have been Mission '89 and Scotland '91, in both of which I have been deeply involved.

When the London office closed in September 1987 I determined to use the knowledge I had as a consultant for the benefit of others. I was sure that the world was waiting for my expertise! The only trouble was that no one had told the world. I discovered that the immediate reaction was to ask me to raise funds. Naively, at first, I accepted because it seemed a means of providing the bread and butter. And I had, after all, had thirty-five years' experience of raising funds for Christian work – many millions of pounds – so I felt that I could do this. But when my PA and I succeeded in raising only seven hundred pounds in eighteen months towards a target of four million pounds, I decided that secular fund-raising was not my forte.

I did discover many people who wanted to learn from my expertise, and a stream of visitors came to my office for advice – until my accountant told me that my knowledge was my stock-in-trade. I was reminded of a story from my church, where a doctor member of the congregation always attended with his prescription pad in his pocket. He found that so many of his friends in the congregation were also his patients. It was convenient for them to ask him after church, 'Could I have a new prescription please?' One day he became anxious that he might be liable if anything went wrong, and that his insurance might not cover him. So he asked a fellow member at the church, who was a solicitor, if he was within the law. He was advised that he was, provided he followed up the church-time consultation with a small bill. The doctor thanked his friend, and determined that in future he would always send a bill to anyone who asked him for a prescription in church.

The next week, in his mail, was a little bill from his solicitor friend 'For advice given in church'!

Throughout the story of these pages, my service to and through Billy Graham has been paramount. He has been the means to enable me to fulfil the burden for evangelism that has always been there. Had Billy Graham not appeared on the scene, I have no doubt that God would have led me into some other fruitful path. In His goodness, however, He gave me this tremendous bonus of association with Mr Graham.

In my experience he is a man of deep spirituality. He is immersed in the Word. He is a man of prayer. His whole concept is centred around finding and doing God's will for his life. Sometimes he agonises over this (as he did before he accepted the Russian invitation). At other times he is quite certain of God's programme for him.

He is a man of great caring capacity. Although he does not emphasise social issues in his preaching, his mind is always concentrated upon them. He demonstrates that he firmly believes that his function is to declare God's Word and to leave the results to the Holy Spirit. Invariably there are those whose lives are changed and who, as a result, become involved in social concern – remember Richard Carr-Gomm?

In practice, in recent years Billy Graham has supported local crusade committees in a Love in Action programme, through which practical help is given to needy areas of society in the crusade city. Indirectly he is deeply involved with the work of his eldest son. Franklin had founded an organisation known as Samaritans' Purse (now Samaritans International), through which he has raised many millions of dollars for relief work in needy parts of the world.

Billy Graham is a family man. His five children have been supportive to his ministry. All of them are in Christian service of one form or another. He declares his good fortune in the person of his wife Ruth. They are a close couple who hate to be apart from one another – yet recognise that the exigencies of the ministry demand it.

He is a concerned leader. He knows each of his team associates intimately. He follows their ministry; he is involved in their families; he rejoices when they rejoice and he mourns when they mourn. When tragedy or anxiety strike, he is among the first to be in touch with them with the assurance of his love and prayers – and when there is an occasion to share in a family rejoicing, he never fails you; remember Jacky's Christmas phone call?

He is a great preacher – not always by the content of his message. Indeed, there have been occasions when some of us who have worked with him have looked at each other and said (at the time of the invitation): 'Surely no one will respond tonight!' But they always do; many thousands of them. Because it is not just *what* he says that counts, it is the immense prayer-backing and the incredible sense of the power of the Holy Spirit which take the message and interpret it to the heart of the listener. It is not Billy Graham who converts them; it is the Holy Spirit. He is faithful in proclaiming the message as best he can – and sometimes through pressure of engagements, tiredness and, on occasion, sickness, that best, by man's standards, may seem less than excellent. But in God's economy, there is no such thing. Billy Graham is the human voice of God speaking through the Holy Spirit – and He never makes any mistakes. Therefore, because of the *source* of Billy Graham's preaching, he is a great preacher!

To us he is, above all, a wonderful friend. We shall never forget the many instances of kindness that have come to our family and to ourselves through his friendship. He is truly the man that God has used to bless us – and we know many others who feel the same way. Many books have been written about him, and many of them make him out to be a complex person. Maybe he is: but he is also a humble and simple man who is deeply dedicated to the task to which God has called him. Sometimes there are pressures upon him which would seek to divert him from his dedication to proclaiming the gospel – political pressures, theological pressures, ecumenical pressures and social pressures. If at times his answer to a question may seem inadequate, or maybe naive, it is because he is concerned that he neither says anything, nor does anything, which might detract from the great ministry to which God has called him. It is a miracle that, with all these pressures surrounding him, he has been able to remain true to his major ministry and calling.

He himself is supported by those around him. His selection of his closest colleagues is his most remarkable skill. He has rarely made a mistake. Every one of them watches over him; prays for him; supports him in the crusade evangelism and upholds him at times of need. He has been surrounded by those who care for him. Unlike many other notorious evangelists, he has been protected from scandal and gossip. He has never, knowingly, been left alone with a person of the other sex. He has never ridden alone in a car with a woman other than Ruth. He has never had a lady visit him in his room unless at least one other of his colleagues was also present. The team will go to great lengths to ensure that such a thing doesn't happen.

Financially, he has always insisted that the accounts of the Billy Graham Evangelistic Association should be impeccable. The association founded an organisation to emphasise financial competence and credence. Many other societies have joined it. He himself has always been on a modest salary, similar to that of a pastor of a large city church in America. Admittedly this would be somewhat more than the pastor of a church in Britain would receive, but then the Americans have a more responsible way of looking at their commitment to their pastor. In effect, the man in the pew looks at the man in the pulpit and says to himself: 'Brother, you are there because I have called you to be there, and you minister to me. It is therefore incumbent upon me to see that I make it possible for you to live at the same standard that I live at.' In contrast the man in the pew in Britain looks at the man in the pulpit and seems to say: 'You chose to do that job, poor fellow: make the best of it' – and if one day the pastor turns up with a new car, the man in the pew says: 'Oh dear, we're paying him too much!'

We once had a dramatic example of this when, many years ago, our membership was at the Olivet Baptist Church in Minneapolis. Miland Knapp, an elder in that church, bought his wife a small car for her to go shopping. The same week, he bought his pastor's wife a similar car, saying: 'It is wrong for me to expect the pastor's wife to struggle without a car, when I have bought one for my wife.'

Of course, Billy Graham also has private earnings which arise from his prolific writings. These he mostly uses for the support of other evangelical enterprises and missionary work. He lives humbly – as humbly as it is possible for a world leader to live, bearing in mind the need these days for adequate security. All his team follow his example in this.

Many books have been written about Billy Graham. Some of the authors have felt it necessary to find *something* which is on the negative side. Occasionally a small and insignificant event has been blown up into great importance and conclusions have been drawn from it. In other cases, the negative aspect has been injected by speculation as to Mr Graham's opinion about something, or an assertion of his alleged views. A few writers have invented circumstances which never happened outside hearsay reports – 'Have you heard that Billy Graham . . .'; but he never had said or done whatever it was, unless it was in an entirely different context to the report quoted. Still others have based their opinion upon newspaper reports which are either inaccurate or erroneous. They build a case around a totally false premise. Why it should always be necessary to include negative reporting, I have never been able to understand. It was that which killed the association's own newspaper, the *Christian*. If there is any area for negative reporting about Billy Graham, then it has been outside my own experience, and this story is confined to my own forty-three years of involvement.

During those years I have listened to countless sermons by him. Always he preaches the gospel; always he seeks a commitment from his listener. This book would be incomplete without his own contribution. This sermonette is taken from his latest book on hope:

The greatest tribute a boy can give to his father is to say 'When I grow up I want to be just like my dad.' It is a convicting responsibility for us fathers and grandfathers. Not too long ago I received a handwritten letter from my youngest son, Ned. It is a letter I will always prize. He expressed appreciation and love for me as his father, and he indicated that he hoped he would be a good role model for his two sons and that he would be able to impact them the way I had been able to impact him. This encouraged me, because I have felt I was a failure as a father due to my extensive absences from home. But Ruth was strong enough and spiritual enough to be both father and mother at the times the children needed it. When I did come home, I tried to spend extra time with them. Now I face the problems and opportunities of trying to be a good grandfather for nineteen grandchildren. Our lives speak loudly to those around us especially the children in our home.

The Son of God reflects the same selfless compassion for the sick, the distressed, and the sin-burdened as does God the Father. It was God's love which enabled Jesus to become poor that we might become rich. It was divine love that enabled Him to endure the cross. It was the same love that restrained Him when He was falsely accused of blasphemy and led to Golgotha to die with common thieves.

When a boy is picked on by a bully, he might call for his big brother or his dad to help him. When I was in grammar school, I was constantly being picked on by a bully who must have weighed one-third more than I did. This older boy went out of his way to give me a beating almost every day. One day as we were getting on the school bus and he was slapping me around, a tiny little guy came up and knocked the daylights out of the bully! My defender had taken boxing, wrestling and karate lessons, and he gave the other boy a sound thrashing. From then on, all three of us were friends.

I remember when my brother, Melvin, was small, and he was picked on by some older boys in our town. I was bigger then and had the chance to defend him. Jesus could have called on a host of angels to defend Him. They could have drawn their swords and come to His rescue at any time. But His love held Him on the cross and made Him, in a moment of agonising pain, stop and give hope to a repentant sinner dying beside Him who said, "'Jesus, remember me when you come into your kingdom.' Jesus answered him, 'I tell you the truth, today you will be with me in paradise'" (Luke 23:42-3).

After terrible torture had been inflicted upon Him by degenerate man, it was love that caused Him to lift His voice and pray, "'Father, forgive them, for they do not know what they are doing'" (Luke 23:34).

From Genesis to Revelation, from earth's greatest tragedy to earth's greatest triumph, the dramatic story of man's lowest depths and God's most sublime heights can be expressed in twenty-five tremendous words: 'For God so loved the world, that He gave His only begotten Son, that whosoever believeth in Him should not perish, but have everlasting life' (John 3:16 KJV).

Billy Graham is a man who is called of God. I am often asked: 'Who will succeed Billy Graham?' I have to reply (using the phrase in its literal, rather than idiomatic, meaning): 'God only knows.' It was God who called and equipped Billy Graham. When his ministry ends, it is God who will appoint his successor. In the bible we read of the urgency that the disciples felt to appoint a successor to Judas. The lot fell upon Matthias – and we never hear about him again. God had already chosen the successor to Judas, and the call of His choice did not come until the Damascus Road. Paul, an apostle born out of due season, was God's choice for the successor. We must beware of choosing a Matthias, and leave it to God to choose the Paul.

If ever that time comes – and there is no certainty that it will (because the Lord may return in glory before the need arises) – we can rest assured that God will equip him in every way as He equipped Billy Graham. I hope that there may be someone who will have the privilege, as I have had, of serving that person in a way similar to that which has been open to me. For if God called the evangelist, he also called the team, of which I had the privilege of being a part. I had no idea, when I rose to my feet at the Keswick Convention, where it would lead me. To God be the glory!

APPENDIX A

The Missing Piece
by Marilyn Rowlandson

My mother-in-law gave me a vase. It was a lovely, long-necked, milk-white vase embossed and edged with gilt. As far as I knew it was not valuable to anyone but me. It had belonged to her aunt, whose goods and chattels were being divided up and disposed of after her death.

As I took my precious possession home I thought of all the places where the graceful line and lovely pattern would be best highlighted. Twenty times a day I moved it during the first week and finally decided that it needed a special place – made just for the purpose of holding and displaying my vase. A nice corner cupboard, I thought, with concealed lighting and black velvet draped across the back; but until it could be made, the vase would have to sit on the mantelpiece.

It certainly wasn't satisfactory: the shelf was too narrow, the wallpaper patterned. But it would have to do for now. And there it sat.

One day a few months later the telephone rang. I left my two small children playing together and went to the next room to answer the call. It was my mother-in-law. To say the least, she was excited. When she managed to calm down she told me that she was in the china department of an exclusive and expensive department store and . . . guess what? There on the table in front of her was a vase like mine, but smaller. It seems that they had been made for some special exhibition. Only a limited number were produced, and they were expensive. She suggested that

I go quickly and put the vase away in a safe place where the children could not reach it. Assuring her I would do so, I put the phone back in its place, rather dazed by the information that my 'precious vase' really was precious!

As I opened the door to the room where my children had been playing I heard a crash! In their play, the vase had 'just happened' to get in their way and had been knocked down and broken. There it lay at the side of the fireplace in tens of pieces. I looked in unbelief; then turned and without a word, went for the dustpan and brush. My vase . . . it was gone . . . broken! What would my mother-in-law say?

My silence didn't last long, and as I swept up the pieces I delivered a few choice words to my children. Oh, it wasn't their fault really, but I was hurt. I guess that is what happens when we are hurt – we hurt others.

I looked at all those pieces of milk-white china lying in my blue dustpan and I cried. I was still crying as I laid a newspaper on the table and sat down with a big tube of china glue. I cried even more as I started the long, frustrating, painstaking task of picking up and sticking together the pieces, in an attempt to recreate my lovely vase. But when the job was finished, I had a milk-white, long-necked vase once more. The only problem was that I had *one piece left over* and a hole in the side of the vase. No matter how hard I tried, I could not make the piece fit the hole so I had to settle for a vase with a hole in it, a vase which was to prove much more precious than before.

I still have the vase. It sits atop a corner cupboard, and the reason it is more precious is because of the lessons I have learned from it.

My vase speaks to me of life. It too is precious and we plan so many things that we are going to do with it. We spend time deciding where to use our lives for the best. Then one day something happens. There life lies, all in broken pieces, never to be the same again. It can happen in a hundred different ways. An illness that curtails our dreams, the breaking up of a marriage that results in the feeling of rejection, an accident, death, whatever the cause the result is still the same: a life broken and in need of repair. In my case it was death that brought my safe, happy, confident world crashing down to lie in pieces. The death of our daughter, almost twenty-one years old, at the threshold of womanhood and her career.

With a simple thing like a telephone bell's ring the world caved in upon us. There had been an accident, and our daughter was dead. No matter how you say that word, it has a finality about it that shakes the foundation of your soul.

Dazed, like spectators sitting on the sidelines, watching but not really involved, we went about the formalities of the funeral, letters, calls, sorting clothes. Then the tears came. I cried as I picked up and began to stick back together 'family life'. I was still crying while I learned that in facing the death of a loved one, all the grief, sadness, questions and shock come through with a sense of having gained something wonderfully more precious than one could think possible.

I learned that the vital part in picking up the pieces and recreating what was there before is the Person of Jesus. All He is, all He did, all He taught. It was the love of God that sent His only begotten Son to die. I started to learn what a great love that is. I couldn't have planned my daughter's death even to save someone! But God did plan His Son's death. He knew all along that many would not think twice about Him, His love, His suffering, His gift. This is Christ Jesus who takes away the sins of a whole world. Perfect love, no strings attached. You can accept this love gift or not, as you choose. But God in love provided it – just in case you will accept it.

I learned that Jesus really means what He says: 'Whatever we ask in His name that would He do.' Oh yes, I had believed in answered prayer as long as I had been a Christian, but this was so personal, so loving.

Then came the long, lonely days that followed the bustle. Yet we were fortunate. I would pray, 'Lord, I can't stand this. Send someone or something to help me over the bad moments.' The doorbell would buzz or the telephone would ring. I even learned to be thankful for an overflowing washing machine because it occupied my mind for a little while. Many times this prayer was answered, always bringing relief, comfort or companionship.

I learned that you can give thanks in every situation, knowing it is God's will concerning you. Not because you understand it all, but because God, with that love that only a heavenly Father can give to His children, plans so perfectly.

Cherylyn and I had sat in church together on the last Sunday she was alive. The minister, Don Bridge, was talking about love – how hard it is for us to say: 'I love Jesus.' Then the minister said, in an impassioned voice, 'Oh, why can't we just tell people we love them?' He had been walking in a churchyard, he said, looking at gravestones. He told us that he had found a stone there which said: 'If you love someone, tell them, tell them loud, and tell them often – because when they are dead, you cannot say "I love you" to them again.'

Those words made me feel uncomfortable at the time. As we walked home after church, my daughter and I shared our love – we forgave each other for not sharing it more, and sorted out all the hurts that needed to be dealt with.

After I had received the news of her death, I asked God if there was anything between her and me. What a wonderful thing it was to know that in His love, our Lord had planned it so that I was able to answer the question with assurance. No! We had made it, just in time. How I praise the Lord for that precious memory.

I think of the pile of belongings sitting in the dining room, tied up in a travel rug, spotted with mud, glass and blood. There on the top was Cherry's *Daily Light*, a little book giving a few verses of scripture for the morning and the evening of each day of the year. There was a rubber band in the page before the day on which she had died. As I read the way in which the Lord had spoken to her that morning, my heart was filled with wonder at the way in which He prepares each of His children for the next step. These are some of the words for that day: 'Sit still, my daughter. Take heed, and be quiet: fear not, neither be faint hearted. Be still and know that I am God. Said I not unto thee that if thou wouldest believe, thou shouldest see the glory of God?'

Today our family is more precious to me. One piece is missing but the ones that are still here have taken on a new meaning. I learned what precious possessions really are. Hearing children quarrel and thanking God that they are fit and well enough to quarrel! The sound of the doors slamming and the sight of a dirty, but happy, youngster tracking mud over a clean floor. The voice of one of the family on the other end of the telephone line. A reunited family around the table after a day at work and school is no longer a thing to be taken for granted. It is a thing for which we give thanks.

Saying 'I love you' often, so there is no doubt about whether or not one loves. Having a pile of dirty socks and untidy rooms to clean. All these things one can take for granted, but I won't any more. They are the precious things of life.

My Saviour is more precious to me, because He showed me that the things I had always said I believed, I did. He took over completely just as He promised.

I still cry, but the tears now are tears of joy when I see God is using my daughter's death to reach people with the gospel message. My broken vase has been mended but the hole will always be a precious memory.

APPENDIX B

A Beginner's Guide to Cricket
by Maurice Rowlandson

The match is played between two teams, each of eleven players. The winner is the team which scores the most 'runs': a 'run' is when the two batsmen exchange places – and there can be from one to three runs scored with each ball bowled. (EXCEPTIONS: four runs are scored for a 'boundary' and six runs for a 'skyed' ball). Generally each team 'bats' twice alternately and if, at the end of the day, both sides have not finished, the match is declared 'drawn'.

TWO TEAMS – One in the pavilion who sends two men out to 'bat'.
One out on the field, including two 'bowlers' (pitchers) and a 'wicket keeper' (catcher).

BATSMEN – One at each end of the 'pitch'. Only one operates at a time, although he is backed up by the other when a 'run' is scored. The batsman plays in an area called the 'wicket', backed by three 'stumps' on which are balanced 'bails'. The line at the front end of the wicket is called the 'crease'.

BOWLER – One at each end of the 'pitch': only one operates at a time, bowling six balls (an 'over') before giving way to the bowler at the other end. When the bowler has bowled his six balls, every man on the field changes place to be in position for the bowler at the other end.

Any member of the team *can* be a bowler, and bowlers change whenever the captain decides. There are spin bowlers, fast bowlers, off-break bowlers, etc., all with different styles to confuse the batsmen.

'OUT' – A batsman (at either end) is said to be 'out' when one of seven things happens:

1. The ball hits the stumps and dislodges the bails.
2. The ball leaves the bat and is caught by a man in the field without the ball touching the ground.
3. Leg before wicket – when the ball would have hit the stumps if the batsman had not put his leg in the way to stop it.
4. Stumped – when the batsman is outside his crease and the wicket keeper hits the stumps with the ball while the batsman is still outside the crease.
5. Run out – when the batsman takes a run, and the man in the field stops the ball, throws it, and hits the stumps while the batsman running to that end is still outside his crease.
6. Obstructing the field – when the batsman tries to prevent one of the fielders from retrieving the ball.
7. Hit wicket – when the batsman hits his own stumps and dislodges the bails.

RUNS – Every time the batsmen hit the ball hard enough (or to a point where there is no man on the field), they can change places, and that scores one run.

If the ball went far enough (or the man on the field fumbles in picking it up), they can exchange places a second time and that scores two runs.

In exceptional cases, they can exchange places yet again and score three runs.

If the ball passes over the extremity line without being stopped by a man in the field, it is a 'boundary' and scores four runs (in that case the batsmen do not have to run, and can return to their own places without penalty).

If the ball passes from the bat and over the extremity line *without touching the ground* it scores six runs.

Bonus runs are scored:
1. When the ball passes wide of the crease – it is a 'wide' (one run).
2. When the ball is not hit by the batsmen, and passes by the wicket keeper (behind the crease) the batsmen can run for a 'bye' (one to three runs – or, if the ball passes over the boundary, four runs).
3. When there is a no ball – when the bowler infringes rules about how he delivers the ball. A batsman cannot be out from a no ball (except by being run out). (One to three runs – or four/six if it is a boundary).

UMPIRES – There are two umpires who keep an eye on the rules. They declare a batsman 'out' or 'not out'; they count the balls in an over; they give decisions on a no ball and on a wide. And they act as a repository for the bowler's sweater, etc. The decision of the umpire is final and it's 'not cricket' to argue with the umpire.

BREAKS – There is usually a break for coffee mid-morning, for lunch at midday and for tea in the afternoon.

INNINGS – When all eleven men in the pavilion have been in to bat, each taking his turn when any batsman is out, then that team replaces those out on the field, and those out on the field return to the pavilion and take their turn at batting. When the last *two* men of a side are batting, when either one of them is out then *both* are out.

DECLARATION – If a captain thinks his side is sufficiently far ahead in the number of runs scored, he can terminate his innings by 'declaring'. The rest of the batsmen do not then bat, but the two sides change over prematurely.

In a major match (called a 'test match'), the game can last five days.

It is a question of tactics – because an early declaration may allow the match to be finished and produce a win rather than a drawn result. But to declare too soon may allow the other side to win.

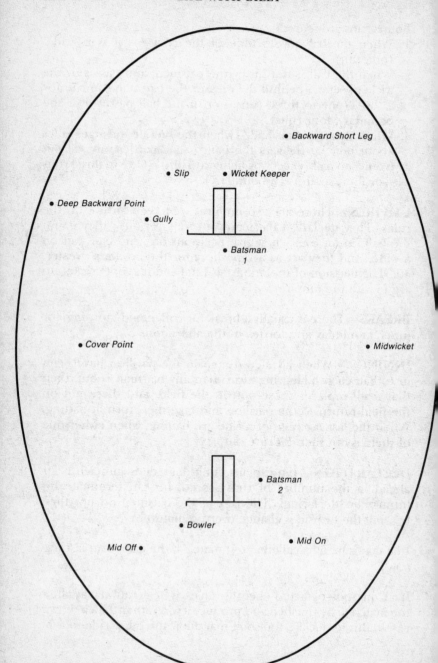

APPENDIX C

Participants in the Various Groups Leading to Mission England, 1984

Select Committee
(first meeting December 3rd, 1975)

Chief Inspector Robin Oake (chairman)

Dr Raymond Brown
The Rev. William Freel
Mr Peter Meadows
Mr P. Derek Warren

The Rev. Eldin Corsie
Mr Garth Hewitt
The Rev. Walter Newby
Miss Rosemary Wheeler

Mrs Jill Dann
Mr Gordon Landreth
Mr Ernest Shippam
Mr Maurice Rowlandson

Working Group

The Rev. Tom Houston (chairman)

The Rev. Howard Belbin
Mr Roger Forster
Mr Gordon Landreth
Mr Brian Mills
The Rev. David Pawson
The Rev. Michael Saward
Mr Maurice Rowlandson

Miss Shelagh Brown
The Rev. Eddie Gibbs
The Rev. David McInnes
The Rev. Lewis Misselbrook
The Rev. John Poulton
Mr Stephen Travis

Mr Michael Eastman
The Hon. Mrs Gill Joynson-Hicks
Mr Peter Meadows
The Rev. Eddie Neale
The Rev. Gavin Reid
Mr P. Derek Warren

The Archbishop of Canterbury's Consultative Group
October 20th, 1976

The Archbishop of Canterbury (chairman)

The Bishop of Southwell
The Rev. Dr Roderick Smith
The Rev. Harry O. Mortin
The Rev. David Pawson
Preb. Cleverley Ford

The Bishop of Chelmsford
The Rev. Dr Kenneth Greet
The Rev. John R. W. Stott
Mr Gordon Landreth
The Rev. John Poulton

The Rev. Arthur Macarthur
The Rev. Dr David Russell
The Rev. Tom Houston
Father Denis Corbishley
Mr Maurice Rowlandson

The Group who met Mr Graham in Copenhagen
April 19th, 1977

Mr Billy Graham (chairman)

The Rev. Richard Bewes
The Hon. C. Joynson-Hicks
The Rev. Gilbert W. Kirby
The Rev. David MacLagan

Dr Bob Evans
The Rev. Michael Cole
Mr Clarence M. Jefferies
Dr Walter Smyth

Mr Eric Delve
Mr Gordon Landreth
Mr Hugh Prest
Mr Maurice Rowlandson

Evangelical Alliance Co-ordinating Committee for Evangelism
October 19th, 1977

The Rev. Michael Cole (chairman)

Mr Clive Calver
Mr Clarence M. Jefferies
The Rev. Wesley Richards
The Rev. Richard Bewes
The Rev. David Holloway
The Rev. Gavin Reid
Dr Walter Smyth

Mr John Fear
The Rev. David MacLagan
Mr Gordon Landreth
The Hon. Mrs Gill
   Joyson-Hicks
The Rev. Gilbert W. Kirby
Miss Rosanne Semple

The Rev. Tom Houston
Mr Hugh Prest
The Rev. Mrs Jean Darnell
The Rev. Brian Hoare
The Rev. David McInnes
The Rev. Derek Tidball
Mr Maurice Rowlandson

The Birmingham Invitational Committee
March 20th, 1980

Mr Kenneth Barnes (chairman)

Mr G. Hopkinson
Dr Peter English
Mr David Mendants
The Rev. Michael Cole
Mr Hugh Prest
Dr Clifford Hill
Mr Bob Dunnert
Mr David Rennie
Mr John Brewster
Mr Stuart Dalgleish

Miss Beryl Graving
Mr Guy Hall
Mr John Wright
Mr Nick Cuthbert
Mr Gordon Landreth
Mr Allan Paines
Mr David Taylor
Mr Everett Oughton
Mr Clarence M. Jefferies
Mr Eric Bell

The Rev. David McInnes
The Rev. Gordon Bridger
Mr Douglas Jackson
The Rev. Gilbert W. Kirby
Mr Philip South
Mrs Monica Hill
Mr Peter Searle
Mr John Earwicker
Mr Martin Culver
Mr Maurice Rowlandson

Signatories to the Invitation prepared at All Souls Church

March 24th, 1980

The Rev. Gilbert W. Kirby (chairman)

The Rev. David Abernethie
Sir Maurice Laing
The Rev. Michael Baughen
Canon T. L. Livermore
Sir Cyril Black
The Rev. Dr Fraser McLuskey
The Rev. David Bubbers
Commissioner J. D. Needham
Mr Clive Calver
Mr David Rennie
The Rev. Mrs Jean Darnall
Mr John Elworthy
The Rev. H. Sealy
Mr John Forrest
The Rev. John R. W. Stott
Canon Michael Green
The Rev. Norman Warren
Mr Richard Walker
Mr Simon Webley
Mrs Mary Whitehouse
Mrs J. W. Hurst
Mr Maurice Rowlandson

Mr Graham Ferguson Lacey
Mr K. W. Bailey
Mr Gordon Landreth
The Rev. Richard Bewes
Dr Brian Mawhinney MP
The Rev. Gordon Bridger
The Rev. Keith Munday
Sir Neil Cameron
The Rev. Kenneth Prior
Mr Stuart Dalgleish
The Rev. Jack Hywel Davies
Mrs S. Saville
Mr Roger Forster
Miss Jill Spink
Mr Nigel Goodwin
Mrs G. Turner
Mrs A. Warren
Major General D. J. Wilson-
   Haffenden
The Rev. David Holloway
Mr Clarence M. Jefferies

Mr C. H. Anderton
Dr John Laird
Mr Michael Bewes
Mr Alan Martin
The Rev. Michael Botting
Mr Brian Mills
Mr Anthony Bush
The Rev. F. G. Nevell
The Rev. Michael Cole
Mr David G. Rivett
Mr Dick Saunders
Dr Peter English
The Rev. John Skinner
Mr Kenneth P. Frampton
The Rev. Eddie Stride
Mr Val Grieve
The Hon. Crispin Joynson-Hicks
Dr Clifford Hill
Sir Timothy Hoare
The Rt Rev. Maurice A. P. Wood
Mr J. Inglis-Jones

The Caretaker Committee

January 14th, 1981

The Rev. David Bubbers (chairman)

The Rev. Tom Houston
Mr Gordon Landreth
Mr Hugh Prest
Mr James Anderton*
Mr Billy Graham
* unable to attend

Mr David C. Rennie
Mr Stuart Dalgleish
Mr Clarence M. Jefferies
Mr Clive Calver
Dr Walter H. Smyth

The Rev. Gilbert W. Kirby
Mr Kenneth Barnes*
Dr Peter English
The Rev. Gavin Reid
Mr Maurice Rowlandson

Steering Committee
(first meeting) March 4th, 1981

Mr David C. Rennie (chairman)

The Rev. Lyndon Bowring	The Rev. Gilbert W. Kirby	Mr Peter Meadows
Mr Clive Calver	Mr Michael Penny	The Rev. Eddie Gibbs
Mr Jim Punton	The Hon. Crispin Joynson-	The Rev. Gavin Reid
Dr Walter H. Smyth	Hicks	Mr Maurice Rowlandson

The Envoys to meet Mr Graham in Nice
July 6th, 1981

Mr David C. Rennie (chairman)

Mr Clive Calver	The Rev. Eddie Gibbs	The Rev. Gavin Reid
Mr Maurice Rowlandson		

They met with

Mr Billy Graham	Dr Walter H. Smyth	Mr Blair Carlson
Mr Fred Dienert		

The Final Invitational Meeting in Manchester
March 5th, 1982

Mr David C. Rennie (chairman)

Mr Billy Graham	Dr T. W. Wilson	Dr Walter H. Smyth
Mr Blair Carlson	Mr Neville Atkinson	Bishop Bill Flagg
Mr Val Grieve	The Rev. Tom Houston	Mr Ian Frith
Mr Brian Mills	The Rev. Alan Boddington	The Rev. Gavin Reid
Mr Tony Dann	Mr Clive Calver	Mr Anthony Bush
Dr Peter English	Mr Clarence M. Jefferies	Mr Victor Jack
The Rev. Ray Skinner	Mr Maurice Rowlandson	

Index